Philosophical Explorations of Justice and Taxation

IUS GENTIUM

COMPARATIVE PERSPECTIVES ON LAW AND JUSTICE

VOLUME 40

More information about this series at http://www.springer.com/series/7888

Helmut P. Gaisbauer • Gottfried Schweiger
Clemens Sedmak
Editors

Philosophical Explorations of Justice and Taxation

National and Global Issues

Springer

Editors
Helmut P. Gaisbauer
Centre for Ethics and Poverty Research
University of Salzburg
Salzburg
Austria

Clemens Sedmak
Centre for Ethics and Poverty Research
University of Salzburg
Salzburg
Austria

Gottfried Schweiger
Centre for Ethics and Poverty Research
University of Salzburg
Salzburg
Austria

ISSN 1534-6781 ISSN 2214-9902 (electronic)
Ius Gentium: Comparative Perspectives on Law and Justice
ISBN 978-3-319-13457-4 ISBN 978-3-319-13458-1 (eBook)
DOI 10.1007/978-3-319-13458-1
Springer Cham Heidelberg New York Dordrecht London

Library of Congress Control Number: 2014958744

Printed on acid-free paper

Springer is part of Springer Science+Business Media (www.springer.com)

Contents

Contributors

Benjamin Alarie Facutly of Law, University of Toronto, Toronto, ON, Canada

Douglas Bamford Department for Continuing Education, University of Oxford, Oxford, UK

Gillian Brock Faculty of Arts, University of Auckland, Auckland, New Zealand

Vittorio Bufacchi Department of Philosophy, University College Cork, Cork, Ireland

Teppo Eskelinen Department of social sciences, University of Eastern Finland, Joensuu, Finland

Helmut P. Gaisbauer Centre for Ethics and Poverty Research, University of Salzburg, Salzburg, Austria

Daniel Halliday School of Philosophical Studies, University of Melbourne, Melbourne, Australia

Arto Laitinen School of Social and Political Philosophy, University of Tampere, Tampere, Finland

Xavier Landes Department of Media, Cognition and Communication, University of Copenhagen, Copenhagen, Denmark

Timothy Mawe Department of Philosophy, University College Cork, Cork, Ireland

Rajiv Prabhakar Faculty of Social Sciences, Open University, Walton Hall, Milton Keynes, UK

Gottfried Schweiger Centre for Ethics and Poverty Research, University of Salzburg, Salzburg, Austria

Clemens Sedmak Centre for Ethics and Poverty Research, University of Salzburg, Salzburg, Austria

Kirk J. Stark School of Law, University of California, LA, Los Angeles, CA, USA

Bruno Verbeek Institute for Philosophy, University of Leiden, Leiden, The Netherlands

Dietmar von der Pfordten Philosophy of Law, University of Göttingen, Göttingen, Germany

Chapter 1
Outlining the Field of Tax Justice

Helmut P. Gaisbauer, Gottfried Schweiger and Clemens Sedmak

Abstract Taxation is one of the most fundamental and influential institutions in all modern societies. This importance of taxation gives rise to crucial normative, ethical, and moral questions—and assumptions about what is just and morally right are closely tied to the discussion, design and implementation of taxation and certain taxes. For that reason a normative examination of taxation, focusing on issues of justice, is of utmost importance. Tax justice is located in the interstices between the traditional tax disciplines of tax law, public finance, and microeconomics and it is connected to approaches from philosophy and some social sciences. It is clearly an inherently interdisciplinary topic. In order to arrive at a sufficiently coherent and defensible set of concepts within the field of tax justice, we propose to clarify at least four key concepts: (i) state, (ii) citizenship, (iii) property, and (iv) social justice.

1.1 Background

Taxation is one of the most fundamental and influential institutions in all modern societies. It fills the coffers of the state and distributes and redistributes income and wealth. Without taxation no modern state could function and fulfill its public duties and, accordingly, there are only few who argue against taxation in general. However, the extent and depth of this public interference with private property is still highly disputed, in academia as well as in the public discourse and in politics. Lay people and theorists alike hold different and contrary views about the proper height

H. P. Gaisbauer (✉) · G. Schweiger · C. Sedmak
Centre for Ethics and Poverty Research, University of Salzburg, Mönchsberg 2a, 5020 Salzburg, Austria
e-mail: helmut.gaisbauer@sbg.ac.at

G. Schweiger
e-mail: gottfried.schweiger@sbg.ac.at

C. Sedmak
e-mail: clemens.sedmak@sbg.ac.at

H. P. Gaisbauer et al. (eds.), *Philosophical Explorations of Justice and Taxation*,
Ius Gentium: Comparative Perspectives on Law and Justice 40,
DOI 10.1007/978-3-319-13458-1_1

and distribution of taxation and about the justification for it. Often such disputes are also influenced not only by personal interest but also moral views about what is just and what is not (Alm and Torgler 2006). Such differences can also be found at the state level, where different tax regimes developed over time, leading to the variety of "cultures of taxation" in today's world (Birger 2008).

The importance of taxation for the social, economic and political functioning of any society gives rise to crucial normative, ethical and moral questions—and assumptions about what is just and morally right are closely tied to the discussion, design and implementation of taxation and certain taxes. The distribution of tax burdens and benefits as well as the usage of the allocated tax revenue is decisive for justice, but like justice itself, these measures are highly disputed (Paul et al. 2006). Especially, in consideration of the ongoing economic crisis and the social, economic and political turmoil it has caused around the globe, the intensification of social inequality and the need to search for measures to overcome the crisis without hurting the most vulnerable, most questions of taxation, particularly regarding tax fairness, who should contribute and how much, have become vital and are widely discussed. Particularly the growing disparities in income and wealth have gained interest and earned criticism, and a change in the tax regime, as well as a higher tax burden on the wealthy, are possible measures against such disparities. Arguments for reducing these inequalities can also be found in their negative effects on the health and well-being of the whole population (Wilkinson and Pickett 2009). Over the course of the last decades a small minority of the super-rich has—looking back in time one has to say: again—detached itself from the rest of the population in terms of income and wealth, and, probably, also political power and influence (Piketty 2014). But how much inequality in income and wealth—within a society and globally—is justified? And on what grounds?

As an effect of the financial crisis sovereign debts are increasing and also pose a significant challenge for intergenerational justice. Some critics argue that the "rich" should simply pay for the crisis in the form of much higher taxes (Crotty 2012), while others are more modest in this regard and warn about the possible negative consequences of excessive taxes on income and wealth (Arnold et al. 2011). Such disputes cannot be settled based on "empirical facts" alone but demand normative reasoning and also political debate (Gaisbauer et al. 2013). A political debate, in which the taxpayers are themselves stakeholders and not to be shut out, is necessary to ground tax politics and give it a wider legitimacy that goes beyond an expert opinion. This is also important for another reason: the functioning of a tax system is to some extent dependent on the cooperation of the taxpayers and on their tax morale and cannot be based on control and power alone (Kirchler et al. 2008).

The individual tax morale and the actual obligations of taxpayers are not always congruent, which can motivate both tax avoidance and tax evasion. Prominent examples like Uli Hoeneß, the former president of the football club Bayern Munich, who was convicted of tax evasion in 2014, are just the tip of the iceberg and it has been estimated by the Tax Justice Network that the super-rich hide between 21 and 32 trillion US-$ in tax havens Henry 2012; Palan et al. 2010). This is money that, as some would argue, should be used for the good, to fight poverty and unemployment.

Again, studies suggest that poorer countries suffer particularly under the illicit money drain, which exceeds by a large amount the development aid they receive from other countries and international organizations (Reuter 2012). The possibilities of international companies avoiding taxes and shifting profits are equally problematic. The ongoing tax competition between states can lead to a rat race that undermines justice domestically and globally (Dietsch and Rixen 2014). It appears—and many chapters in this volume come to this conclusion—that the current tax regimes and the international tax order is not just—at least not in some important aspects—and that it is necessary to tax some people and some companies more than others. But how much taxation is justified? Are there certain limits to taxation? Such limits can certainly be found not only in pragmatic and economic arguments but they are also demanded by justice itself and inherent in basic concepts of desert, property or respect.

It is for these reasons that a normative examination of taxation focusing on issues of justice is of utmost importance, especially in times of disagreement, conflicts of interest, scarce state revenues and economic and financial globalization, as they create additional pressure on the nation state. Such a discussion on taxation and justice takes place on different levels, which we reflect in this volume. On the principal level such a discussion investigates the justification and grounding of taxation as such and the role taxation plays and should play in the design of justice, be it for a just society or a just world order. But these general reflections have to be considered further and there is also a need to discuss different types of taxation, tax systems and their design and implementation on a less abstract level. The current tax systems are the result of a long history and developed out of conflicts, compromises and political agendas. Furthermore, certain taxes, such as wealth and inheritance taxes, are especially contested (Prabhakar 2008). This also reflects the current situation of social stratification and inequalities in power. Whether or not a certain tax should be favoured, and for what reasons, has to be discussed, as well as why it is just to target certain kinds of assets or income. Finally, in times of a globalised world and the wide spread of severe poverty in poorer states, taxation can no longer be viewed as simply a national matter but has to be discussed on the international and global level (Kohonen and Mestrum 2009). How can taxation contribute to a more just world and what obstacles need to be overcome in this regard?

1.2 Key Concepts

Reflections on taxation for a more just world do not come as an agenda for one single academic discipline. Tax justice is not an academic concern that lies at the heart of a single discipline or academic tradition but cuts across a multitude of disciplines like public finance, law, philosophy, political science, fiscal sociology etc. (cf. Musgrave 1996/1997; Leroy 2011). Thus outlining the field of tax justice requires introducing the relevant questions, discussing the appropriate methodological approaches and clarifying the main concepts involved in tax justice reasoning.

The most prominent question in tax policy debates is the one which asks whether our share of the burden which the fiscal authorities impose is fair (Slemrod 2004). On a more abstract level this develops into two central questions of tax justice: whether and on what grounds a given overall tax burden, as well as taxation in general, is justified and whether this burden is fairly distributed among the taxpayers. Normative tax theory proposes two main concepts to justify tax liabilities in general and the specific level and distribution of a given tax burden (Musgrave 2005). The benefit view conceptualizes taxes as the price of public services rendered to everybody and paid by every 'consumer' of these services—according to some specified calculation of individual benefit. The benefit principle connects the fiscal side of the picture directly with the output side of a political and social system. This idea would imply, for example, that taxpayers could refuse to pay taxes for services they neither need nor want. On the other hand, its followers argue that a benefit concept of taxation allows for strong incentives to effectively control the growth of a 'leviathan' state and a potentially byzantine bureaucracy and is therefore in line with democratic standards (Buchanan 1997). The ability-to-pay perspective limits this picture to the input side by proposing only a standard for fair distribution of a given overall tax burden. Consequently, it is in line with the political tax principle of non-affectation which means that the fiscal authorities collect money that is not linked to some special policy programs but instead the political authorities are free to finance policy programs according to their democratic agenda (Brunner 1989). According to the ability-to-pay principle, every taxpayer should make the same (absolute, relative or marginal) sacrifice. Since modern (and all other real-world) tax systems are built upon a multitude of different types of taxes and not upon a single tax the question for practitioners is less one of whether to apply the benefit or the ability-to-pay principle than rather what principle gives better answers to detailed problems of (de-)legitimizing tax policy decisions on different levels (Musgrave 2005). Evidently the benefit principle is normatively closer to economic liberalism while the ability-to-pay principle feeds better into welfare economics and their respective political, i.e. social-democratic, world views. Obviously from a social ethics perspective the normative underpinnings of these two principles are not sufficiently structured grounds on which to build an elaborated theory of taxation and social justice. Such principles must be accompanied by clarified concepts of statehood, citizenship, property and some other conceptualized ideas of social justice.

As to preferential methodological paradigms to investigate such issues, tax justice is clearly a topic which is interdisciplinary in nature. It falls in the interstices among the traditional tax disciplines of tax law, public finance and microeconomics and it connects with approaches from philosophy and some social sciences. Additionally, tax justice is not the first concern of practical philosophy or social ethics. Accordingly, a focus on tax justice may help to mobilize enormous intellectual resources which have been rather fenced in within disciplinary gardens in the cause of greater and more profound rationality in tax justice thinking and discourse. Since conceptual confusion is one of the major fallacies of interdisciplinary research, major effort is to be made to clarify central concepts of the field. In order to arrive at a sufficiently coherent and defensible set of concepts in the field of tax justice, we propose to clarify at least four key concepts: (i) state, (ii) citizenship, (iii) property, and (iv) social justice.

1.2.1 The State

According to eminent scholars like Norbert Elias or Joseph A. Schumpeter the development of the modern system of taxation is part and parcel of the process of civilization and the establishment of modern statehood (Elias 1988). The modern capitalist state is first and foremost a tax state (Schumpeter 1918[1991]). Thus, studies in taxation could be key to a broad range of analytical perspectives from state building (Ardant 1975; Tilly 1975), political rebellion and revolution (Goldstone 1991; Adams 1984), to economic organization, labour force participation or philanthropy, as a fiscal sociological approach suggests (Campell 1993). However, this potential is widely ignored. On the other hand, analytical attempts to shed light on the socio-political processes and constellations that determine taxation could fertilize political sociology considerably. Pressures for transformation from geopolitical, economic, or fiscal crises motivate political elites to respond by altering tax policies. However, the effect of crises on taxation is mediated in complex ways by a variety of additional factors. Such factors might be classes and other social groups with different levels of tax tolerance and interests in different forms of taxation; the balance of power among these groups; the system of political representation; the institutional arrangement of the state apparatus (Campell 1993). Again, these roads are largely still to be travelled. A fiscal-sociological perspective on the state can also be instructive for tax justice theorizing. Awareness of the socio-economic cleavages and the asymmetry of power complete the concept of a state as a polity of common value that is aiming for the common good. The state is an instrument to realize tax justice considerations, but it is never a neutral ground for the competition of the best tax ideas. Statehood and taxation are narrowly intertwined, and so are taxation, poverty alleviation and social justice.

However, in taxation the state is not everything. A lot of issues important for tax justice considerations are located at the international, the supranational, and the global level. Perversions like tax havens, the difficulty of adequately taxing international corporations and capital, issues of international tax competition and 'location factors', the lack of transparency in global (legal and illicit) financial flows are all of major importance for tax justice considerations as well as for handling questions of global and local poverty and justice. One major difficulty arises from the fact that social justice is mostly understood as a matter within a given (national) society. For such an understanding, concerns of redistribution, the financing of public goods and other welfare and poverty considerations, including tax justice, are expressions of an exclusive citizenship.

1.2.2 Citizenship

There is a rich tradition in philosophical debate that focuses on ideas of membership or citizenship, and the relation between the individual and the community. In a nutshell, the modern idea of citizenship means membership of a political community with a given set of duties and access to equal fundamental rights and the conditions necessary for their realisation. In the context of tax justice, duties are often equated with the duty to pay taxes and rights to access a publicly financed framework of goods and services that enables self-realisation on an equal basis and that protects the fundamental rights of citizens. A closer look reveals that the picture is more complex since there is not a clearly defined community of citizens but a given constellation of transactions that involves citizens as well as non-citizens or non-resident citizens. In other words: the community of taxpayers, unified through the same liability, is not identical with the community of formal citizens or the *de facto* inhabitants of a given politico-geographical area since even tourists or economic actors who visit a place or make transactions there—maybe by 'virtual' means, via the internet—are liable to taxes. The same holds true for people who are excluded from society because of poverty, homelessness etc., who still pay taxes when paying for the most basic requirements for survival. On the other hand, the picture of the taxpayer-citizen is not reliably descriptive since there are a lot of possibilities and a far ranging practice of free riding, i.e. tax avoidance and tax evasion, that deprives the community of liable means to raise revenue. In some philosophical traditions, citizenship is sometimes portrayed as an evil rather than a legitimate and desirable state. This, at least, is an impression that one can get from reading R. Nozicks (1974) ideas on taxation and community.

1.2.3 Property

Property is another key concept for philosophical attempts to conceptualize taxation. Taxation, it is often argued, interferes with the private property of the taxpayers and such interference must be justified. Taxpayers—whether it be natural or juridical persons—have some kind of right to their property, one that ought not to be violated by others and the state. Many important questions arise here. Firstly, to what extent and on what grounds is private property justified? When can a person or a company be said to own a certain good—why can some things, such as another human being, never be owned—and what are the limits to ownership and property? Some would want to argue that private property itself is the problem and is only a social construct to legitimise inequalities, others would say that the state's very existence is first and foremost justified to protect private property (Paul et al. 2010). Secondly, it has been observed that the relation between private property and taxation is often viewed as if there existed something like a pre-tax world, in which goods were distributed without the interference of taxation (Murphy and Nagel 2002). On the contrary, the process of acquiring property itself is taking place in a world of taxation and it is shaped by the state. This can lead to a line of argument that grants the state certain property rights over private property, concluding that taxation is the legitimate way to exercise this right. Such concepts of property can be used to justify and to criticise taxation and certain taxes—for example wealth taxes—equally. Thirdly, it can be questioned what possible higher goods than property exist, goods and values that might even allow expropriation by taxation. Tax justice is then the attempt to find a balance that respects private property but limits it.

1.2.4 Justice

Justice is a key concept to delineate the relations between the state and the taxpayers as well as between taxpayers and non-tax-payers (so far as they exist). John Rawls has used the famous words, that "[j]ustice is the first virtue of social institutions, as truth is of systems of thought. A theory however elegant and economical must be rejected and revised if it is untrue, likewise laws and institutions no matter how efficient and well-arranged must be reformed or abolished if they are unjust." (Rawls 1972, p. 3) Taxation is surely such a social institution and one that is of utmost importance for the distribution of income and wealth as well as other goods. Their distribution ought to be just and for that to happen, all attempts to conceptualise tax justice have to specify what rules of justice should be applied and what goods of justice should be targeted. Should the tax system be designed to make the distribution of income and wealth more equitable and to what extent? Should it be designed to respect market outcomes to the greatest possible degree or should it be designed to redistribute resources from the wealthy to the poor? Can taxation be a measure to achieve other goals of justice too, like equality of opportunity or basic liberties? The many different attempts to achieve social justice will most likely produce different answers to those questions and that makes it even more necessary to debate the grounds of justice as well as its application.

Furthermore, recent discussions about global justice have raised new and highly important questions (Pogge and Moellendorf 2008). Persons and companies are now active in different states with different tax laws. We already mentioned that tax avoidance and tax evasion are severe problems since many different and domestic answers to tax justice appear to be outdated in view of these developments of globalisation. It is no longer the task to delineate the relations between one state and its taxpayers just because other states are also involved and taxpayers can move from one to another. If income and wealth can simply move away from one state to another and escape justice, tax justice needs to find answers to these questions.

1.2.5 Trust

One fruitful line of inquiry into the relationship between taxation and justice is to focus on the concept of the fiscal contract. A fiscal contract is agreed by citizens to governs the fiscal (and public policy) authorities that are held responsible for a legitimate use of public money. A fiscal contract is contracted amongst citizens (as a kind of social contract) and governs the fiscal and political authorities (as a kind of political contract). From an economics perspective, contracting requires trust. Trust is a societal resource necessary for all kinds of economic relations. We propose understanding trust as part of the "intangible infrastructure" of a society, an infrastructure of societal intangible resources. A focus on intangible infrastructures like values, knowledge, ideas, and especially the concept of trust allow investigations into the connection between taxes and the common good. Taxation is based on intangible infrastructures and at the same time trust is an important tool to maintain those foundations of a well-ordered society. Intangible infrastructures need to be built and maintained as much as tangible infrastructures. Analytically, trust can be based on four specific sources: (i) confidence (in competence), (ii) a shared ontology of rationality (mode of calculation), (iii) (perceived) resource security, (iv) order security in terms of a reliable and effective frame for agency. In the context of fiscal contract consideration clearly (iii) and (iv) are constituted by or resulting from the contract. Both dimensions of the fiscal contract (constitution of fiscal authorities; social contract between the citizens) involve the sources of trust in a different way and are open to different pathologies or toxic regulations. Beyond that all four sources of trust allow for further considerations of the concept of trust as a pre-economic societal resource and as part of the intangible infrastructure of society.

1.3 About the Chapters in This Volume

This book has three parts. The first part is devoted to questions about the grounding and justification of taxation in general. The second part contains chapters that discuss certain types of taxes and their benefits and disadvantages in relation to justice. The chapters in the third part move the discussion from the domestic to the international level and discuss taxation against the background of the aspiration of global justice.

In the opening chapter, "Fiscal Justice and Justified Trust", *Clemens Sedmak* and *Helmut P. Gaisbauer* are particularly interested in the relationship between formal (legal, political) frameworks and informal networks. There seems to be a culture of suspicion vis-à-vis the former and a culture of trust regarding the latter. This asymmetry in the readiness to trust leads to a way of thinking that supports the idea: "the lower the tax burden, the better". On the other hand, the idea of a fiscal contract is based on an idea of mutual trust (tax authorities trusting the tax payers, i.e. through limited controls, tax payers trust the tax authorities in terms of tax fairness and the appropriate use of the fiscal income). The thesis we will develop here has three elements: (1) Formal frameworks (F) and informal networks (N) are interdependent and mutually linked; trust in F implies trust in N and vice versa. Social networks operate within structural frameworks and need "institutional framework trust" or "trust in systems" in order to be able to flourish. (2) The generation of income and wealth is based on trust—people need social capital and networks as well as legal and political frameworks and public infrastructure in order to generate incomes, in other words: non-communal money or capital independent of structure does not exist. (3) On the basis of this culture of trust as the centre of wealth-generation and common-good tax justice, justified trust can be linked via an "ability to trust" principle and a "responsibility to trust" principle.

In the second chapter, "Taxation and the Duty to Alleviate Poverty", *Gottfried Schweiger* aims to show that taxation in general and progressive taxation in particular are justified by the duty to alleviate poverty in the context of welfare states. He argues that sufficient access to basic capabilities and functionings is an aim that is feasible and a worthy aspiration for welfare states and that it demands comprehensive measures to reduce and to alleviate poverty. Taxation is one important means to achieve those goals in at least two ways: first, it provides the state with the necessary revenue to fund public goods, social services and benefits from which all citizens benefit, but especially for those worse-off who profit the most. Programmes to provide better schooling, housing, health care and social inclusion should be funded publicly because they are not humanitarian aid but the demands of justice. Taxation is a visible expression of this duty of justice. Second, the reduction of tax burdens on those who are poor leaves them with more funds and therefore better opportunities to achieve certain capabilities and functionings. This argument is in favour of progressive taxation which exempts those who are less well-off and burdens more those who are better-off. The reduction of inequalities in income and wealth that is produced by progressive taxation and special taxes on wealth and capital income is a favourable side-effect.

Dietmar von der Pfordten argues in his chapter, "Justice, Equality and Taxation", that the justice of taxation depends first on the distribution being made possible. For him the principle of normative individualism/humanism is fundamental: only individuals can be the ultimate point of reference of moral obligations and hence the justificatory source of ethics, politics and law. In order to balance conflicting interests the "principle of the relative dependence of individual concerns on others" is proposed. The more the origins or the realization of the concerns or the interests of a morally considerable individual depend on others or a community, the more the respective concerns and interests have to be relativized in the process of deliberation, and the more the community may decide according to its common goals. This principle is applied to the justice of taxation. As a basic principle of taxation, a limited equivalence/benefit-principle is defended. The ability principle can only provide some additional considerations. Income can be taxed more extensively than consumption and wealth. A progressive income tax is defended.

The fourth chapter, "'You did not build that road'—Reciprocity, Benefits, Opportunities and Taxing the Extremely Rich", written by *Bruno Verbeek*, examines a typical strategy that is used to argue for increases in the marginal tax burden for the extremely rich by stating that they amassed their wealth by taking advantage of economic opportunities that they had not created themselves. He shows, first, that these arguments commit what could be called a 'fallacy of composition'. They assume that, since an entrepreneur's efforts would be in vain had those public goods and services not been provided, all economic gain therefore is attributable to these goods and services—a conclusion that does not follow. Secondly, he argues that this type of 'Warren argument' appeals to a principle according to which taxation is the price a citizen pays for the enjoyment of the benefits the state provides. Third, he wants to show that such a principle not only undercuts the 'Warren argument', but also that it mandates a completely flat tax rate with no marginal rates at all. In the final part of this chapter, Verbeek discusses an argument for taxing the extremely rich that does not appeal to a benefit principle. This argument proceeds from the idea that justice demands that taxation is levied according to the ability to pay. Social-democrats and left liberals who are concerned about the extremely high incomes at the top end of the income distribution are better advised to adopt such a strategy.

Benjamin Alarie's chapter, "The Challenge of Tax Avoidance for Social Justice in Taxation", aims to explain that the obvious tax policy prescriptions for social resource inequality are not without complications. More specifically, he is concerned with the question of why the most salient of such ideas—increasing tax rates—is not on its own a solution. The problem is that increasing tax rates leave those confronting those higher tax rates with greater incentive to engage in various activities in order to legally avoid those taxes. It also increases the return to lobbying for tax changes that make avoiding that burden more possible. Thus increasing tax rates is not the clear-cut effective policy prescription one might reflexively think it should be. The example of the Bush tax cuts for individuals and certain kinds of capital income illustrates that cutting tax rates is also not the right approach. In many countries claims that cutting taxes will increase tax revenues (i.e., that we "are on the wrong side of the Laffer curve") are incorrect. If tax rates are increased it is not necessarily the wealthiest that will bear the greatest burden, and if tax rates are cut, it is not certain—or even particularly likely—that it will be the least well-off who will benefit. The proper reform is one of base broadening and increasing international tax cooperation. Responding intelligently to the demands for a more progressive tax system that promotes the realization of social justice will confront difficult practical and political challenges. These good tax policy starting points are available if the political will can be found to sustain their introduction and implementation.

Xavier Landes' chapter, "Why Why Taxing Consumption. Justifications, Objections and Social Cooperation", opens the second part of the book. He analyses Robert Frank's proposition of an incremental tax on consumption that is motivated by the control of positional externalities, i.e. the costs that individuals impose on each other when they consume goods for securing or acquiring social status. A close analysis of Frank's proposition identifies three justifications for a tax on consumption: efficiency, paternalism and equality. This chapter has two purposes. Firstly, it reviews these justifications, highlighting some objections and possible replies. As such, it suggests that reasons based on equality or paternalism are controversial while the invocation of efficiency is actually grounded in an underlying view of social cooperation. Secondly, this chapter advances the idea that an ultimate justification for the choice of specific tax base (consumption, income and wealth) expresses such an underlying view. In other words, the choice of a specific tax base is not totally instrumental, it has some intrinsic moral value too. In this respect the chapter ends with a comparison between taxing income and taxing consumption. It is shown that a tax on consumption raises questions that should be answered by political philosophers.

The second chapter of this part, "Egalitarianism and Consumption Tax", is written by *Daniel Halliday*. He examines the criticism of consumption taxes on grounds that they discriminate against the poor: consumption taxes are 'regressive', insofar as they require poor persons to pay a larger fraction of their income per consumed unit of consumed good. After an attempt to spell out exactly what this objection asserts, Halliday attempts to respond to it. The apparently egalitarian complaint about regressive taxation can be countered by other egalitarian worries about the vulnerability of low-income groups to the harms resulting from the type of consumption being taxed. This calls for the redesign of consumption taxes rather than abolition. Further progress can be made by recognizing there are ways of taxing consumption other than the standard model of a sales tax that is typically assumed in these debates. One is to hypothecate the revenues from ways that aid the poor, mitigating the regressivity of the tax burden. Another is to replace sales taxes with licences or permits. Hypothecation and licensing can also be combined in ways that can eliminate regressivity altogether.

Douglas Bamford argues in his chapter, "Ethical Taxation: Progressivity, Efficiency and Hourly Averaging", that calculating taxation on an hourly average basis is an ethical requirement. In order to reach this conclusion the author first presents an argument that tax policies should be guided by the requirements of distributive justice. Bamford takes an ecumenical position on distributive justice, merely showing that most prominent approaches to justice would support a taxation system with two broad features. The first is that the system would be progressive in nature and thereby provide transfers from the economically fortunate to the less fortunate. The second feature is that the system would retain economic incentives and thereby encourage an effective and efficient economy. These two requirements are commonly considered to go against one another, and so proposals that deliver both of these would be attractive in terms of all the approaches to distributive justice set out. A recently proposed form of tax calculation—hourly averaging—is presented and in the final two sections. Bamford shows that this is attractive for its progressivity and for providing economic incentives.

The chapter of *Rajiv Prabhakar*, "Why do the Public Oppose Inheritance Taxes?", is concerned with the common wisdom that inheritance taxes are very unpopular among the public. This public opposition seems puzzling as these taxes typically apply to a minority of estates. Usual explanations for this are that people are poorly informed about the extent of these taxes or that there is a lack of a compelling moral case for such taxes. He argues that current approaches do not go far enough and suggests public attitudes to inheritance taxes are better understood as a specific case of discontent with wider taxes. Addressing this means tackling a disconnection the public feel over the taxes they pay as well as exploring public reactions to different combinations of taxes. Greater public support for inheritance taxes is important for building public compliance with these taxes as well as improving the chances for policy reform.

In the chapter, "The Role of Expressive versus Instrumental Preferences in U.S. Attitudes toward Taxation and Redistribution", *Kirk Stark* connects the debate over U.S. tax attitudes with research on the role of expressive preferences in electoral choice. An expressive account of political behaviour emphasizes the low likelihood that any one voter's views will influence policy outcomes and thus locates her cost-benefit calculus in the expression itself rather than its effect on policy outcomes. Expressive considerations include the reputational consequences of taking sides in popular debates, especially as those consequences bear on the voter's effort to portray herself to the people that matter in her life—her family, friends, co-workers, and most of all, herself. The author explains how an expressive account resolves the supposed "paradox" of popular opposition to redistributive tax policies and discusses the implications of this view for U.S. tax politics.

The third section is opened by a chapter of *Gillian Brock* on the question, "What Burden should Fiscal Policy Bear in Fighting Global Injustice?" She examines how improvements in our fiscal arrangements could be an important vehicle for realizing key aspects of global justice. Her chapter begins by outlining some of the important principles that orient her account of global justice (and, moreover, should be part of any plausible account of what we should aim at in pursuing global justice). Improved institutional quality at both the state and global level has a crucial role to play in achieving global justice goals. Then she outlines some of the challenges that must be met to deliver the necessary institutional quality in the area of taxation. Effective and legitimate states, tax morale, and an appropriate fiscal contract are all highly important for creating and sustaining an environment conducive to beneficial development, as she explains. She discusses some positive proposals for levying global taxes that could assist enormously with realizing global justice. Currency conversion taxes seem especially worthy of serious consideration, as do carbon taxes and expansions of the air-ticket tax. Finally, her chapter briefly reviews some of the features that make the global taxes discussed both normatively desirable and politically feasible.

Vittorio Bufacchi proposes in his chapter, "The Global Luxuries Tax", a new solution to the problem of global poverty. He focuses on Thomas Pogge's Global Resources Dividend (GRD), arguably the most ingenious solution to the problem of global poverty currently on the table. In particular, it will be argued that GRD falls victim to two challenges: the Implementation Objection (it is very hard to implement the GRD in practice, as it is, for example, unclear how to ensure that the GRD applies universally and without exceptions) and the Unintended Consequences Objection (the GRD may not be as effective as it may seem at first, since the policy would inevitably have inflationary pressure, which would wipe out the funds raised by the GRD for its targeted benefactors). Bufacchi then introduces the idea of a Global Luxuries Tax (GLT), and in particular how it overcomes some of the potential limitations of the GRD. The GLT is collected whenever a person, wherever they happen to live (bar a few exceptions), accesses a certain luxury item. One of the advantages of this scheme is that the tax in question is progressive, to the extent that those who frequently access luxuries will repeatedly contribute more to the GLT than those who do so seldom. It is important to distinguish between a Universal GLT and a Partial (or Restricted) GLT. A Universal GLT applies to everyone across the globe who enjoys certain luxuries, even if the person in question lives among the global poor. A Partial GLT applies only to certain areas of the world, namely those countries where the GDP is above a certain threshold. In his view, a GLT entails both Universal and a Partial component, depending on the luxury. The luxuries to be taken into account include Air Travel, Academic Conferences, New Cars and Boats, Financial Transactions (all Universal GLT), as well as Procreation and Mobile Phones use (both Partial GLT). Finally, Bufacchi considers some objections to GLT. In particular, the GLT fares better than the GRD on the Implementation Objection and the Unintended Consequences Objection. He aims to show that the most effective approach to the problem of global poverty requires tackling the problem via a whole range of different measures, from reforming the international tax regime to taxing natural resources. The GLT is simply one measure amongst many others that can deliver for the global poor.

The chapter of *Teppo Eskelinen* and *Arto Laitinen*, "Taxation: Its Justification and Application to Global Contexts", focuses on the justification of taxation, in other words the principled rather than the technical aspect of taxation. They first show how, on the one hand, democracy is required for taxation to be legitimate, and how on the other hand democratic communities are dependent on taxation, and then argue there is no vicious circle. Based on that, they present a typology of ways of justifying taxation, according to which taxation can base its legitimacy on (1) meeting basic needs, (2) financing public goods, (3) redistribution, or (4) (dis) incentivising certain types of conduct. The authors then discuss the applicability of each of these types of justification, arguing that all of them do apply at a global level. This chapter further concludes that different normative justifications guide us towards different designs of taxation in practice, so the background justification has to be made clear, especially when designing new taxation systems.

References

Adams, James R. 1984. *Secrets of the tax revolt*. New York: Harcourt Brace Jovanovich.

Alm, James, and Benno Torgler. 2006. Culture differences and tax morale in the United States and in Europe. *Journal of Economic Psychology* 27 (2): 224–246. doi:10.1016/j.joep.2005.09.002.

Ardant, Gabriel. 1975. Financial policy and economic infrastructure of modem states and nations. In *The formation of National States in Western Europe,* ed. Charles Tilly, 164–242. Princeton: Princeton University Press.

Arnold, Jens Matthias, Bert Brys, Christopher Heady, Åsa Johansson, Cyrille Schwellnus, and Laura Vartia. 2011. Tax policy for economic recovery and growth. *The Economic Journal* 121 (550): F59–F80. doi:10.1111/j.1468-0297.2010.02415.x.

Birger, Nerré. 2008. Tax culture: A basic concept for tax politics. *Economic Analysis & Policy* 38 (1): 153–167.

Brunner, Johann K. 1989. *Theory of equitable taxation: Normative foundation and distributive consequences of income taxation*. Berlin: Springer.

Buchanan, James M., and Richard E. Wagner 1977. *Democracy in deficit: The political legacy of Lord Keynes*. (The Collected Works of James M. Buchanan), Vol. 8. Indianapolis: Liberty Fund.

Campell, John L. 1993. The state and fiscal sociology. *Annual Review of Sociology* 19:163–185.

Crotty, James. 2012. The Great Austerity War: What caused the US deficit crisis and who should pay to fix it? *Cambridge Journal of Economics* 36 (1): 79–104. doi:10.1093/cje/ber029.

Dietsch, Peter, and Thomas Rixen. 2014. Tax competition and global background justice. *Journal of Political Philosophy* 22 (2): 150–177. doi:10.1111/j.1467-9760.2012.00419.x.

Elias, Norbert. 1988. *On civilization, power, and knowledge: Selected writings*. Chicago: University of Chicago Press.

Gaisbauer, Helmut P, Gottfried Schweiger, and Clemens Sedmak. 2013. Ethical obligations of wealthy people: Progressive taxation and the financial crisis. *Ethics & Social Welfare* 7 (2): 141–154. doi:10.1080/17496535.2013.779003.

Goldstone, Jack A. 1991. *Revolution and rebellion in the early modern world*. Berkeley: University of California Press.

Henry, James S. 2012. The cost of offshore revisited. Tax justice network. http://www.taxjustice.net/cms/upload/pdf/Price_of_Offshore_Revisited_120722.pdf. Accessed 26 Sep 2014.

Kirchler, Erich, Erik Hoelzl, and Ingrid Wahl. 2008. Enforced versus voluntary tax compliance: The 'slippery slope' framework. *Journal of Economic Psychology* 29 (2): 210–225. doi:10.1016/j.joep.2007.05.004.

Kohonen, Matti, and Francine Mestrum, eds. 2009. *Tax justice: Putting global inequality on the agenda*. 1st ed. London: Pluto Press.

Leroy, Marc. 2011. *Taxation, the state and society. The fiscal sociology of interventionist democracy*. Bruxelles: Peter Lang.

Murphy, Liam B., and Thomas Nagel. 2002. *The myth of ownership: Taxes and justice*. 1st ed. Oxford: Oxford University Press.

Musgrave, Richard A. 1996/1997. Public finance and finanzwissenschaft traditions compared. *FinanzArchiv/Public Finance Analysis* 53 (2): 145–193.

Musgrave, Richard A. 2005. Fairness of taxation. In *The encyclopedia of taxation and tax policy*, eds. Robert D. Ebel, Joseph J. Cordes, and Jane G. Gravelle, 135–138. Washington D.C.: The Urban Institute Press.

Nozick, Robert. 1974. *Anarchy, state, and utopia*. 1st ed. New York: Basic Books.

Palan, Ronen, Richard Murphy, and Christian Chavagneux. 2010. *Tax havens: How globalization really works. Cornell Studies in Money*. 1st ed. Ithaca: Cornell University Press.

Paul, Ellen Frankel, Fred Dycus Miller, and Jeffrey Paul, eds. 2006. *Taxation, economic prosperity, and distributive justice*. 1st ed. Cambridge: Cambridge University Press.

Paul, Ellen Frankel, Fred Dycus Miller, and Jeffrey Paul, eds. 2010. *Ownership and justice. Social philosophy and policy 27*. 1st ed. Cambridge: Cambridge University Press.

Piketty, Thomas. 2014. *Capital in the twenty-first century*. Trans: Arthur Goldhammer. Cambridge: The Belknap Press of Harvard University Press.

Pogge, Thomas, and Darrel Moellendorf, eds. 2008. *Global justice: Seminal essays*. 1st ed. St. Paul: Paragon House.

Prabhakar, Rajiv. 2008. Wealth taxes: Stories, metaphors and public attitudes. *The Political Quarterly* 79 (April): 172–178. doi:10.1111/j.1467-923X.2008.00917.x.

Rawls, John. 1972. *A theory of justice*. 1st ed. Cambridge: Harvard University Press.

Reuter, Peter, ed. 2012. *Draining development? Controlling flows of illicit funds from developing countries*. 1st ed. Washington D.C.: World Bank.

Schumpeter, Joseph A. 1918 [1991]. *The economics and sociology of capitalism*, (Edited by Richard Swedberg). Princeton: Princeton University Press.

Slemrod, Joel, and Jon Bakija. 2004. *Taxing ourselves. A citizen's guide to the debate over taxes*. 3rd ed. Cambridge: MIT Press.

Tilly, Charles. 1975. *The formation of National States in Western Europe*. Princeton: Princeton University Press.

Wilkinson, Richard, and Kate Pickett. 2009. *The spirit level: Why equality is better for everyone*. 1st ed. London: Penguin.

Part I
Grounding Taxation

Chapter 2
Fiscal Justice and Justified Trust

Clemens Sedmak and Helmut P. Gaisbauer

Abstract In the following essay we are particularly interested in the relationship between formal (legal, political) frameworks and informal networks. There seems to be a culture of suspicion vis-à-vis the former and a culture of trust regarding the latter. This asymmetry in the readiness to trust leads to a way of thinking that supports the idea: "the lower the tax burden, the better". On the other hand, the idea of a fiscal contract is based on an idea of mutual trust (tax authorities trusting the tax payers, i.e. through limited controls, tax payers trust the tax authorities in terms of tax fairness and the appropriate use of the fiscal income). The thesis we will develop here has three elements: (1) Formal frameworks (F) and informal networks (N) are interdependent and mutually linked; trust in F implies trust in N and vice versa. Social networks operate within structural frameworks and need "institutional framework trust" or "trust in systems" in order to be able to flourish. (2) The generation of income and wealth is based on trust—people need social capital and networks as well as legal and political frameworks and public infrastructure in order to generate incomes, in other words: non-communal money or capital independent of structure does not exist. (3) On the basis of this culture of trust as the centre of wealth-generation and common-good tax justice, justified trust can be linked via an "*ability* to trust" principle and a "*responsibility* to trust" principle.

2.1 The Key Question

Let us begin by analysing the idea of inheritance tax as it represents one of the most contested types of tax (Gaisbauer et al. 2013). Inheritance tax provides a window into fiscal ethics because it is by its very nature embedded in the question of

C. Sedmak (✉) · H. P. Gaisbauer
Centre for Ethics and Poverty Research, University of Salzburg, Mönchsberg 2a, 5020 Salzburg, Austria
e-mail: clemens.sedmak@sbg.ac.at

H. P. Gaisbauer
e-mail: helmut.gaisbauer@sbg.ac.at

H. P. Gaisbauer et al. (eds.), *Philosophical Explorations of Justice and Taxation*, Ius Gentium: Comparative Perspectives on Law and Justice 40,
DOI 10.1007/978-3-319-13458-1_2

redistribution and common-good considerations. The actual process of inheriting can be reconstructed as follows (Sedmak 2013a)—A inherits x from B:

1. B is in a "right holding" position vis-à-vis x (Rx),
2. Rx is transferrable,
3. Rx is regulated by a ("thin") legal, political and social framework F,
4. A and B are members of a social network N,
5. N is usually "thick", i.e. characterized by personal acquaintance, special obligations, and face-to-face interactions,
6. B transfers Rx to A after B's death (or: Rx is transferred to A after B's death),
7. Step 6 constitutes the difference between A's pre-inheritance and A's post-inheritance position, i.e. Rx changes A's position both in F and in N,
8. By accepting Rx, A accepts the new position in F and N,
9. Step 6 can be justified on the basis of expectation fulfilment within "family rules" of N.

A standard argument against inheritance tax is often expressed as follows: x is N's (or B's) property, based on merits and/or achievements and/or efforts by N-members (or B) and inheritance tax is akin to robbery by an unrelated agent (F). Seen in this light, the key question to be asked is the following: What is the relationship between ("thin") F and ("thick") N? (e.g., what is the relationship between "System" and "Life world", between "group" and "grid"?). There are three possible answers to this one question: (a) F-N are parallel social constellations with occasional points of contact that can (and should perhaps) be minimized or can at least be forged *ad libitum*; (b) F-N are mutually dependent on each other, thus the relationship is characterized by reciprocity; (c) the relationship F-N is asymmetrical (characterized either by F-predominance or by N-predominance). "N" is a set of personal contacts based on personal acquaintance and face-to-face interactions. N provides special levels of interpersonal trust and trustful relationships with a component of special obligations. N is based on "face-based trust", that is trust connected with persons in their respective particularity. "F" is a ("thin") legal, political and social framework based on a type of trust that is formal, institutional and follows the dynamics of "trust in systems".

The question: "What is the relationship between ('thin') F and ('thick') N?" can be assumed to be the key question in the justification of any tax. Taxation as a process by which individuals, institutions, and communities are forced to make a contribution, via tax, to the authorities for the administration and development of society refers primarily to the 'thin' framework F. F is financed through taxes, i.e. through the compulsory exaction of money by a public authority for public purposes. Two core points of view are fundamental in motivating tax avoidance or even tax evasion: (1) Income is basically self-made and people should be free to support N as a preferential capital-commitment option; (2) Representatives of F will squander the money, and F is not an economically viable way of working with resources. These points relate to issues of trust: (1) either points to a form of self-trust that could be described as unjustified self-trust based on self-deception (see Govier 1993, p. 115 f.), or on the idea that, because of their bonds with N, people are prepared to contribute more capital towards N than towards F—and feel justified in doing so. In other words: greater trust in N than in F justifies a corresponding allocation of resources. (2) points to a culture of suspicion of state authorities; based on such lack of trust in any policies outlining careful and prudential spending, people will justify tax avoidance or even tax evasion by arguing: "I could make better use of the money, even better use for the sake of the common good".

In the following contribution, we will address this question of the relationship between taxation and trust with special reference to the relationship between thick networks ("N") and thin frameworks ("F").

2.2 What is the Relationship Between ('Thin') F and ('Thick') N: Two Examples

The idea of "self-made" wealth is prominent in debates about the myth of a pre-tax income and the myth of "self-made wealth", i.e. wealth without framework or community support (Collins et al. 2004). We will examine two examples in this section on the premise that an example transcends the function of mere illustration. Examples can "tell" us something, especially how to close the gap between a rule and its application (Kroß 1999). Examples can serve as "windows into contexts" (cf. Chambers 1984, p. 66 f.). Examples can reject universally held truths and they can pinpoint crucial issues that can be used for further analysis. (Sedmak 2013b, pp. 11–18). In the light of these observations, let us take a look at two examples. In his autobiography (Sugar 2011; abbreviation: SWS) Alan Sugar (Lord Sugar of Clapton) describes his business success in terms of the self-made man: "No one actually started me off" (SWS 84). He describes his childhood as having laid the foundation stone for his ambitions: "My parents did their best, but not being able to have what I wanted made me determined to do something for myself—to be self-sufficient" (SWS 11). He engaged in business activities at an early age, identifying seemingly useless waste in a textile factory as something which could be put to good use elsewhere: "Basically, I'd spotted some stuff in one place and seen another place to sell it. And what's more, I really enjoyed doing it" (SWS 13). His keen sense of recognizing opportunity made him realize the potential value of old wooden blocks destined to be dumped after street renovation: "Bingo! It occurred to me that these discarded wooden blocks could be made into fire-lightning sticks"; (SWS 15). In addition, Sugar soon proved he had a nose for business, or more precisely, marketing, in the store where he was working part time: "I introduced one of my marketing ideas … When asked by the customer for a bottle of, say, Milk of Magnesia, if you were to reply, 'Small or large?' most punters would say, 'Small'. Much better to ask, 'Do you want the small 1s 6d one or the extra-value 2s 6d one?' I applied this to lots of things in the shop … and it worked nine times out of ten"; (SWS 29). Thirdly, apart from a keen sense of opportunity and marketing acumen, he demonstrated the courage to initiate business and accept the risks involved, e.g., by starting up a shampoo production business with Steve Pomeroy and Geoff Salt.

"Steve's family business was lemonade, so they knew where to buy bottles and labels. I could source the ingredients to make the hair lacquer and the shampoo—a soap detergent with a little bit of perfume in it" (SWS 51). Soon he left his government job (much to the disappointment of his father) and became a sales person in electronics. The turning point came when he accidentally spotted some broken TV sets: "I thought of my mate Malcolm, who was a TV Engineer. He could fix the sets and I could flog them. I said, 'I'll take them.'" (SWS 74). Here we can clearly see Alan Sugar's sense of opportunity at work, but we can also see how he found help in realizing opportunity by means of an informal, thick network of friends. He developed a simple business model: you take a discarded, broken item, fix it and then sell it—he followed this model for TV sets then record players and went on to found his own company. When he handed in his notice, his employer warned him: "Let me tell you, you haven't got very good contacts", (SWS 83) which plainly indicates the magnitude of the informal and thick network, N. Alan Sugar started up his own brand by putting a label on imported cigarette lighters: "I decided that I would use my own brand name on some products, even though I bought them from an importer"; (SWS 87)—"AMS Trading" was born. Obviously, Alan Sugar owed the possibility for implementing this business strategy to the fact that there were legal provisions in place to make that possible. At some point—here again, we see a personal trait in his inventiveness—Sugar had a break-through idea: "Ann and I visited my mum and dad's for tea and I noticed they had a plastic butter dish—a red-tinted one. As I lifted the lid up, I saw a moulding mark, known to me now as a sprue mark—the place where the plastic is injected—and in that moment, something clicked in my brain. Here we had a coloured, see-through plastic butter lid, and all I needed to do was to make a similar item but much bigger, also see-through, with a nice grey tint to it" (SWS 107). He ordered a factory to produce the goods and sold them at a high price—"That was it—the start of the big time for me", (SWS 109). After that he produced amplifiers, where success depended on sourcing the right technicians and managing to get into a mail order catalogue; and finally, he managed to enlarge his network, N, by establishing direct contacts with Japanese business partners. This was the basis for the huge economic success of Alan Sugar's companies.

What does this story tell us about the relationship between "F" and "N"? (a) Alan Sugar's capabilities can be identified as key elements in the process of wealth creation (creativity, persistence, flexibility, openness, ability to learn and adapt, and to make and maintain contacts, marketing and sales skills, inventiveness, sense of opportunity). While we do not want to underestimate the importance of those character traits, they alone would not have brought him the business success he experienced without the appropriate environment. We could compare the dynamics at work here with a Wittgensteinian observation on the importance of the appropriate surroundings for meaningful linguistic devices and communicative acts (Wittgenstein 1972, p. 250, 584). Similarly, Alan Sugar could not have developed his skills without the appropriate context; this is not only a developmental statement about the basis of his self-trust but also refers to the flourishing of his capabilities: capability-building is based on informal and structural conditions (cf. Sedmak 2011). (b) N turns out to be a necessary condition in Sugar's business journey (his parents and friends provide him with a start-up loan, his parents' flat serves as his first storage space, his friends support him as business partners, business mediators as well as mentors; his friends together with their expertise and contacts are crucial to his success. In other words, Alan Sugar needed social capital to be able to build his business existence. "Social capital", as a set of social connections based on access to networks, norms, and trust, enables people who control them to pursue their goals more effectively. Social capital consists of trust-based connections with an expectation of reliability and reciprocity (cf. Putnam et al. 1993). Alan Sugar made ample use of his social connections thus investing trust. (c) F can be shown to be a necessary element in Sugar's success story: (i) Alan Sugar uses both tangible infrastructures (e.g. transportation, communication) and intangible infrastructures (e.g. education, access to credit) to build his business empire. A significant moment in his business life is the miners' strike in 1972 with the ensuing electricity cuts as a consequence: this taught him a lesson about dependency on a thin framework F. (ii) Sugar operated and still operates in a legally structured space (import and labelling freedom, little quality control mechanisms in place, no price regulation, possibility to hire and fire, possibility to found enterprise with little capital). He could not have started his business on the basis of N alone; without larger structural and infrastructural conditions in place he would not have had the environment and he would not have been able to convert his social capital into any operation, let alone large scale operations.

Alan Sugar's story is the story of a self-proclaimed "self-made" man whereby a close reading of his autobiography unambiguously reveals a twofold dependence on N and F. Sugar could trust his family and his friends and he could also trust the structural systems (transport, communication, legal system) in place.

A second example could be the rise of the House of Rothschild in the eighteenth and early nineteenth centuries. The economic and social rise of Mayer Amschel Rothschild (1744–1812) was the beginning of the wealth of the House of Rothschild (cf. Ferguson 1998; Backhaus 2012, pp. 80–96; Elon 1996, Chap. 3; Wilson 1988, pp. 38–44). Mayer Amschel Rothschild came from a family of small textile merchants and grew up in Frankfurt's *Judengasse*. He learned the basics of commerce in the business of Wolf Jakob Oppenheimer where he worked as an apprentice in Hannover, a position mediated by relatives. After that he started his own business dealing in rare coins. The basis for this branch of business was twofold: expertise in numismatics and social capital, i.e. good contacts with the aristocracy. It was crucial for Rothschild that he won the patronage of Crown Prince William of Hesse (for whom his father had also worked). Access to the Court and gaining the title "Court Factor" in 1770 were major stepping-stones. In the same year, Rothschild entered into a strategic marriage with Gutle Schapper, another Court Factor's daughter, who provided him not only with access to economic capital but also access to social capital and contacts. Hence, even at this stage, we can see that three factors played a major role in the business success of Mayer Amschel Rothschild: social capital (access to the Court and other strategic social contacts), access to economic capital, and personal skills such as reliability, discretion, learnedness. He was also known for his detailed catalogues and accommodating flexibility in pricing policy. On the basis of these three factors alone, Rothschild was able to enlarge his portfolio and enter the market of antiques. The business expanded and increasingly included established figures of a high social background. The business thus far made Rothschild prosperous, but he was by no means a man of fortune. His major breakthrough was his entering the world of finance through the provision of banking services to Crown Prince Wilhelm. The "smooth" transition took place on well-prepared ground and according to Niall Ferguson's analysis: "In some ways, the transition was a natural one. An antique-dealer with a growing circle of suppliers and customers naturally would extend credit to some of these", (Ferguson 1998, p. 45). By 1797 Mayer Amschel Rothschild was definitely well-off. In the throes of the French Revolution, business rapidly expanded, Rothschild handled payments from Britain for the hire of Hessian mercenaries, thus profiting from the war. He built up a position as an international banker to Wilhelm IX and was thus able to gain profitable contracts. In 1798 he sent his son Nathan to England so that Nathan could get first-hand experience of the textile business—this was the first foreign branch of his business. Nathan entered a strategic marriage to the daughter of a leading merchant as well, thus gaining social and economic capital in London. Soon after 1807 Nathan was forced to work illegally, entering the smuggling business: "in October 1807 he was sending a consignment of coffee to Sweden via Amsterdam, using an American registered ship and fake Dutch documents", (Ferguson 1998, p. 58; see also Morton 1962, pp. 45–48). At the same time, Mayer Amschel Rothschild benefited from the growing egalitarian consciousness; he entertained strategic friendships, e.g. with Karl Friedrich Buderus, obtained insider knowledge and established a network of allies by strategically placing his sons in various European locations. Part of Rothschild's business model was the categorical exclusion of daughters and sons-in-law from his business (Ferguson 1998, p. 74).

If we were to take a moral philosophical reflection on this well-known story what could we say? What does this story tell us about the relationship between F and N? (a) Again, personal skills, capabilities and features were key: Mayer Amschel Rothschild's willingness for delayed imbursement, his sense of long-term business relationships, his sense of opportunity and his expertise in various quarters. (b) A second factor was the "thickness" of his family network, order and unity, the concentration of sons, strategic marriages. The fact that the Rothschild family could use Hebrew script to convey messages was crucial in a business that called for a high degree of confidentiality. Connected with this inner network of family ties was Rothschild's social capital in a wider sense—which gave him access to information and closeness to political powers. Social capital was the basis for access to financial and economic capital: "Mixing with members of the aristocracy was essential if it was they who governed, and almost as much political information came from informal socialising as from formal meetings with ministers" (Ferguson 1998, p. 8). This is a clear understanding of the importance of "N", networks in various degrees of "thickness". (c) A third factor touches upon the framework "F": Niall Ferguson identifies "political confidence" as a decisive factor in the history of the rise of the House of Rothschild (Ferguson 1998, p. 5). This is to say that investors need to trust the states with which they do business; they need to trust states to honour their contractual obligations. This is a matter of political and legal frameworks. Representatives of these frameworks (Princes, Kings) were part of the Rothschild network. In other words, part of his success was the fact that he bridged the gap between N and F by entering network relationships with F-authorities.

Again, we see the dependence of an individual person's economic success on N and F and the key role of "trust". Mayer Amschel Rothschild could trust his family, his business friends and he could also base his business on "political confidence" including trust in the communication and transport systems. What does that tell us about the relationship between F and N?

2.3 What is the Relationship Between ('Thin') F and ('Thick') N? The Idea of Reciprocity

The stories told in the two examples above confirm normative considerations presented by Thomas Nagel and Liam Murphy (Murphy and Nagel 2002). A legal and political framework including the idea of property and property rights enables economic activities and network formation. "Private property is a legal convention, defined in part by the tax system; therefore the tax system cannot be evaluated by looking at its impact on private property, conceived as something that has independent existence and validity. Taxes must be evaluated as part of the overall system of property rights that they help to create" (Murphy and Nagel 2002, p. 8). Both informal networks and individual efforts towards wealth-generation are based on a framework including infrastructural features that have been produced by communal efforts. Networks can only prosper on the basis of reliable frameworks. Networks need to be cultivated and maintained, and in order to do that we need certain tangible as well as intangible infrastructures such as values, knowledge, trust. F provides tangible infrastructures such as communication and transportation and the infrastructure of public space. Informal networks provide intangible infrastructures such as ideas, trust, knowledge, values, and beliefs. These value and knowledge systems are formed on the basis of conversations. The proper place for conversation is encounter within networks. Whereas the political framework provides a legal system, networks N provide the "sense of justice" necessary for the legal system (Sedmak 2013b, pp. 126–129). Tangible structures as provided by F depend on intangible structures as provided by N. Katie Warfield, Erin Schultz and Kelsey Johnson regard intangible infrastructures as a: "soft infrastructure that facilitates the functioning and management of a tangible infrastructure" (Warfield et al. 2007, p. 2). One could perhaps illustrate "facilitating" thus: a tangible road network infrastructure can only achieve what it is meant for if those using it abide by the rules of the highway code i.e., stick to a standard code of conduct, have a keen sense of obligation and willingness to work together with other road users. In the public space intangible and tangible infrastructures come together, F and N are inextricably linked; one example in this regard is cultural infrastructures: "The cultural infrastructure is partly tangible and partly intangible. Architecture is the most visible example of the tangible cultural infrastructure, while all cultural ideas (what we could call the 'recipes' of culture) constitute the intangible infrastructure." (Andersson 2006, p. 5). Ideas are a core ingredient of intangibles and manifest themselves in the tangibles of architectural structures, office blocks, schools and/or other works of art. "In many instances, the intangible infrastructure is a precondition for the tangible: think of Modernism and its effect on architecture and industrial design in the nineteenth and twentieth centuries. Intangible ideas, expressed as creativity or innovations, facilitate the transformation of infrastructure" (Keane 2009, p. 79). Frameworks, on the other hand, provide the context within which networks can flourish: Orwell's dystopia *Nineteen Eighty Four* presents a scenario where a totalitarian framework undermines network building and a culture of trust necessary for friendships. Ismail Kadare's novel *The Palace of Dreams* or Franz Kafka's works, to name but two other literary examples, would give us similar accounts. Networks need a climate of trust that is also based on the reliability of the wider political framework (Kadare and Bray 2008). Networks cannot flourish within a climate of suspicion. On the other hand, particularistic trust, as shown in networks, is the basis for general trust required for the functioning of F (Luo 2005). There seems to be reciprocity at work here: F provides the context for N to flourish, F would soon lose credibility without supporting networks following an Aristotelian thought of the importance of civic friendships for a vital political life (Scorza 2004).

An important contribution towards a deeper understanding of the mutual connectivity between F and N can be found in the documents of the Catholic Social Teaching tradition. Catholic Social Teaching operates within the assumption of permeability between micro categories and macro structures (see Sedmak 2014): Categories describing face-to-face interaction are relevant in shaping structures: "Respect" and "Love" can be reconstructed as political categories (cf. Paul VI 1965, p. 28). "Respect" enables a culture of conversation which can serve as a model for doing politics and for establishing a framework F (cf. Williams 2000, p. 4 f.). "Friendship" (again following the Aristotelian model) is a relevant political category (John Paul II 1991, p. 10). The third chapter of *Caritas in Veritate* presents economics and civil virtues as a unity, making use of ideas developed in the civil economy approach (cf. Bruni 2007). "The Church's social doctrine holds that authentically human social relationships of friendship, solidarity and reciprocity can also be conducted within economic activity, and not only outside it or 'after' it" (Bendedict XVI 2009, p. 36). N and F are presented in a way that the one could not exist without the other. Another aspect of such permeability is the relationship between community and society; particular communities are necessary for an inclusive society, i.e. networks that need to be nourished and sustained (John XXIII 1961, p. 146; Leo XIII 1891, p. 51; John XXIII 1963, p. 89), the right to "associate" is a key feature of Catholic Social Thought (cf. Fleckenstein 2002); hence, particular networks are necessary for wider frameworks to be built. Consistency between the various social spheres can be illustrated by the fact that we find the claim in Catholic Social Teaching that "interpersonal relations" and "inter-structural relations" follow the same "grammar", the same regulatory patterns: "History shows with ever-increasing clarity that it is not only the relations between workers and managers that need to be re-established on the basis of justice and equity, but also those between the various branches of the economy, between areas of varying productivity within the same political community, and between countries with a different degree of social and economic development" (John XXIII 1961, p. 122). One element of the claim here is that the meaning of the terms used to characterize interpersonal relationships can be transferred to the structural level thus adding depth to the understanding of the macro dimension of frameworks.

If we accept the idea that F and N are mutually connected, their mutual dependence will have tax policy implications: "Individual citizens don't own anything except through laws that are enacted and enforced by the state. Therefore, the issues of taxation are not about how the state should appropriate and distribute what the citizens already own, but about how it should allow ownership to be determined." (Murphy and Nagel 2002, p. 176; see also Murphy 2005; Maultzsch 2004; Zelenak 2003). The point of taxation is the safeguarding of societal and communal infrastructures. This dimension of reciprocity between F and N motivates the idea of a fiscal contract regulating a balance between taxpayers' input and the output provided by the fiscal authorities. This brings us to the concept of trust.

2.4 Taxation and Trust

We assume "trust" to be a basically rational attitude that accepts our own vulnerability and need for cooperation, and makes us enter relationships characterized by a certain irreducible risk (cf. Hartmann 2011, p. 56). If x trusts y, x hands over A to y. A is important to x, but y may damage or destroy A, and there is no guarantee that A will not be damaged or destroyed. In this sense, trust is based on recognition of vulnerability. Vulnerability is the position of a person who cannot protect herself from events that threaten that which she takes to be important to her (Anderson 2014, p. 135). "Trust" is psychologically based on the recognition of integrity, competence, benevolence, and reliability (Bierhoff and Rohmann 2010). Trust is a basis for knowledge claims and knowledge chains as well as for conversations (Hardwig 1991; Cockburn 2014). Trust reduces social complexity and transaction costs (Luhmann 1973). If someone is trusted, this changes her moral status as well as her self-understanding (Hertzberg 2010).

Trust is a necessary element both at the F-level and at the N-level. Jerry Evensky has shown at the macro level that trust can be reconstructed as the foundation of economic activities in Adam Smith's thought (Evensky 2011). The quasi-magical energy of markets that coordinate production and consumption is "unleashed by human freedom in almost magical ways… only where trust prevails" (Evensky 2011, p. 250). Without trust, there can be no culture of private property, no incentive to accumulate or re-invest capital, no mechanism to obtain credits, in fact no monetary culture at all. Trust is a necessary element in imperfect markets (Gilbert 2007). A free market system depends on the fact that citizens trust that their fellow citizens share a moral sense of values and respect the legal framework F. The framework for market-enabling trust is provided by governments and a shared sense of law and order. In his Theory of Moral Sentiments, Adam Smith reminds us that justice is: "the main pillar that upholds the whole edifice [of society]. If it is removed, the great, the immense fabric of human society… must in a moment crumble into atoms" (Smith 2002, p. 86). There is also a political meaning of trust in the sense that: "lack of confidence in government increases the cost of maintaining social stability and decreases the productivity of society" (Evensky 2011, p. 260)—if there is no trust, rules will not be respected. A good (however atrocious) example of the political meaning of trust can be found in the Chinese famine 1958–1962: more than 36 million people died due to the destructive spiral of mistrust and dynamics of self-deception (Yang et al. 2012; Dikötter 2010). The importance of trust for the level of networks has been illustrated above with reference to social capital theories. Trust requires a particular "climate" to flourish, even in the political sphere (cf. Hartmann 2011). One element of this climate are soft factors such as N-aspects. Now, if F and N are both necessary for the generation (and maintenance) of tax-relevant income or capital, there can be no doubt that the issue of trust is key to considerations of tax justice in particular or the idea of taxation in general.

However, there seems to be a certain crisis of trust. Onora O'Neill discussed this crisis in both her Gifford and her Reith Lectures using the National Health Service (NHS) as her UK-based example (O'Neill 2002). O'Neill discusses the phenomenon of misplaced mistrust which has lost recognition over the debates about misplaced trust. She reminds readers (if we continue in the "signs" we have used so far in this article) that the N-dimension of personal relationships cannot be reduced to the F-dimension: if F is a legal framework providing contractual relationships and if N is the level of networks with personal relationships based on trust, it can clearly be shown that contracts cannot be entered in a trust-less atmosphere. Trust is valuable social capital; we need trust to understand a contract, to allow for contingencies and the proper application of a contract which cannot be realized by drawing up and implementing yet another contract. Hence, there is a primacy of trust over contract. Without trust no institution and no profession can offer areas of cooperation. O'Neill states that we find ourselves in a crisis of trust and a culture of mistrust and suspicion because of deception, terrorism, new hazards, higher levels of information, an increased sense of rights and entitlements, etc. Whereas trust often invites reciprocal trust thus triggering a 'virtuous' spiral, mistrust can trigger the dynamics of increased and recursive mistrust. One standard answer to counter the culture of suspicion is the introduction of a culture of accountability and mechanisms of auditing (O'Neill 2002, pp. 129–134; see also Power 1997). A culture of accountability, however, can lead to even higher levels of mistrust, i.e., not only in terms of "who will guard the guardians", but also in terms of more contractualizing (including relationships), especially if there is no "intelligent accountability" allowing for judgement to be made or a rational discussion of indicators and criteria. A second solution O'Neill puts forward to counter the culture of suspicion is to introduce higher levels of transparency which, again, is not bad in itself, but does not help to reduce mistrust if we are simply confronted with "more information". Here again, we need "intelligent transparency" with a sense of judgement. The real enemy of trust is "deception" (rather than "secrecy"). Hence, the target of a culture of transparency will have to both avoid and unveil deception, thus establishing a culture of truthfulness. O'Neill's suggestion points towards a concept of "reasonable trust" or "justified trust"—a culture of trust based on moral standards and rational justification as "reasonably placed trust". This kind of trust is justified and not "blind", but still needs to recognize human vulnerability and the fact that we have to accept risks and cannot fully control the world around us. The basis for reasonably based trust is also the reasonable insight into the need for cooperation.

So, what is the connection between these discussions about trust for and against institutions and the question of taxation? We could identify several points: (i) there is a culture of suspicion regarding both tax compliance on the side of the taxpayers (and new arrangements with financial institutions to reduce tax evasion) and tax spending on the side of the debt-incurring public budgets. (ii) There is a tendency to move towards more tax transparency and tax accountability as mechanisms to counter this culture of suspicion. (iii) There is a tendency to see the relationship between taxpayer and fiscal authority as a contractual relationship. The term "fiscal contract" is indicative. It is a normative tool to capture the balance between the taxpayers' input and the output provided by the fiscal authorities and to illustrate or assess the 'ethics' of this balance according to normative standards. Normative tax theory offers two key principles for fair taxation: the benefit principle and the ability-to-pay principle (Musgrave 2005). The benefit principle states that each individual's tax burden ought to be commensurate to the benefits he or she receives from the government. The ability-to-pay principle states that the tax burden ought to be related to the taxpayer's level of economic well-being (Slemrod and Bakija 2004, p. 59). The benefit view sees taxes as the price for public services, and fair taxation as the 'correct'—cheapest possible—price, and is therefore *prima vista* normatively 'complete'. It rests on a natural order where, as suggested by John Locke and Adam Smith, the invisible hand of the market yields a result that is both efficient and just. Furthermore the claim of fair benefit taxation requires the premise that the distribution of income must also be just, as first articulated by Knut Wicksell (Musgrave 2005). Be that as it may, the ability-to-pay principle demands normative completion since it focuses on the tax side of the picture only. The taxpayer incurs a loss and taxation should spread that loss in a fair and equitable fashion, hence according to their 'ability to pay'. These principles are framed within contractual models of the fiscal authority-taxpayer relationship. This is important and well justified—as much as a culture of transparency and a culture of accountability.

However, if we take the primacy of trust (over contract) and the significance of trust both for F and for N seriously, we cannot stop there. The basic element to shape the relationship between fiscal authority and taxpayer needs to be: trust. Thomas Aquinas famously suggested a common-good orientation as a basic condition for public trust and just laws. "A law, properly speaking, regards first and foremost the order to the common good." (Aquinas 1981, I–II 90,3 resp). Unjust laws undermine the common good (Aquinas 1981, I–II 96,4, resp). Taxation is just to the extent that it constitutes a fair contribution towards the common good (cf. Meredith 2008) good. The basis for "reasonably placed trust" in the State or "justified trust" in the fiscal authority has to be its common good orientation. Common good orientation can mean two things: (1) Individual tax payers recognize their own vulnerability and their "need to trust" based on their need for cooperation. This has been illustrated above in the dependence of individual wealth generation *on* F and N and the mutual dependence *of* F and N. Recognizing one's need for cooperation implies a common good orientation on the part of the tax payer. Trusting that others pay their taxes (thus showing a common good orientation) will increase tax compliance levels (Schaltegger and Torgler 2008, p. 426). If citizens believe that others are honest taxpayers their willingness to pay taxes will increase. (2) Common good orientation on the side of fiscal authorities can be understood in Aquinas' sense of a *bonum commune*–orientation of tax spending. The point of public expenditure can be linked to the common good. Slemrod and Bakija state that the ability-to-pay principle is nothing more than an intuitively appealing defence of linking tax liability to some measure of well-being rather than to an estimate of the benefits from government activities (Slemrod and Bakija 2004, p. 59). We have analysed this difference in the normative range as reflecting different traditions of conceptualizing the welfare state, with the benefit principle proving typical for the individualistic Anglo-Saxon and US-public reasoning and the ability-to-pay view, with a demand for an ethics of welfare being more representative for the continental 'European' tradition of the welfare state (Gaisbauer 2014). While the benefit view allows for controlling government expenditure structures and is therefore in line with requirements from democracy it fails to accurately conceptualize citizenship, i.e. membership of a political community with *on modus operandi* that is by no way explained sufficiently by invisible-hand considerations. F and N, as we have attempted to show, are mutually connected, with individuals depending on both F and N for their economic success. Thus, an ethics of taxation built on conceptions of the self-interested individual is not convincing for welfare state policies. On the other hand, the ability-to-pay view is normatively incompatible to (fiscal) contract theory. Such a perspective asks for benefit considerations to be at the core of the theory. Our proposition is to view taxation as contribution-tax to public action that realizes the common good. Clearly such a concept understands benefit in terms of consent over a certain set of public policy, as contribution to this realization beyond (but not totally neglecting) self-interest considerations. Such a concept of taxation defines taxation as a citizen's participation in general interest programmes. From a socio-political perspective it allows one to grasp the establishment of the tax state as a kind of socio-financial democratic contract that establishes mass taxation in return for social protection, public health and education (Leroy 2011).

Against this background of a common-good orientation as the basis for justified trust, we propose the "ability to pay" and the "benefit principle" be complemented by two additional principles, namely: an "ability to trust" principle (adapting levels of taxation to the level of the justification of trust) and a "responsibility to trust" principle making representatives of F or N as well as individuals recognize the social feature of dependence, the human factor of vulnerability, and the need for mutual cooperation. "Trust" then, is not a "nice to have" factor—but (as "justified trust") the basis for tax justice as such. There will have to be further discussions about issues such as: What does it mean for fiscal authorities to accept their own vulnerability? or How does recognizing vulnerability and the need for cooperation influence tax compliance? Such debates would complement the discourse on the fiscal contract with a discourse on "fiscal trust".

References

Anderson, Joel. 2014. Autonomy and vulnerability intertwined. In *Vulnerability*, ed. Catriona Mackenzie, Wendy Rogers, and Susan Dodds, 134–161. New York: Oxford University Press.

Andersson, Ake E. 2006. *The economics of experiences, the arts and entertainment*. Cheltenham: Edward Elgar.

Aquinas, Thomas. 1981. *Summa Theologica. Complete English ed.* Westminster: Christian Classics.

Backhaus, Fritz. 2012. *Mayer Amschel Rothschild: Ein biografisches Porträt. Originalausgabe. Herder Spektrum 6232*. Freiburg im Breisgau: Herder.

Bendedict XVI. 2009. 'Caritas in Veritate'—Encyclical Letter of His Holiness Benedict XVI. http://www.vatican.va/holy_father/benedict_xvi/encyclicals/documents/hf_ben-xvi_enc_20090629_caritas-in-veritate_en.html. Accessed 17 Sept 2014.

Bierhoff, Hans-Werner, and Elke Rohmann. 2010. Psychologie des Vertrauens. In *Vertrauen—Zwischen sozialem Kitt und der Senkung von Transaktionskosten*, ed. Matthias Maring, 71–89. Karlsruhe: KIT Scientific Publishing.

Bruni, Luigino. 2007. *Civil economy: Efficiency, equity, public happiness. Frontiers of business ethics v. 2*. Bern: Peter Lang.

Chambers, Robert. 1984. *Rural development: Putting the last first*. 1st edn. London: Longman.

Cockburn, David. 2014. Trust in conversation. *Nordic Wittgenstein Review* 3 (1) (June).

Collins, Chuck, Lapham, Mike, and Scott Klinger. 2004. I Didn't Do It Alone: Society's Contribution to Individual Wealth and Success. Boston: United for a Fair Economy. http://www.faireconomy.org/files/pdf/notalonereportfinal.pdf. Accessed 15 Sept 2014.

Dikötter, Frank. 2010. *Mao's great famine: The history of China's most devastating catastrophe, 1958–1962*. London: Bloomsbury.

Elon, Amos. 1996. *Founder: A portrait of the first rothschild and his time*. New York: Viking.

Evensky, Jerry. 2011. Adam Smith's essentials: On trust, faith, and free markets. *Journal of the History of Economic Thought* 33 (2): 249–267.

Ferguson, Niall. 1998. *The house of rothschild*. New York: Penguin.

Fleckenstein, Marilynn P. 2002. The 'right to associate' in catholic social thought. *Journal of Business Ethics* 38 (1/2): 55–64. doi:10.2307/25074777.

Gaisbauer, Helmut P. 2014. Steuergerechtigkeit, Prinzipien der Besteuerung und die steuerethische Begründung des Europäischen Wohlfahrtsstaates. In *Gerechtigkeit. Vom Wert der Verhältnismäßigkeit Grundwerte Europas*, ed. Clemens Sedmak 4:93–112. Darmstadt: Wissenschaftliche Buchgesellschaft.

Gaisbauer, Helmut P., Otto Neumaier, Gottfried Schweiger, and Clemens Sedmak, eds. 2013. *Erbschaftssteuer im Kontext*. Wiesbaden: VS.

Gilbert, Dirk Ulrich. 2007. Vertrauen als Gegenstand der ökonomischen Theorie. *Zeitschrift für Management* 2 (1): 60–107.

Govier, Trudy. 1993. Self trust, autonomy, and self-esteem. *Hypatia* 8 (1): 99–120.

Hardwig, John. 1991. The role of trust in knowledge. *The Journal of Philosophy* 88 (12): 693–708. doi:10.2307/2027007. (December 1).

Hartmann, Martin. 2011. *Die Praxis des Vertrauens. Suhrkamp Taschenbücher Wissenschaft 1994*. 1. edn. Berlin: Suhrkamp.

Hertzberg, Lars. 2010. On being trusted. In *Trust, sociality, selfhood. Religion in philosophy and theology 52,* ed. Arne Grøn and Claudia Welz, 193–204. Tübingen: Mohr Siebeck.

John Paul II. 1991. Centesimus Annus, Encyclical Letter on the Hundreth Anniversary of Rerum Novarum, 1 May 1991, John Paul II. http://www.vatican.va/holy_father/john_paul_ii/encyclicals/documents/hf_jp-ii_enc_01051991_centesimus-annus_en.html. Accessed 17 Sept 2014.

John XXIII. 1961. John XXIII—Mater Et Magistra. http://www.vatican.va/holy_father/john_xxiii/encyclicals/documents/hf_j-xxiii_enc_15051961_mater_en.html. Accessed 17 Sept 2014.

John XXIII. 1963. Encyclical Pacem in Terris of John XXIII, 11 April 1963. http://www.vatican.va/holy_father/john_xxiii/encyclicals/documents/hf_j-xxiii_enc_11041963_pacem_en.html. Accessed 17 Sept 2014.

Kadare, Ismail, and Barbara Bray. 2008. *The palace of dreams*. London: Vintage Classic.

Keane, Michael. 2009. The capital complex: Beijing's creative cluster. In *Creative economies, creative cities. Asian-European perspectives,* ed. Lily Kong and Justin O'Connor, 77–98. Heidelberg: Springer.

Kroß, Matthias. 1999. Philosophieren in Beispielen. Wittgensteins Umdenken des Allgemeinen. In *Mit Sprache Spielen. Die Ordnungen und das Offene nach Wittgenstein,* ed. Hans-Julius Schneider and Matthias Kroß, 169–187. Berlin: Akademie Verlag.

Leo XIII. 1891. Leo XIII—Rerum Novarum. http://www.vatican.va/holy-_father/leo_xiii/encyclicals/documents/hf_l-xiii_enc_15051891_rerum-novarum_-en.html. Accessed 17 Sept 2014.

Leroy, Marc. 2011. *Taxation, the state and society. The fiscal sociology of interventionist democracy*. Bruxelles: Peter Lang.

Luhmann, Niklas. 1973. *Vertrauen: ein Mechanismus der Reduktion sozialer Komplexität.* 2nd edn. Stuttgart: Lucius und Lucius.

Luo, Jar-Der. 2005. Particularistic and general trust: A network analysis in Chinese organizations. *Management and Organization Review* 1 (2): 437–458.

Maultzsch, Felix. 2004. Morals and markets: The significance of pre-tax ownership. *The Modern Law Review* 67 (3): 508–523.

Meredith, Christopher Todd. 2008. The ethical basis for taxation in the thought of Thomas Aquinas. *Journal of Markets and Morality* 11 (1): 41–57.

Morton, Frederic. 1962. *The rothschilds: A family portrait*. New York: Atheneum.

Murphy, Liam. 2005. Taxes, property, justice. *NYU Journal of Law & Liberty* 1 (2): 983–986.

Murphy, Liam, and Thomas Nagel. 2002. *The myth of ownership. Taxes and justice*. Oxford: Oxford University Press.

Musgrave, Richard A. 2005. Fairness of taxation. In *The encyclopedia of taxation and tax policy,* ed. Robert D. Ebel, Jane G. Gravelle, Joseph J. Cordes, 135–138. Washington D.C.: The Urban Institute Press.

O'Neill, Onora. 2002. *Autonomy and trust in bioethics. Gifford Lectures 2001*. Cambridge: Cambridge University Press.

Paul VI. 1965. Pastoral Constitution on the Church in the Modern Word-Gaudium Et Spes. http://www.vatican.va/archive/hist_councils/ii_vatican_coun-cil/documents/vat-ii_const_19651207_gaudium-et-spes_en.html. Accessed 17 Sept 2014.

Power, Michael. 1997. *The audit society: Rituals of verification*. Oxford: Oxford University Press.

Putnam, Robert D, Robert Leonardi, and Raffaella Nanetti. 1993. *Making democracy work: Civic traditions in modern Italy*. Princeton: Princeton University Press.

Schaltegger, Christoph A., and Benno Torgler. 2008. Direct democracy, decentralization and earmarked taxation: An institutional framework to foster tax compliance. *Intertax* 36 (10): 426–433.

Scorza, Jason A. 2004. Liberal citizenship and civic friendship. *Political Theory* 32 (1): 85–108. doi:10.2307/4148170. (February 1).

Sedmak, Clemens. 2011. Fähigkeiten Und Fundmentalfähigkeiten. In *Der Capability-Approach in Sozialwissenschaftlichen Kontexten,* ed. Bernhard Babic, Reinhold Bauer, Christian Posch, and Clemens Sedmak, 29–52. Wiesbaden: VS Verlag für Sozialwissenschaften.

Sedmak, Clemens. 2013a. Erben, Privilegien und Gesetze. In *Erbschaftssteuer im Kontext,* ed. Helmut P. Gaisbauer, Otto Neumaier, Gottfried Schweiger, and Clemens Sedmak, 23–40. Wiesbaden: VS Springer.
Sedmak, Clemens. 2013b. *Armutsbekämpfung: Eine Grundlegung*. Wien: Böhlau.
Sedmak, Clemens. 2014. Katholische Soziallehre und Politische Vorstellungskraft. In *Der gesellschaftliche Mensch und die menschliche Gesellschaft,* ed. Elisabeth Kapferer, Gertraud Putz, Clemens Sedmak, and Mario Wintersteiger. Innsbruck: Tyrolia-Verlag.
Slemrod, Joel, and Jon Bakija. 2004. *Taxing ourselves. A citizen's guide to the debate over taxes*. 3rd edn. Cambridge: MIT Press.
Smith, Adam. 2002. *The theory of moral sentiments. Cambridge texts in the history of philosophy*. Cambridge: Cambridge University Press.
Sugar, Alan. 2011. *What you see is what you get my autobiography*. London, Basingstoke and Oxford: Macmillan Pub Ltd.
Warfield, Kate, Erin Schultz, and Kelsey Johnson. 2007. Framing infrastructure in a cultural context. Creative City Network of Canada. Working Paper 3. Simon Fraser University
Williams, Fiona. 2000. Claiming and Framing in the Making of Care Policies. The Recognition and Redistribution of Care. Gender and Development Programme Paper Number 13, November 2010, United Nations Research Institute for Social Development. http://www.unrisd.org/80256B3C005BCCF9/(httpAuxPages)/F0924AD817FE8620C125780F004E9BCD/$file/Williams.pdf. Accessed 17 Sept 2014.
Wilson, Derek. 1988. *Rothschild: The wealth and power of a dynasty*. 1st American edn. New York: Scribner.
Wittgenstein, Ludwig. 1972. *Philosophical investigations*. Oxford: Blackwell.
Yang, Jisheng, Edward Friedman, Jian Guo, and Stacy Mosher. 2012. *Tombstone: The untold story of Mao's great famine*. London: Allen Lane.
Zelenak, Lawrence. 2003. The myth of pretax income. *Michigan Law Review* 101 (6): 2261–2274.

Chapter 3
Taxation and the Duty to Alleviate Poverty

Gottfried Schweiger

Abstract In this chapter I aim to show that taxation in general and progressive taxation in particular are justified by the duty to alleviate poverty in the context of welfare states. I want to argue that sufficient access to basic capabilities and functionings is an aim that is feasible and a worthy aspiration for welfare states and that it demands comprehensive measures to reduce and to alleviate poverty. Taxation is one important means to achieve those goals in at least two ways: first, it provides the state with the necessary revenue to fund public goods, social services and benefits from which all citizens benefit, but especially for those worse-off who profit the most. Programs to provide better schooling, housing, health care and social inclusion should be funded publicly because they are not humanitarian aid but the demands of justice. Taxation is a visible expression of this duty of justice. Second, the reduction of tax burdens on those who are poor leaves them with more funds and therefore better opportunities to achieve certain capabilities and functionings. This argument is in favour of progressive taxation which exempts those who are less well-off and burdens more those who are better-off. The reduction of inequalities in income and wealth that is produced by progressive taxation and special taxes on wealth and capital income is a favourable side effect.

3.1 Introduction

In modern societies taxation is present everywhere in daily life and is a heatedly debated political issue. Everyone has to pay taxes and it would seem that many people are not very happy about the actual tax systems, whether it be that they think that they pay too much taxes or that the tax burden is unjustly distributed or that the tax revenue is wasted by the state. It is therefore no surprise that political

G. Schweiger (✉)
Centre for Ethics and Poverty Research, University of Salz-burg, Mönchsberg 2a, 5020 Salzburg, Austria
e-mail: gottfried.schweiger@sbg.ac.at

H. P. Gaisbauer et al. (eds.), *Philosophical Explorations of Justice and Taxation*,
Ius Gentium: Comparative Perspectives on Law and Justice 40,
DOI 10.1007/978-3-319-13458-1_3

philosophy and ethics has produced some literature about the justification and distribution of individual taxation as well as such issues as the ethics of global taxation, corporate taxation and methods used to avoid taxes. My own attempt in this chapter is situated within the capability approach—understood as a partial theory of justice—and is mainly concerned with the triangle of social justice, taxation and poverty. I attempt to justify taxation in general within the framework of the state's duty of justice to alleviate poverty. Obviously, such an argument about why taxation is justified is intertwined with and based on an argument about how the state should use the tax revenue and some ideas about how the tax system should be designed. Taxation is to be used for the common good and to set-up and sustain justice and the tax system and the distribution itself of tax burdens and benefits should be just. Unfortunately, I will not have space in this chapter to say anything about why there is poverty in today's world and I will also not say anything about how the current tax systems and the production of poverty are intertwined, for example by tax competition between states or tax avoidance by international corporations or rich individuals (Dietsch and Rixen 2014). Both pose several questions of justice that need to be addressed and I can only argue on a much more abstract level.

If taxation is connected in this way to justice it means that I view taxes not primarily as the price taxpayers pay for the public goods they consume. Such a benefit principle would restrict taxation to a kind of a mutual beneficial contract between a taxpayer and the state, which implies that taxpayers even have the right to resist paying taxes if they do not receive equivalent goods for it or if they do not need those goods (Feld and Frey 2007). The first problem of such an approach to justify taxation is that it is almost impossible to calculate the prices for several public goods such as security, parks and a clean environment, education or health care. The second problem is that it appears to give justification for a voluntary social exclusion of the rich and to an involuntary social exclusion of those who are not able to pay taxes, which would leave them without access to public goods. Both would negatively affect those who are poor, because they heavily rely on public goods and have less material resources to contribute to the state's revenue and to pay privately for social services. The same is true for more vulnerable groups such as the elderly, people with special needs or people who are chronically ill.

In the first section I will present a very brief and imprecise sketch of a capability theory of justice to ground my later elaborations. In the second section I will then argue that poverty is a violation of justice because it deprives the poor of their central capabilities deprived and because those who are affected by it have justified claims towards the state to help them overcome their situation. In the third section I will then argue in favour of progressive taxation which exempts those who are less well-off and burdens more those who are better-off. The reduction of inequalities in income and wealth that is produced by progressive taxation and special taxes on wealth and capital income is a favourable side effect.

3.2 Capabilities and Social Justice

Every theory of social justice has to clarify at least five things: the metric of justice (what type of goods should be distributed), the rule or rules of justice (how they should be distributed), the context of justice (in which social context this distribution takes place), the agents of justice (who has certain claims or duties of justice), and the institutions of justice (who is responsible for justice actually happening). Obviously all are highly contested in the sense that there are many possible alternative theories which can be used to clarify them. My modest aim here is to present a sketch of answers to the first two questions from the perspective of the capability approach. I will do this with the aim of establishing the ground for my main objective which is to argue that poverty is a violation of social justice and that the state has the responsibility and duty to intervene. My guideline is that the goal of justice is to put all members of society, and eventually all humans, in a position to live their lives as autonomous and respected persons as far as it is possible for a society to do so. This orientation on autonomy and respect is driven by the importance to the individual of both aspects and by her ability to live a good life in the sense of a life that she views worth living. Autonomy in the sense I want to point out is closely tied to self-realization, which is not a mere individualistic project of modernity but has certain intersubjective and social preconditions that make it possible (Honneth 2014). The goal of justice is not an atomised society but one in which the individual and the social are in balance and respect is the hinge which links them. Without being respected by others individuals might be free but isolated and abandoned.

The first and most prominent contribution of the capability approach to discussions about justice is surely the presentation of an alternative metric of justice, namely capabilities and functionings (Robeyns 2005; Nussbaum 2011). Capabilities describe the real freedom to achieve functionings, and functionings are all possible beings and doings of a person, for example being healthy, being well nourished or being able to move from one place to another. This allows a focus on what people are really able to do and be in their lives and also allows evaluation of their objective well-being in this regard. But there are also certain difficulties that come with such a focus on capabilities and functionings. On the one hand capabilities and functionings are not easy to distribute and some people are just not able to reach some of them but for reasons that are not relevant for social justice. For example, the capability to be healthy can be made impossible by many reasons that are not controllable such as genetic variation, accidents or natural disasters. It is therefore not unjust, in all cases, that some people suffer from ill-health or are less healthy than others and it is not always possible to distinguish those cases which are neutral to justice from those which involve real injustices. In comparison a strict egalitarian resourcist approach would be satisfied if all persons receive the same amount of resources or basic goods. On the other hand the relation of capabilities and functionings is not uncomplicated itself and it is not always clear whether capabilities or functionings or both are the best metric of justice. Most capability theorists argue that capabilities are to be preferred because of the high value of autonomy and the ability to choose they entail (Nussbaum 2011). If one wants to fast, and for that reason not realize the functioning to be well nourished, then this is not a case of injustice but rather the expression of this person's freedom. On the contrary a society would be unjust if it prohibited such autonomous decisions and forced its members to be well nourished even if some of them wished to fast. The major problem with capabilities as the metric of justice is that they are very difficult to measure and that it assumes a highly demanding concept of autonomy and freedom that a considerable number of people fall short of in real life. The functionings that a person is actually well nourished or healthy can be measured objectively but the respective capabilities cannot and it is highly speculative to try to decide whether persons do actually have a capability and choose not to realize the according functioning or if there are hidden or subtle constraints, such as cultural pressure, that limit their freedom to realize it. Also for those members of society who have only limited functionings to act autonomously, for example children or people with mental disabilities or severe dementia, the metric of capabilities is not adequate. For this reason, a fully comprehensive theory of justice will have to use capabilities and functionings to evaluate well-being and to guide the distributional pattern depending on the particular context to which it is applied.

Despite these difficulties an orientation on capabilities and functionings appears to be the right choice for the metric of justice for several reasons of which I would like to highlight two (Anderson 2010). On the one hand, they are sensitive to what people can actually achieve with the goods and resources they command. For example, a person with chronic illness can have a very different level of capabilities and functionings from a healthy person even though they both command the same amount of resources such as income. The chronically ill person may have to spend all her money to adapt her house or to get help to move from one place to another, while the healthy person does not have to spend extra money on her accommodation or mobility. Such differences are relevant for justice and can only be detected if one looks at what people can actually do and be. On the other hand, the capability approach circumvents the problem that subjective welfare can be misleading in that people adapt their preferences and their experiences to their own circumstances. For diverse reasons such as cultural habits or ideological pressure or lack of knowledge and education people are capable of feeling well and free and happy even under the worst and harshest living conditions. Under such conditions it is misleading to take the subjective view as sufficient and it is instead necessary to objectively evaluate how people are actually living (Sen 1983). If people suffer from ill-health where it is not necessary and if they are oppressed, then there is injustice no matter how well these people adapt to their situation and how high their subjective well-being might be. The capability approach is concerned with how people actually live and not so much with how many resources they command or how well they feel. Capabilities and functionings are ends and not means of justice.

Most capability theorists employ a sufficientarian rule of justice and argue that at least as a minimal condition of justice all humans are entitled to reach a certain threshold of central capabilities (Nussbaum 2011). On the one hand, sufficiency claims that it does not ultimately matter how people fare in comparison to each other so long as they are able to live a good life. A society in which all are sick and die young, and in which all are poor and cannot meet their basic needs, might be an equal one but it is still not a good one and, if it could be different, it is also unjust. Poverty is not unjust because others are richer but because people in poverty are not able to live a good life in the sense that they fall short of those central capabilities and functionings. To fulfil this task, it is necessary to specify the relevant capabilities and functionings but also the relevant thresholds that need to be reached. This opens the discussion about a list of central capabilities and functionings and their justification. Still, no method to select capabilities and functionings will be perfect and no list will be exhaustive. Justice should inform and guide the societal framework and the design of its institutions and for that it is neither necessary to draft a full list out of theory nor can empirical evidence be enough but such evidence has to be interpreted before the normative goals of justice. If we want to design justice in the context of the education system a more refined and tailored list of capabilities and functionings is needed than if justice is discussed on the level of a whole society. For the latter, I would view an orientation on the goal of justice to enable people to become and be autonomous and respected persons as a guiding principle.

On the other hand, sufficiency is only concerned with setting the minimum bar of justice and questions of justice and injustices also frequently arise above the threshold. For example, the huge inequalities in income and wealth in a society without poverty would still be problematic but their critique seems to demand a different rule of justice from that of sufficiency. Likewise, a society would be unjust in which all children have access to an adequate minimum of education but only the members of a specific racial group have access to higher education. A possible strategy to solve such problems above the threshold is either to argue for a plurality of rules of justice—like for example David Miller does, when he distinguishes the principles of need, desert and equality (Miller 1999)—or to interpret the sufficiency rule in a way in which it becomes a rule of equality with regard to at least some capabilities and functionings. I favour the first approach and want to distinguish not only different rules of justice—depending on the capability and functioning in question and the social context in which justice is to be applied—but also different levels of justice—a minimum floor, a medium floor and a maximum—in which the maximum of justice serves as an ideal that is never likely to be realized in full. This idea has a prominent example in the theory of Avishai Margalit who argues that we should first aim for a decent society and that the world would already be a much better place if we reach this goal (Margalit 1996).

As an example, I want to emphasize respect as a particularly important aspect of justice and the functioning to be respected as a worthy and autonomous person. This functioning—and not only the capability—is central for each and every human and reflects the core idea of the capability approach that the individual, her freedom and her objective well-being, is what ultimately matters. Being respected by others (persons and institutions) is not only relevant for the individual self-respect but for self-efficacy and the realization of other capabilities and functionings. I do not see any good reasons to determine different thresholds within this functioning that would allow a differential respect of persons in this sense. Therefore, sufficient respect is an equal respect, despite the difficulty that the functioning to be respected is hard to narrow down and disrespecting behaviour comes in many different forms. Recent activities from capability oriented researches to develop measures of shame and humiliation in the assessment of well-being and poverty underline that importance (Zavaleta Reyles 2007).

To sum up, a social context is just insofar as all its members have access to a minimum threshold of central capabilities and functionings that allow them to live their lives as autonomous and respected persons. This social context can be a small community, a region, a state or the whole world but in my following deliberations about poverty, justice and taxation I will be mostly concerned with poverty and taxation within a state and not touch upon issues of global justice. This is not to suggest that the capability approach in general, or my own take of it, is nationalistic rather than cosmopolitan. The simpler and more pragmatic reason is that taxation today is, with only a few exceptions, an issue of states who make their own tax laws and use the tax revenue as they see fit. There are good reasons for global taxation, especially against the background of global poverty, but I will not discuss them in this chapter. I will also not distinguish different types of agents of justice, such as children, women, non-citizens or disabled persons, and discuss their particular duties and claims of justice within a state, whether it be due to natural or socially produced differences.

3.3 Social Justice, Poverty and Taxation

What does such an account of social justice imply for taxation? How should the tax system be designed? Additionally, how can taxation and particular taxes be justified as just? I will not be able to answer all these questions but rather present one line of argument to justify taxation, in particular progressive taxation of income and wealth, based on the duty to alleviate poverty. Social justice in general demands a state and an institutional framework that is able to guarantee the just distribution of capabilities and functionings and the needed conversion factors. This can also be applied to the tasks of poverty alleviation. Certainly, the state should not only be concerned with poverty alleviation and justice is also demanded beyond the thresholds of poverty. But a minimal just society will be one in which poverty is alleviated and, to the most possible extent, reduced. A basic understanding of poverty alleviation means that the state directs its funds and adapts its institutions to help those living in poverty. Poverty alleviation makes their lives better and has the goal of helping them to overcome their poverty. But why is such poverty alleviation a duty of justice? As a first step I want to bring forward some arguments for that claim. After that I will return to the question of taxation.

I want to focus on poverty in modern welfare states in contrast to absolute poverty as can be found in less developed countries. This distinction between relative and absolute poverty also reflects different methods of measuring poverty (Alcock 2006). The threshold for relative poverty is set in relation to the level of welfare within a certain country or state and typical examples are the relative poverty line in the European Union of 60% of the equivalised median income or indicators of material deprivation which are chosen to reflect those goods and services than are seen as normal to be able to acquire in a certain society (Whelan and Maître 2008). A wider concept to capture poverty is that of social exclusion, which focusses on key areas of social life (work, cultural life, politics etc.) from which people are involuntarily excluded (Millar 2007). The capability approach used as a method for poverty measurement and research is applied in different contexts but favours an absolute approach that aims to uncover poverty and ill-being and not mere inequality (Sen 1983). Nevertheless, there are overlaps between those different conceptualisations and measurements of poverty (Hick 2012).

In a nutshell, poverty is a condition of limited freedom and this lack of freedom is unjust (Graf and Schweiger 2014). It interferes with the justified claims towards central capabilities and functionings such as to be healthy, to enjoy well-being, to be socially included, and to be respected. This does not imply that poverty only violates those particular capabilities and functionings, rather I suggest that it is not necessary to have anything like a full and exhaustive list to show the injustice of poverty. For example, health and poverty are connected through various channels such as the environment, occupation, stress, behavioural patterns, food, knowledge and health literacy and access to health care. Inequalities in socio-economic positions kill people (Wilkinson and Pickett 2009).

The limitation of freedom and autonomy caused by poverty happens in many different aspects of social, political, cultural and economic life. In addition, many of those disadvantages that are connected to poverty are corrosive, which means that they lead to further disadvantage in other areas (Wolff and De-Shalit 2007). Insufficient health or education makes it harder to be productive in the labour market; insufficient income makes it harder to live in a green and healthy environment. Poverty as it is usually understood is a living condition of less material resources and goods which translate into fewer opportunities to achieve valuable capabilities and functionings. Although the capability approach views income, wealth and other resources and goods only as means, as conversion factors, it is clear that having less of them affects the capabilities and functionings a person can have. This limitation of freedom affects both the local and global autonomy of a person (Franklin-Hall 2013). I take local autonomy to mean the ability to make choices that affect you immediately (e.g. like going out for dinner or what movie you want to watch) and global autonomy as the ability to make life plans (e.g. if you want to marry, what job you want to have). The limitation of global autonomy and the effect of poverty on future life chances and opportunities to pursue the life course one wants are particularly well studied. Growing-up poor gives children less chances in education, it negatively affects their health and their subjective well-being, self-esteem, confidence and trust in others (Vleminckx and Smeeding 2003). In this regard, income poverty and other poverty measures are therefore indirect approaches to the lack of freedom and injustice they cause. Poverty is also a condition of having less political power and opportunities to participate and to be heard in decision making processes. It is a condition of anxiety and stress and of stigma and shame which makes it difficult to appear in public (Walker et al. 2013). People living in poverty are more vulnerable and insecure and they are involuntarily dependent on other persons and institutions to help them. Furthermore, it is not something people choose but something that happens to them for structural reasons that they cannot control. This is the case both in poorer countries, where the living conditions are very low and people are trapped, and in richer countries and welfare states in which the main reasons for poverty are connected to involuntary unemployment, low education, chronic illness, disability and care duties (Alesina and Glaeser 2006). Poverty is embedded in and shaped by various social, political, economic, and cultural environments and the institutional framework such as social protection, health care, public services and labour market policies and regulations. That a certain living condition, such a being unemployed or sick, is converted into one of poverty with all those limitations and disadvantages is not something that happens naturally.

These brief remarks should be sufficient to explain the case that poverty is a violation of social justice and I now want to turn my attention to taxation. If poverty is a state of lack of freedom, then poverty alleviation financed by taxation is an act of deliberation. I understand taxation as the legal extraction of financial funds belonging to a natural or a juridical person by the state. Taxation is first and foremost justified insofar as the state is in need of these funds to fulfil its tasks, which consist of those tasks of justice and those tasks that the citizens have agreed upon. This implies that I view taxation as not necessary and even unjustified if it is not needed to secure social justice or other necessary tasks that are demanded from the state by the will of its citizens. Obviously such power to articulate and to express one's will is also highly unequally distributed among citizens, which poses serious questions for the justificatory power of democratic decision making processes and their ability to determine tax policies. In theory and practice a state without or with only very low taxation could exist, for example if a state gains sufficient funding through the selling of natural resources. Since poverty is a violation of justice its alleviation is not something that the citizens have to agree upon and it seems implausible that they could vote not to alleviate poverty—especially not in the form of a simple majority vote that overrules the minority of those in need. Hence, the freedom of self-determination is restricted in this matter.

Poverty alleviation needs funding and that should come from taxes rather than private charity even if this would generate enough revenue. On the one hand, if the funding of poverty alleviation is put in private hands the danger of instability is higher. Private persons or charities could stop funding because they run out of money or simply because they decide to stop giving. After all, it is still private money. On the other hand, it makes a difference for those who are dependent on that support whether it is given to them because they have a right to it as citizens or whether they receive it because they are a charity case. This is a certain form of inequality that should be avoided because it makes it impossible for those who receive and those who give to meet as equals. It interferes with the capability to be respected as a valuable member of society. These arguments in no way forbid richer people to spend their money on those who are worse-off—on the contrary there are certain duties of justice to do so as long as the state is inadequate—but wherever possible and feasible poverty alleviation should be put in the hands of the state and its institutions and the poor should not be dependent on the pity of others. Taxation is then the best way to fund it.

Poverty alleviation is not a single measure but rather a set of measures that are embedded in an existing infrastructure and set of institutions that benefit—to a varying degree—all citizens. A good system of public transportation is not something that only benefits poorer people, even if they are more dependent on it because they do not have the resources to switch to a private car. The same applies to schools or health care or clean and safe neighbourhoods. Only a small minority of the rich can opt out and finance these services and goods privately to achieve the same level of capabilities and functionings. The vast majority, including those worse-off, benefits from those public goods and that they are provided to them by the state and financed by taxation. They are the prerequisite of equality of opportunity, which justice demands in order to enable all citizens to participate to the greatest possible degree. Poverty alleviation is also not only concerned with material resources and institutions but also with issues of discrimination, disrespect and exclusion. It is equally important to create a society of mutual respect in which poverty and a lower social status is no longer deeply connected with experiences of denigration, humiliation and stigmatisation. Poverty alleviation that aims at strengthening capabilities and functionings is therefore not restricted to the benefits given directly and only given to those in need. And poverty alleviation is also valuable to those who do not need it. The safety net of social protection, the knowledge of solidarity, provides the security and stability that one will not lose everything because of sickness or unemployment or the wrong choices. Such security is an important prerequisite of freedom and autonomy to pursue one's own life plans. Without it people's lives become precarious and stressful.

If taxation is needed and justified, how should the tax burden then be distributed to be fair and to support the goals of justice? I will argue in the next section in favour of progressive taxation in contrast to a flat tax and I will also be concerned with the limits of taxation.

3.4 The Case for Progressive Taxation

In principle every member of society should contribute to a just society and institutions should be designed in a way that makes this possible. Equality might be understood as supporting some kind of flat tax, a system in which everyone pays the same tax rate. The concept of social justice I have presented is oriented towards the goal of enabling all members of society to live with certain central capabilities and functionings and one in which all members are equally respected. One could argue that it is not a question of justice, then, with which tax system these tasks are fulfilled, whether it is a flat tax or a progressive tax system or a combination of both as it is most common. Still, I want to argue that progressive taxation should be preferred, even in those cases where a flat tax system would also be sufficient to fund poverty alleviation. Progressive taxation is the idea that the tax rate increases as the tax base does. For example, if one earns under 1000 € the tax rate is 0%, the tax rate for all incomes between 1000 € and 2000 € is 20% and the tax rate for all incomes above 2000 € is 30%. I view two important arguments in favour of such progressive taxation versus a so-called flat rate: the idea of the ability-to-pay and the idea of limiting inequalities.

The ability-to-pay principle spells out the idea that each taxpayer should contribute to the extent that she is not overburdened and that leaves her as much of her income or wealth as possible. This is based on the assumption that the income and wealth is deserved and well earned. If that is the case then the state is only allowed to interfere with that income and wealth to a limited extent as far as its duties of justice demand. In most cases one has to acknowledge that the idea of desert is distorted and that, based on unequal chances and luck, most people are not responsible for their socio-economic position in a strict sense (Duncan and Murnane 2011). While a flat tax would leave that distribution by luck untouched, a progressive taxation does correct those arbitrary market outcomes to some extent. Furthermore, the ability-to-pay principle suggests that income and wealth have a decreasing value as they increase (Layard, et al. 2008). Not only the subjective well-being, also the level of central capabilities and functionings is less lowered if someone has to pay 1000 € in taxes from an income of 5000 € compared to someone who has to pay 100 € from 500 €. Under a flat tax model it would only be possible to implement a certain threshold above which taxation begins but the dynamic above that threshold would be ignored.

This is relevant especially for a concept of social justice that is concerned with providing a minimal threshold. Social justice as I have discussed it allows for lowering the level of welfare support if that is necessary to support others to reach the social minimum. For a society in which some have higher earnings while others live in poverty this implies progressively taxing those with higher earnings and wealth. The state is limited in its right to tax only insofar as it violates other, equally important claims of justice of those taxed, which in my case here is first and foremost that the state is not allowed to make people poor through its taxation. Above this threshold a more detailed account of tax justice is needed than I have presented here. Another implication of the ability-to-pay principle is that it should exempt those who are living in poverty from paying taxes to leave them more funds. This principle could—and actually is—extended to other groups that are disadvantaged like people with disabilities, chronically ill persons or one-parent families. They are already facing challenges and it would be unjust to burden them even more and to add another concern to their problems.

The idea of lowering inequalities is inherent in the concept of social justice I have sketched at the beginning of this chapter in two respects. Firstly, inequalities that refer to people living in poverty while others are not are unjust because they interfere with the righteous claims for certain central capabilities and functionings that are distorted by poverty. As long as there is poverty, there has to be redistribution. However, secondly, inequalities above the threshold of poverty are also problematic as far as they interfere with the idea of all members of society being equally respected (Anderson 2010). A society in which a small minority is far better-off, and controls economic, social, political and cultural power and resources, is unjust because it violates this fundamental idea. It does not allow its members to interact on an equal footing and it is very likely that those in power will use it for their own benefit and to pursue their own interests exclusively. The close relation of material wealth and political power in particular has to be criticised in this regard in that it makes it nearly impossible for people with a lower socio-economic position to be represented in political decision making processes (Lister 2004). This also influences the design of tax policies which are in favour of the richer minority. Progressive taxation is one—by itself not sufficient—tool to limit such inequalities in income and wealth and to redistribute them to make society more equal. The other option would be to equalise the pre-tax distribution which would demand more comprehensive measures from the state in order to regulate incomes and other opportunities to enhance an individual's socio-economic position. A flat tax model would have a far less redistributive effect. Hence, of special concern for the relation of taxation and justice, is to limit the opportunities for tax avoidance and tax evasion of those who should contribute to a larger extent, such as rich individuals and companies. They are getting richer at the expense of the majority and of the states where they work and live. (Crotty 2012). From the perspective of poverty alleviation, such acts deprive the state of the necessary funding which affects all its citizens.

A concept of social justice of capabilities and functionings demands poverty alleviation to a large extent and that needs funding by taxation. The concept of progressive taxation implies that those who are better-off contribute more without being overburdened. They have a particular obligation not in a sense of charity but in a sense of equal citizenship (Gaisbauer et al. 2013). The limits of taxation are reached when the tax burden would violate the claim of the taxpayer to social justice, which means in those cases where taxation would interfere with the ability to reach the necessary threshold of capabilities and functionings. Or to put it in other words: the most basic limits of taxation are where it would make people poor. Another limitation is that taxpayers are treated equally, so that no one person or minority is taxed extensively while others are left alone. This would possible not violate any claims for sufficient capabilities and functionings but it would be an act of discrimination that violates the demand for equal respect. Other limitations might be developed from a more detailed approach, but that is beyond my concern in this chapter. The same applies to questions regarding how tax compliance can be achieved, which is not only a means to an end but also has its own value since it reflects the relation between a state and its citizens. The task of poverty alleviation and to provide social protection is one that has its support within the population but it appears more extensive redistributive measures are far more contested (Hennighausen and Heinemann 2014). Also the question of why those who do not benefit from the current system are often in support of it is one that I cannot answer here. The capability approach, which supports an objective measure for justice in terms of capabilities and functionings, is more prominent here.

3.5 Conclusions

In this chapter I have examined the relation between justice, poverty and taxation from the perspective of a capability approach to justice. I have argued that the state has a certain duty to alleviate poverty and that this implies that taxation is justified and that the tax system should be designed in a way to support that. As I have said, my arguments were based within state borders and refer to the existence of a more or less functioning welfare state in which basic institutions of social protection exist. For the majority of the world's poor and especially those who are extremely poor this is simply not the case and they live in failed states, in refugee camps or as illegal immigrants. For them there is no state that would use the tax funds for their benefit. Furthermore, there are very good reasons to assume that global poverty is not something that can be solved by the poorer states themselves because they are trapped in unfavourable agreements with richer states, they are helpless against the power of transnational companies and organisations, they suffer from the tax avoidance and tax evasion of a small rich minority, and bad governance and corruption. Under such circumstances it seems naïve to call for solutions at a state level and to argue that it is the main responsibility of the state to secure social justice for the poor. These are powerful arguments for global or international taxation, and to design the tax system in a way that supports global justice in order to make social justice possible. Nevertheless, the state will be an important player for taxation as well as for poverty alleviation. It should be one goal to reform the global agenda and another—also necessary one—to make the tax systems within states better and more just. This is particularly true in those richer countries in Europe or North America which suffer from tax systems that favour a rich minority and in which problems of poverty and inequality are intensified through the financial and economic crisis of recent years where such reforms are demanded.

References

Alcock, Pete. 2006. *Understanding poverty*. 3rd ed. Basingstoke: Palgrave Macmillan.

Alesina, Alberto, and Edward L. Glaeser. 2006. *Fighting poverty in the US and Europe a world of difference*. 1st ed. The Rodolfo Debenedetti lecture series. Oxford: Oxford University Press.

Anderson, Elizabeth. 2010. Justifying the capability approach to justice. In *Measuring justice: Primary goods and capabilities,* eds. Harry Brighouse and Ingrid Robeyns, 1st ed., 81–100. Cambridge: Cambridge University Press.

Crotty, James. 2012. The great austerity war: What caused the US deficit crisis and who should pay to fix it? *Cambridge Journal of Economics* 36 (1): 79–104. doi:10.1093/cje/ber029.

Dietsch, Peter, and Thomas Rixen. 2014. Tax competition and global background justice. *Journal of Political Philosophy* 22 (2): 150–177. doi:10.1111/j.1467-9760.2012.00419.x.

Duncan, Greg J., and Richard J. Murnane, eds. 2011. *Whither opportunity? Rising inequality, schools, and children's life chances.* 1st ed. New York: Russell Sage Foundation; Spencer Foundation.

Feld, Lars P., and Bruno S. Frey. 2007. Tax compliance as the result of a psychological tax contract: The role of incentives and responsive regulation. *Law & Policy* 29 (1): 102–120. doi:10.1111/j.1467-9930.2007.00248.x.
Franklin-Hall, Andrew. 2013. On becoming an adult: Autonomy and the moral relevance of life's stages. *The Philosophical Quarterly* 63 (251): 223–247. doi:10.1111/1467-9213.12014.
Gaisbauer, Helmut P., Gottfried Schweiger, and Clemens Sedmak. 2013. Ethical obligations of wealthy people: Progressive taxation and the financial crisis. *Ethics & Social Welfare* 7 (2): 141–154. doi:10.1080/17496535.2013.779003.
Graf, Gunter, and Gottfried Schweiger. 2014. Poverty and freedom. *Human Affairs* 24 (2): 258–268. doi:10.2478/s13374-014-0224-y.
Hennighausen, Tanja, and Friedrich Heinemann. 2014. Don't tax me? Determinants of individual attitudes toward progressive taxation. *German Economic Review*, April, Early View. doi:10.1111/geer.12050.
Hick, Rod. 2012. The capability approach: Insights for a new poverty focus. *Journal of Social Policy* 41 (2): 291–308. doi:10.1017/S0047279411000845.
Honneth, Axel. 2014. *Freedom's right: The social foundations of democratic life*. 1st ed. Cambridge: Polity.
Layard, Richard, Guy Mayraz, and Stephen J. Nickell. 2008. The marginal utility of income. *Journal of Public Economics* 92 (8–9): 1846–1857. doi:10.1016/j.jpubeco.2008.01.007.
Lister, Ruth. 2004. A politics of recognition and respect: Involving people with experience of poverty in decision-making that affects their lives. *In the politics of inclusion and empowerment*, eds. John Andersen and Siim Birte, 1st ed., 116–138. Basingstoke: Palgrave Macmillan.
Margalit, Avishai. 1996. *The decent society*. 1st ed. Cambridge: Harvard University Press.
Millar, Jane. 2007. Social exclusion and social policy research: Defining exclusion. In *Multidisciplinary handbook of social exclusion research,* eds. Dominic Abrams, Julie Christian, and David Gordon, 1st ed., 1–16. Chichester: Wiley.
Miller, David. 1999. *Principles of social justice*. 1st ed. Cambridge: Harvard University Press.
Nussbaum, Martha. 2011. *Creating capabilities: The human development approach*. 1st ed. Cambridge: Belknap Press of Harvard University Press.
Robeyns, Ingrid. 2005. The capability approach: A theoretical survey. *Journal of Human Development* 6 (1): 93–114.
Sen, Amartya. 1983. Poor, relatively speaking. *Oxford Economic Papers* 35 (2): 153–169.
Vleminckx, Koen, and Timothy M. Smeeding, eds. 2003. *Child well-being, child poverty and child policy in modern nations: What do we know?* revised edition. Bristol: Policy Press.
Walker, Robert, Grace Bantebya Kyomuhendo, Elaine Chase, Sohail Choudhry, Erika K. Gubrium, Jo Yongmie Nicola, and Ivar LøDemel, et al. 2013. Poverty in global perspective: Is shame a common denominator? *Journal of Social Policy* 42 (2): 215–233. doi:10.1017/S0047279412000979.
Whelan, Christopher T., and Bertrand Maître. 2008. Poverty, deprivation and economic vulnerabilty in the enlarged EU. In *Handbook of the quality of life in the enlarged European Union,* eds. Jens Alber, Tony Fahey, and Chiara Saraceno, 201–217. London: Routledge.
Wilkinson, Richard, and Kate Pickett. 2009. *The spirit level: Why equality is better for everyone*. 1st ed. London: Penguin.
Wolff, Jonathan, and Avner De-Shalit. 2007. Disadvantage. 1st ed. *Oxford political theory*. Oxford: Oxford University Press.
Zavaleta Reyles, Diego. 2007. The ability to go about without shame: A proposal for internationally comparable indicators of shame and humiliation. *Oxford Development Studies* 35 (4): 405–430. doi:10.1080/13600810701701905.

Chapter 4
Justice, Equality and Taxation

Dietmar von der Pfordten

Abstract Taxation needs justification. Therefore, it is subject to arguments about justice and equality. In terms of normative ethics, justice takes the lead. The article is divided into four parts: I. Formal Relations of Justice. II. Material Principles of Justice. III. Consequences for the Justice of Taxation. IV. International/Global Justice of Taxation. The justice of the contribution/taxation depends first on the distribution of goods made possible by the particular community in which taxation takes place. Fundamental for any ethics is the principle of normative individualism/humanism: *Only individuals can be the ultimate point of reference of moral obligations and hence the justificatory source of ethics, politics and law.* In order to balance conflicting interests the "principle of the relative dependence of individual concerns on others" is proposed: *The more the origins or the realization of the concerns or the interests of a morally considerable individual depend on others or a community, the more the respective concerns and interests have to be relativized in the process of deliberation, and the more the community may decide according to its common goals.* This principle is applied to the justice of taxation. As a basic principle of taxation, a limited equivalence/benefit-principle is defended. The ability principle can only provide some additional considerations. Income can be taxed more extensively than consumption and wealth. A progressive income tax is defended.

4.1 Introduction

Taxation needs justification. How could such a justification be achieved? Apart from considerations of efficiency, two notions are ethically crucial to achieve this aim of justification: *justice and equality*.[1] However, one has to notice from the start

[1] See also, for an initial main evaluation according to equality and proportionality (that is justice), Adam Smith (1776, 350 ff.). Apart from these ethical requirements one needs to take into account

D. von der Pfordten (✉)
Philosophy of Law, University of Göttingen, Platz der Göttinger Sieben 6, 37073 Göttingen, Germany
e-mail: dpfordt@gwdg.de

H. P. Gaisbauer et al. (eds.), *Philosophical Explorations of Justice and Taxation*, Ius Gentium: Comparative Perspectives on Law and Justice 40,
DOI 10.1007/978-3-319-13458-1_4

a fundamental difference between these two notions. From a *descriptive perspective*, the qualification of humans and actions as equal or non-equal is basic. However, from a *normative perspective*, justice is more important and takes the lead. This has consequences regarding our search for a justification of taxation, because justification is a normative aim. So in order to avoid the is-ought-fallacy one has to link the question of taxation to the question of justice.

We believe that human beings and their actions and institutions can be just or unjust. Justice, therefore, is a property of the human character (a virtue) and a property of human actions and institutions, that is, collective human actions or rules, including the intended or unintended results of these actions and institutions. What, then, distinguishes justice from other properties of the human character like prudence, modesty or bravery, and other properties of human actions and institutions like rationality or efficiency? The main distinguishing feature is this: these listed properties are understandable entirely *without relations to others*. In situations which concern only oneself, one can be modest, prudent, brave, rational and efficient but not just—at least, not in the ordinary sense of the concept. One can be modest, prudent or brave while facing an earthquake. Moreover, we can act rationally or efficiently in repairing a bike. By contrast, justice in the ordinary sense of the concept—Plato, Aristotle, Thomas Aquinas and others had already noticed it (Plato 1990a, p. 12e6–8, 1990b, p. 507a10; Aristotle 1984, V 3, p. 1129a25 ff.; V, 15, 1138a4 ff.; Thomas Aquinas 1987, II-II, qu. 57, 1, 58, 2)—is always *related to others*, that is, to other entities which deserve moral and ethical consideration. Therefore, justice is always a virtue or an action, including its results in relation to others, and is thus a relational property. Institutions when they carry out collective actions or when they employ rules imply such a *relational property* to others.

Besides this necessary relation to another person, justice always comprises two other relational features: (1) Justice is always related to some *object*, that is virtue or action. (2) Justice is always related to some *scheme of evaluation/measurement*. So justice is at least triple-relative. The same holds for all human actions which are ruled by justice, e.g. taxation. We have in any taxation system an entity, which taxes another entity, for a cause (income, consumption, wealth), according to some measurement. Because of this relational character, one has to start every discussion of justice with considerations about the different types of justice-relations.

4.2 Formal Relations of Justice[2]

1. The most basic type of justice-relation is the type of relation between two human beings, e.g. between human being A and human being B. The most fundamental requirement of justice is that A should develop character traits and perform actions which are just in relation to B and vice versa. Previously Aristotle identified this

other requirements like certainty, efficiency in collecting taxes etc.

[2] For the relations of justice, see von der Pfordten (2008).

basic relation of justice (Aristotle 1984, p. 1130b6 ff.). It was later named "*iustitia universalis/generalis*" (Thomas Aquinas 1987, II-II, qu. 58, 6, 7).

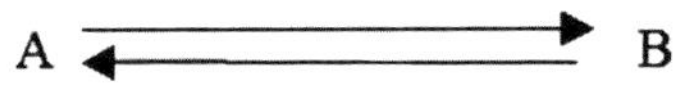

2. Beyond *iustitia universalis*, we can distinguish some more specific relations of justice: The two relations between A and B can be related via the ideal of equality, so via a second order relation.

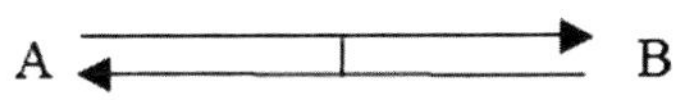

We then get the more specific justice of exchange (1)=*iustitia commutativa*/inter-subjective justice. One example is when A buys a car from B, is the exchange just?

A more simple visualization is by a double-arrow:

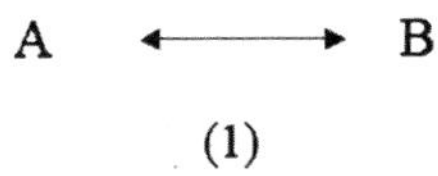

The equity consideration is in this case limited to the pure worth/relation of equal exchange. E.g., it does not matter whether A or B are rich or poor.

3. More complex and decisive for our question concerning the justification of taxation are justice relations if one adds a third *relatum*/element. There are two fundamentally different possibilities. One could add (1) another individual C or (2) a community of individuals A and B. We will consider the first possibility initially, that is the addition of another individual C:

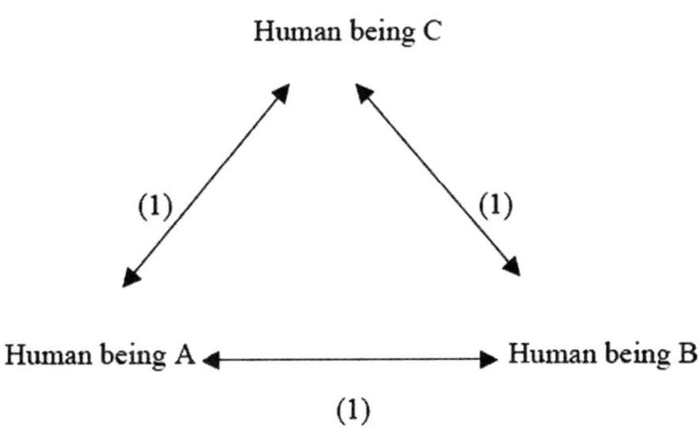

With the integration of a third *relatum* C we face an additional problem of interpersonal equality. Is C obliged to treat A and B equally?

The obligation of C to treat A and B equally depends on the status of their relationship. Imagine C is a private participant in an economic exchange. She buys her bread always from baker A and never from baker B. So she treats A and B unequally, but—according to our assumptions—she is not being unjust.

Imagine now C was the mother of A and B. She gives a piece of a cake only to A, but not to B. So she treats A and B unequally and her action is therefore unjust. What is the reason for this different evaluation? As a mother, C has the responsibility for her children, but not for specific bakers, because the family is a community with relations of mutual responsibility. Therefore, the obligation to treat others equally here depends on being responsible for them. In the economic market, the obligation to treat others equally is reduced or—under certain conditions—even abolished.

4. What changes occur when adding a community consisting of A and B? There are two main particularities emerging in this setting. First of all the treatment of A and B has to be principally equal because they are part of a community. The community is obliged to treat all members *prima facie* equally because they stand in a relation of mutual responsibility to each other.

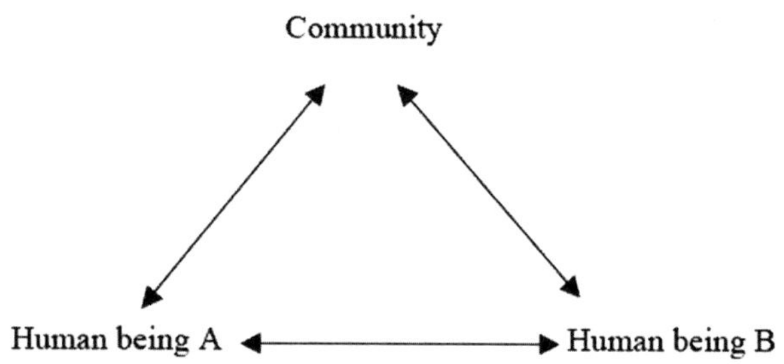

Secondly, the new type of relation between the community and the human being differs in one main respect from the basic type of relation between two human beings A and B since the *relata* are different. So non-symmetry arises in these relations even at a structural level. Therefore, we could split the communal relation into two different types of relations: a relation of contribution from a human being to the community (2) and a relation of distribution from the community to a human being (3).

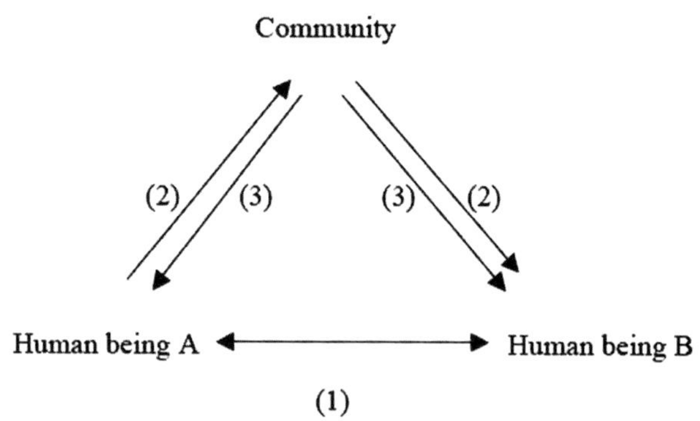

We can identify the relation (2) of the single members to the community. This relation can also be found in Plato. (Plato 1990c, p. 161b5 ff., 1990d p. 370a4, 433a1 ff., 1990e I 127a14 ff.; Aristotle 1984, V 2, p. 1129a33 f.). It was named "*iustitia legalis*" in the middle ages (Thomas Aquinas 1987, II-II, qu. 58, 6, 9 ad tertium; Thomas Aquinas 1993, p. 293 ff.). More appropriate would be "*iustitia contributiva*", or "contributive justice" instead, because not only is obedience towards laws (legal justice) a matter of this relation but also the deliverance of contributions (contributive justice) and acts of legitimisation of the community. The relation of contributive justice is the kernel of our main question, which taxation is just. E.g. are inequalities of income, wealth or consumption decisive? Which form of measurement is justified? A head tax? A proportional tax? A progressive tax?

However, we cannot limit our considerations to this contributional relation because the contribution is only one aspect of the more encompassing view of justice.

The relation (3) of the community to the single member is also mentioned by Plato, (Plato 1990d, p. 433e12 f.), but was first carefully developed by Aristotle (Aristotle 1984, V 5, p. 1130b33 ff.). It was named traditionally "*iustitia distributiva*" (Thomas Aquinas 1987, II-II, qu. 61, p. 1 ff.; Thomas Aquinas 1993, p. 284 ff.). It comprises the main question about the distribution of tax revenues in order to sustain political projects and redistribute goods.

5. The distinction between the relations of contributive and distributive justice opens up the space for three different meta-questions of equality.

(1) One can ask *intrapersonally*: do a person's contributions and her gain from distribution stand in a justified relation? Example, do the taxes and individual gains show an equality relation, e.g. the pensions in a public pension-system and the contributions to this pension-system?

(2) One can ask, for two or more human beings involved, e. g. A and B, but restricted to one type of justice relation (contribution or distribution), that is interpersonally isolating, are the isolated contributions and distributions of different individuals just? This question has two parts: (a) Do A and B contribute justly, in a manner that is *prima facie* equal? (b) Do A and B get a just share of the distribution that is *prima facie* equal?

(3) One can finally ask, for two or more human beings involved and for all justice relations (contribution and distribution) that are interpersonally non-isolating, are the joined contributions and distributions of several individuals just, in a manner that is *prima facie* equal?

6. In one special case, a unification of two of the later relations deserves special structural consideration, if the community directs one action to two members with

respect to their basic relation (1). We then get a fourth fundamental type of justice-relation within a community:

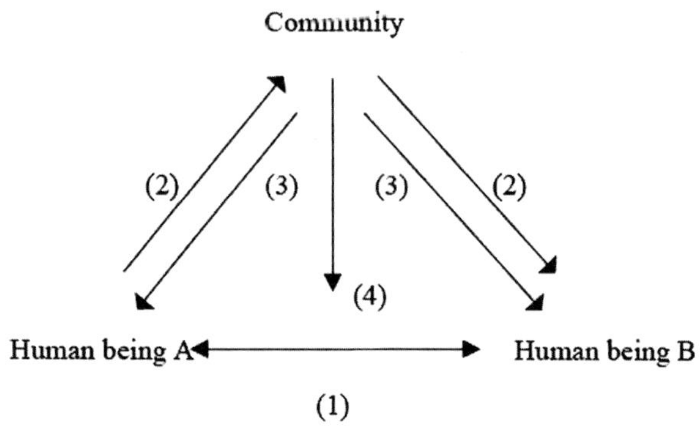

This relation (4) could be named corrective or commutative justice (*iustitia correctiva vel commutativa*). The wider name "*iustitia correctiva*", "corrective justice", is preferable because an exchange does not always take place. This relation comprises the correction of every form of unjust interactions, e.g. in civil law and penal law. It also comprises the correction of historical injustice by the individual members, e.g. through slavery or suppression by private persons or communities. It is not limited to the correction of intended or negligent wrongdoing. It is also not limited to the correction of actions by identifiable members of the community. However, in these cases the distinctions between corrective justice and distributive as well as contributive justice become blurred. In some cases, taxes do not only aim at collecting revenues but also at correcting or limiting private interactions, e.g. the excessive consumption of alcohol, tobacco or fuels.

4.3 Material Principles of Justice

All four types of relations need some material principle as a complement. However, and importantly, not all relations need the same principle as a complement!

In the literature one finds a lot of material relating to principles of justice: the principle of equality, the maximizing principle of Utilitarianism, the Pareto principle, the difference/maximin principle of Rawls etc. (Rawls 1973; see von der Pfordten 2010, p. 168 ff.). Usually the problem is this, many theories of social justice mainly pay attention to distributional relations, e. g. within Rawls, thereby narrowing the concept of justice. The justice of exchange, of contribution and of correction are seldom covered or at least not covered extensively. It is clear that this is not acceptable. Moreover, it is certainly not justified in a theory of taxation, where contributional justice is at stake.

2. Robert Nozick formulated a fundamental critique of taxation in *Anarchy, State and Utopia* (Nozick 1974, 161 ff.). He used the basketball-star Wilt Chamberlain as an example and asked, rhetorically, why should the state be allowed to tax the extra 25 cents everybody pays to see Wilt Chamberlain play? Nozick assumes that everybody who pays the 25 cents originally owns the money paid and that the transfer to Wilt Chamberlain is just. Therefore, he can see no justification in taxing Chamberlain's income.

However, this is not convincing. The taxation of Chamberlain's income is justified because the community provides some conditions that are necessary for attaining this income: public roads, stadiums, police forces, a law-system, education, etc. Without all these partly publicly financed goods it would be impossible for Wilt Chamberlain to become a basketball-star and earn the money. However, we have to formulate this concept of justice more carefully.

3. A first step is to realize that in most cases the distribution (of money obtained from taxes) by the state is factually impossible without any contributions (from taxpayers). Today, the main source of revenue is taxation. Therefore, there is a *factual link* between distribution and contribution. This factual link leads to a first partial and negative justification of taxation. If the political project, which is financed by taxation, is in a fundamental way unjustified, then the taxation to finance this project cannot be justified. Therefore, a criminal regime cannot claim that its taxation is justified. Everybody can ethically refuse to pay taxes to sustain this regime. This rationale was invoked when Henry David Thoreau refused to pay taxes as long as the practice of slavery was not abolished by the American state (Thoreau 1993, pp. 1–18).

However, the positive relation does not hold. The justification for the distribution is not sufficient to justify the contribution and one needs additional reasons instead.

The next step is to ask which material principle can possibly justify taxation. For an answer, I will refer to other work (von der Pfordten 2010, p. 23 ff., 2012, pp. 449–471.). Fundamental for any ethics is the principle of normative individualism/humanism which states that *only individuals can be the ultimate point of reference for moral obligations and hence the justificatory source of ethics, politics and law. Collective entities such as nations, peoples, societies, communities, clans, families, communicative groups or eco-systems, etc. cannot fulfil this function.*[3]

After accepting normative individualism, one has to ask what the decisive normative qualities of the individuals are. Here we see a continuum between purely corporal *strivings*, corporally based *needs*, mostly mental *needs* and purely mental *aims*. These four normative qualities can be summarized under the label of *concerns/interests*.

[3] For an early expression, see Henry David Thoreau (1993, p. 18): "There will never be a really free and enlightened State, until the State comes to recognize the individual as a higher and independent power, from which all its own power and authority are derived, and treats him accordingly."

This leads to a first conclusion with respect to the factual link between contributions and distributions and the first partial justification founded upon this link. Projects of the political community are partially justified if and only if there is (1) some sort of assumed general constitutional agreement of all members to finance common projects/distributions and (2) a majority agreement (or their representatives agree) on the specific projects which are undertaken.

4. Beyond this, what can the main principle to reach a just system of contributions be? A solution is offered by the following "principle of the relative dependence of individual concerns on others", which has been explained and defended on another occasion (See: von der Pfordten 2010, p. 210 ff., 2012, pp. 449–471):

> The more the origins or the realization of the concerns or the interests of a morally considerable individual depend on others or a community, the more the respective concerns and interests have to be relativized in the process of deliberation, and the more the community may decide according to its common goals.

What does it mean to say that the origins or the realization of one's concerns depend on others or a community? There may be two reasons for such a dependency: (1) historically and retrospectively, a certain shared practice serves as a necessary condition for the development of a certain concern, e.g., the emergence of a certain sport such as jogging as a condition for the desire to go jogging; (2) instrumentally and prospectively, a certain practice can only be realized with others or within a particular community with its particular institutions, e.g., the interest to communicate with others or to make use of certain infrastructural facilities.

Ideally, the relative dependence of individual concerns on others takes the form of a continuum. At the one end, there are concerns that depend on others only to a minor degree or not at all. At best, they may be supported by others, such as life, physical integrity, thinking, etc. These interests can be realised all over the world, in all cultures and societies. For them, in particular, the principle of equality holds. The interest not to be tortured, for instance, combines the interest in one's own physical integrity and the interest in self-determination—both of which are not dependent on any community, thus increasing their strong dependency on the individual. For that reason, the interest not to be tortured must remain unaffected by relativising deliberations as much as possible (Cf. von der Pfordten 2006, pp. 149–172).

At the other end of the continuum, there are concerns which are almost totally dependent upon others or the social community, such as, e. g., an interest in communicating with others, working together with others, visiting public institutions, such as museums and in making use of the public transport system, and one's interest in social aid, a common economy, in natural resources, such as oil or coal, and in sustaining the community. For these concerns—all strongly dependent on a community—the maximizing principle notably holds because each concern's dependency on the community justifies the common decision. Single individuals have, in these cases, no legitimization to veto the aim of collective maximization. In between the two extremes there is, e.g., an interest in being treated with respect, in being informed about facts of personal relevance, interests in employment, freedom of speech and the use of one's own goods, etc. In these cases, it is much more difficult to choose a single principle. Several factors are decisive for the choice, like the relative dependence of the interests of the individuals in respect to the community and the importance for the bearer of that particular principle, but also the content of the interests. Many principles are candidates for such application. Moreover, even a combination of principles is possible. What might be a justification of the principle of the relative dependence of individual concerns on others?

The ethical solution of conflicts by norms is an act of collective decision-making, that is, an act of collectivization in respect to the individual person, who has to limit his or her own decisions or life-plans (i.e., his or her freedom) in order to ensure a reconciliation of interests in the community. It is justified that the individual should accept this collectivization in order to ensure peaceful co-existence, and more so when these decisions or life-plans are not his or her own but are dependent on the community.

4.4 Consequences for the Justice of Taxation

1. What now are the consequences for the justice of taxation? We have to ask which taxes are justified according to these considerations. I will limit my discussion here to three main types of taxes: income tax, wealth tax and consumption tax.

At the beginning, it is helpful to notice a factual relation. These three types of tax occur in the following temporal order for the normal actions of a taxpayer:

Income	→	Wealth	→	Consumption
(In-Relation)		(Property)		(Out-Relation)

How do the interests related to these three types of human actions depend on the community?

The most dependent on the community is one's interest concerning income (in-relation), because only the specific conditions of a specific community (e.g. industrialized, good infrastructure, good educational system, police and law-system, safe, peaceful, well-ordered) allow a certain amount of income above a baseline of primitive economy in a state of nature. This applies to all types of income, and also to capital gains. Without all the institutions of a developed society or state, the income could only be that of a farmer, fisherman or hunter having his subsistence wage. This approximately equal income of a subsistence farmer, fisherman or hunter is the measure that provides the baseline for comparison. The justifying relation between income above this baseline and the support by the institutions of a developed society can be called the *equivalence principle*. This principle will shortly be discussed and defended in a limited and special form, leading to a progressive income tax.

The interest related to consumption (out-relation) depends, to a lesser degree, on a specific community, e.g. how somebody could spend his money, buy goods, rent an apartment. Additionally consumption is made by free choice out of the wealth which belongs to each individual. Therefore, the taxation of consumption is less justified than the taxation of income.

The interest to keep one's wealth as assets depends least of all on the specific community, namely only insofar as the stability of a certain currency has to be guaranteed and the police/law protects material goods like houses, cars etc. If somebody has acquired his wealth legally, using money which was already subject to income-tax, it is *prima facie* his free decision to save it, spent it, or transfer it to other people or another country.

Therefore, we get the following order of justified taxation: (1) Income, (2) consumption, and (3) wealth. Following these considerations, the result is that the state is most justified in taxing income, to a lesser degree consumption and to the least degree wealth.

2. A general justification for taxation is given by the *equivalence principle* mentioned. This principle is old (See Black 2010, p. 36 f.). It can be traced back to antiquity. Its basic idea is that there must be some equivalence/proportionality between contribution and distribution.[4] Aristotle mentioned that the contribution of a singular individual is decisive for the distribution (Aristotle 1984, p. 1131b30 f.). Moreover, in the Bible in the 2nd Epistle to the Thessalonians (3, 10) we find the bold prescription: "*Anyone unwilling to work should not eat.*" Thomas Aquinas justified a fair payment to the sovereign for services rendered (Thomas Aquinas 1987, II-II, 66, 8). For John Locke property is justified by labour (Locke 1991, § 28 ff.). The state is legally allowed to tax because of its protection of property (Locke 1991, § 140). Some newer authors have named this principle of equivalence—unfortunately, as I think—the "benefit principle." (Weston 1903, p. 160 ff.; Murphy and Nagel 2002, p. 16 ff.).

What are the arguments for the equivalence principle? Even in modern political communities, the relationship between the individual and the community preserves the original character of the basic justice-relation of justice of exchange. Contributions/taxes are generally justified because of the agreed distributions. However, without this link to the distributions by the community there seems to be no reason why the state should be allowed to coerce individuals to pay taxes.

Some newer authors have criticized the equivalence/benefit-principle. For Murphy and Nagel the equivalence/benefit-principle suffers from a fundamental problem (Murphy and Nagel 2002, p. 18) in that it does not suggest what the tax rate or rates should be because it does not give guidance as to the appropriate level of government expenditure. It takes expenditure as given and allocates taxes in proportion to the resulting benefit. Murphy/Nagel make the point that the issue of the nature and extent of government services does itself raise questions of justice.

[4] See for a formulation by a law-commentary for practitioners: Kirchhof (2013, p. 1 f.).

"Once we acknowledge those questions, it is clear that the benefit principle cannot serve as a standard of tax justice." However, this is a *non sequitur*. It is true, that the question of distribution raises questions of justice. However, this does not hinder the application of the equivalence principle as one principle to link distributions and contributions. The distribution of welfare to persons with no or low income is justified by an additional principle of solidarity which holds in respect of all members of close communities. The existence and realization of such an additional principle of solidarity does not exclude the application of the principle of equivalence towards those who have significant income. Some other arguments of Liam/Murphy against the equivalence-principle will be discussed later on.

3. Another proposed principle is the *ability principle* (See Murphy and Nagel 2002, p. 20 ff.). We find it in an early limited form in Plato: "Everyone should do/contribute his own in the polis." (Plato 1990d, p. 433a.). It was promoted by the Utilitarians to maximize utility (See Black 2010, p. 37). Karl Marx has given it another formulation and linked it with a need-principle of distribution: "From each according to his ability, to each according to his need." (Marx 1974, p. 21). Stephen Weston defended the principle at the beginning of twentieth century (Weston 1903, p. 171 ff.). In our days, the Social Democratic Party in Germany has given the principle a more metaphoric formulation, saying that strong shoulders can/should carry more than weak ones. Applied to taxation one could formulate the principle like this: "He who is able shall pay taxes! He who is more able shall pay more taxes."

How should one evaluate the ability-principle? The ability-principle is strictly limited to the human property of ability but a description is not a justification. If somebody can do something, this does not imply that he *should* do it. Such a conclusion would be a clear example of the is-ought-fallacy. 'Ought to' implies 'can', but not vice versa. Therefore, the ability principle is no more than another additional factual condition. It lacks the necessary normativity.

One could conclude that all three principles, the equivalence principle, the principle of solidarity and the ability principle, are necessary to provide a justification for taxation, but they stand in a relation of asymmetry to each other. The ability principle only limits taxation. One has to be able to pay taxes in order to be obliged to pay taxes. The principle of solidarity secures a tax-free minimum and gives a claim for welfare. There must be a tax-free minimum of income and some welfare-support, because one needs a minimum wage and living together in a community produces an obligation for solidarity. However, the general normative justification of taxation can neither result from the ability principle nor from the principle of solidarity. It results from the equivalence principle. The whole existence of government is only justified because it provides certain distributions of goods.

4. A more fundamental consideration is this. The ability principle is a concretization of some sort of normative collectivism. If somebody can contribute, he should do and do so as much as he can. Therefore, the collective efficiency is the main purpose. Beyond the ability, there is no limit for contributions. The equivalence principle takes instead the individual as the decisive last focal point of justification. It relies on normative individualism. Because the individual gets some distribution from the community, he or she has to contribute. As we saw, normative

individualism is preferable. Only individuals can be the last source of justification. Therefore, they must be its last focal point. Consequently, the equivalence principle is normatively basic. The ability principle adds only some limiting conditions.

5. What can the measurement of taxation be? There are three main possibilities: (1) Strict absolute equality, that is taxation per capita/head, the so-called poll tax. (2) Proportionality/Linearity, the so-called flat tax. (3) Progression, the so-called progressive-tax.

Today, most countries have a progressive tax system with respect to income tax. E.g. the highest percentage of income tax in the EU averages now at 38.8%. Some Eastern European Countries have a flat tax, e.g. Bulgaria, Romania, Lithuania, Estonia and Latvia.

What is justified as the rate of income tax, a poll tax, a flat tax or a progressive tax? The equivalence principle gives the following answer which justifies a progressive system of income tax. The higher the income progressively is, the more the specific conditions of a community can be assumed to be necessary to achieve this higher income. These conditions are means like roads, infrastructure, educational system, health system, police, law-system etc. but also the relative evaluation of different types of work by specific communities, e.g. an arbitrary higher evaluation of legal, economic or medical advice in comparison to religious, spiritual or philosophical advice in modern western societies. The personal contribution of the individual to attain his or her income is necessary and justifies leaving some amount after taxation. However, the increase of the individual labour effort is limited. An individual cannot work more than 12, 14 or 16 h a day permanently. He/she cannot invent more than a limited number of problem solutions and give personal advice only to a limited amount of persons. On the contrary, the external conditions to gain a higher income can rise without personal limitations until a general limit of the nation or nowadays even the world is reached. An enterprise could use public roads with 10, 100, 1000, 10,000 or even 100,000 trucks. It can employ 10, 100, 1000, 10,000 or even 100,000 labourers who acquired their skills at least partially through a public system of education. A progressive scheme of income tax is justified because, at least typically with higher incomes, the possible personal contribution decreases and the contribution of others and *a fortiori* state and society, and therefore the dependence on others, increases.[5]

6. Now it is necessary to come back to the critique of Liam Murphy and Thomas Nagel. They have suggested five arguments against the equivalence/benefit principle of taxation, which will be criticized in what follows (Murphy and Nagel 2002, p. 17 ff.):

(1) It sustains a flat tax.

However, this is not the case as we saw before. It sustains a progressive tax, because with increasing income the part contributed by the society rises progressively.

(2) It does not give us guidance as to what the tax rate should be, because it does not give us guidance as to the appropriate level of government expenditure.

[5] For a formulation by a law-commentary for practitioners, see Kirchhof (2013, p. 3).

Yes, but this is the case for all contribution principles, because the expenditure of the government is subject to questions of distribution. The expenditure is not only an overall decision of ethics/justice, but also to some extent a contingent political decision of every individual community. Therefore, we have to do both. We have to reason ethically about the appropriate level of expenditure and we have to take up the political decisions of every individual community in order to decide how high the tax rate has to be in each particular case. However, this does not destroy the general justification of the equivalence principle for a progressive tax-scheme.

(3) The poor benefit greatly from the government via welfare/health services. This would justify their contribution/payment, which would be, according to Murphy/Nagel, pointless.

However, the very poor are exempted from contributions because of the ability principle. Welfare/health services is a special issue which is justified by the different principle of humanitarian solidarity. Therefore, they have to be left out of consideration with regard to the equivalence/benefit-principle. So welfare/health services for the poor do not hinder the justification of taxation in general by reference to the equivalence principle, i.e. by reference to gains via public projects and general distributional advantages.

(4) The equivalence/benefit principle assumes that the initial pre-tax distribution is just and at the same time changes this distribution. This is said to be self-contradictory. However, there is no assumption by the equivalence/benefit principle that the pre-tax distribution is just. There is only the assumption of an income without society and government and the necessity of contributions to make possible collective projects. There might be some additional reflections about the justice or injustice of the initial pre-tax distributions which might lead to some additional taxation, e.g. according to luck egalitarianism (Kok-Chor Tan 2012). Nevertheless, these additional reflections do not hinder the application of the equivalence principle to justify a basic and general taxation of the income.

(5) The equivalence/benefit principle is not an overall distributive principle.

Yes, that is true, but the equivalence principle as a principle for the justification of taxation mainly addresses contributive justice, not the distinct relation of distributive justice. An overall distributive principle is moreover firstly questionable and secondly—if one holds such a principle—it can be added to the results of the application of the equivalence principle. There is no need to assume that the equivalence principle uniquely determines all justice relations. On the contrary it can be supplemented by additional considerations, e.g.—as we saw—the principle of solidarity, the principle of ability, luck egalitarianism or other political and distributional reasons (See for some: Wingert 2012).

7. Another counter argument was formulated by Verbeck (See his contribution in this volume). Do all people not have the same *opportunities* to use public resources like roads or bridges? Yes, but it is the actually taken opportunities, not the mere opportunities alone, which are decisive. Moreover, the people with higher income, e.g. Bill Gates with Microsoft, use the opportunities *not only theoretically*, but also *in reality* progressively more.

Compare these two examples. We do not pay for the mere opportunity to go to the cinema. Only if we actually take that opportunity and buy a ticket, do we have to pay. So mostly we only have to pay if we transfer the mere opportunity into reality. Alternatively, think of the water or electricity supply. We pay for the amount of water or electricity we use.

8. What about other forms of income tax? Income tax on capital should be equally high as income tax on labour because capital gains are only possible under the same conditions as income through labour. Huge differences between the income tax of individuals and corporations are not justified. Nevertheless, additional reasons of competition and efficiency are allowed. In this respect, there exists a justice gap in many countries today.

How should other forms of income be evaluated?

For inheritance/gift (See general: Gaisbauer et al. 2013), the initial contribution of the benefitted person is nil or much smaller in comparison to the investment of labour and capital. Therefore, the tax can be in principle higher than the normal income tax on labour-income and capital-income. However, there is also a counter-argument: the freedom of the testator must be respected, a person who has often abstained from higher consumption and saved his fortune not the least to sustain his widow, children and grandchildren. This intention has to be taken into account to a certain degree. This is the reason why it does not seem to be justified to tax inheritance/gifts higher than labour- and capital-income. Additionally the inherited property was already, as income, subject to income tax. Therefore, inheritance tax does tax the property for a second time. The consequence must be a lower inheritance tax which can nevertheless be progressive in respect of the amount of the heritage and the distance of family-relations.[6]

For a lottery prize there is normally a very small contribution from the prize-winner, so the tax can be higher than the normal income tax on labour- and capital-income.

9. How high should the maximum income tax be? In Austria, the highest rate is currently 50 %, in Germany 47.5 %. The maximum rate of income tax depends firstly on the amount of agreed distribution which has to be produced by the tax. The decision for a large or a small government is a political decision but within certain limits also an ethical one. Labour is already a contribution to the community. Therefore, it is clear that an income tax on labour of 70, 80 or 90 % will not only cause practical problems, but does not honour individual achievement. The same holds for such a tax rate on capital income.

10. Here, we do not see that the necessary contribution of the community to the individual interest (see the "principle of the relative dependence of individual concerns on others" above) is higher if higher amounts of money are spent. Therefore, the *prima facie* measurement of taxation should be an absolute figure that is a flat tax which exists in nearly all countries. There seems to be no reason for differentiation. Only according to secondary political aims or projects can a differentiation

---

[6] See for a defense of a progressive inheritance tax: Koller (2013).

be justified, e.g. a price support on the vital goods for daily life like bread etc., on books, on ecological behaviour etc.

11. Concerning wealth tax there is only a small taxation justified to compensate the protection by sustaining a stable currency and a police- and law-system because the individual interests in private property depend only to a low degree on the actual community.

12. A last question which has to be discussed is this: what about the consequences of taxation? Do they play a role? This is mainly a question about the role of efficiency. These consequences, such as efficiency, provide only one aspect of the overall consideration of justice, but not the most decisive one. Therefore it is not justified to structure the tax system only or mainly according to consequences/efficiency-considerations, e. g. in order to sustain savings and investments and suppress positional externalities, as proposed by Robert Frank (Frank 1999, 2007, 2008, 2011, see the contribution of Xavier Landes in this volume). Therefore, it is from a justice perspective not justified to e.g. punish the free decision of individuals for consumption instead of savings by a massive progressive consumer tax.

4.5 International and Global Justice of Taxation

1. In reality, we do not only have one but a multitude of communities. These communities can be related to each other in two fundamentally different ways: (1) in simple relations like individuals or (2) as part of a greater community. The difference leads to the *iterative* application of either the justice relation (1) between mere individuals (relation 5) or the justice relations (1)–(4) between individuals and communities (relations 6–8), that is a horizontal (level 1) or vertical extension (level 2).

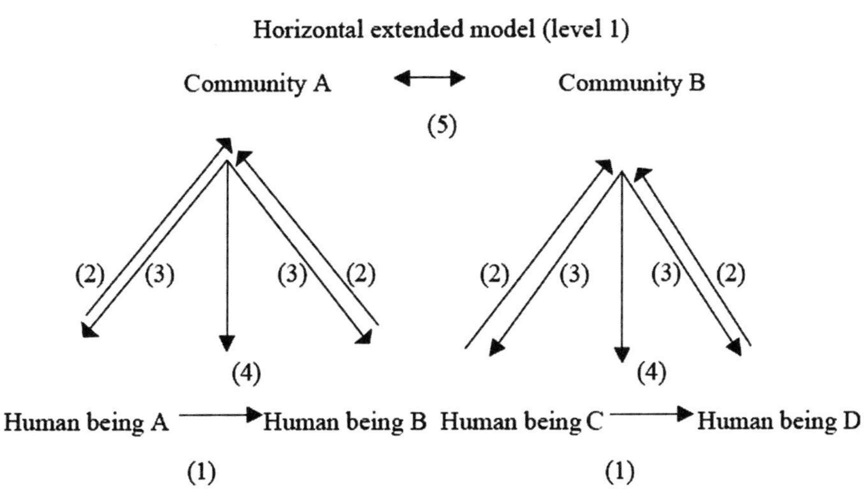

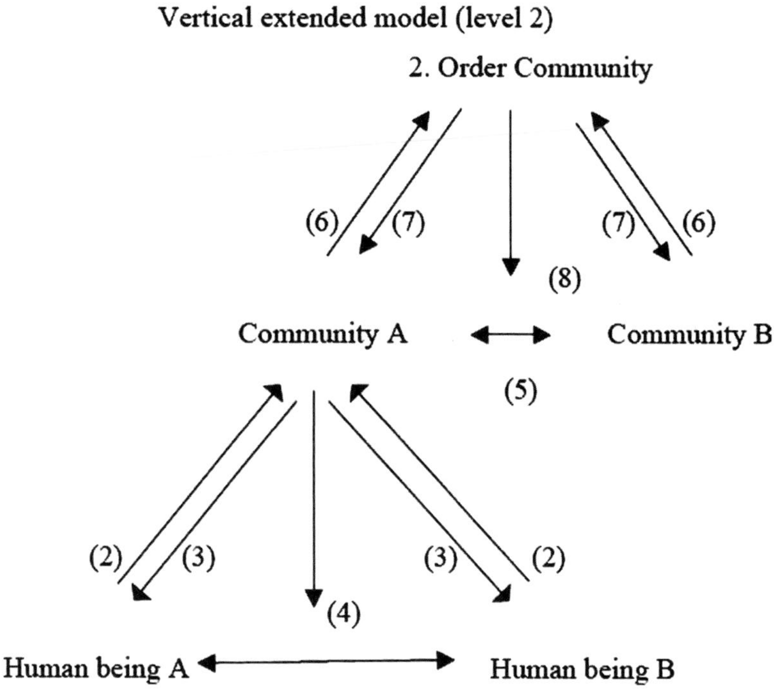

The justice relation (5) between communities resembles the simple justice-relation (1) between individuals.

Theoretically, the building of communities can happen without limitation. Therefore, we get a cascade of communities. This already takes place in singular political communities. We see the gradual development of an increasingly complicated multi-layered system of private communities (clubs, enterprises), municipalities, regional and federal governments. In addition, it takes place on the international and global level.

2. This picture is quite complicated already. However, it is becoming even more complicated because the different levels are *permeable*. The individuals can have a direct relation to the first-order community as well as to the second- or higher order communities (level 3). Moreover, the same is true for communities in relation to higher order communities. For only two levels, we get a picture like this:

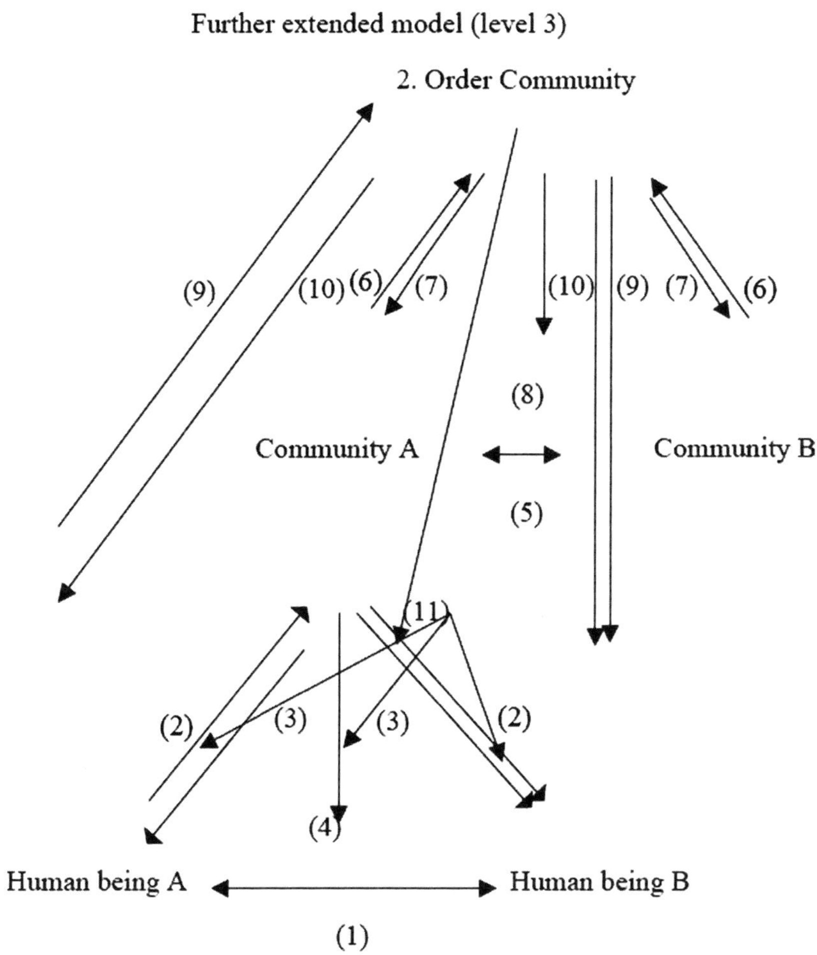

The second-order community can correct all first-order *relata* in respect of their justice-relations directly (relation 11).

Both significant phenomena—*iteration* and *permeability*—lead to an important consequence for the material question of justice. The material question has second- and higher order dimensions. We not only have to ask if we ought and how to build up the first order relations (1)–(4), but also if we ought and how to institutionalize iteration and permeability at the second and higher levels.

2. For the international/global justice of taxation, the decisive question is this: has the transition from level 1 (horizontally extended model) to level 2 (vertically extended model) and further on to level 3 (further extended model) already taken place? Equally, and normatively: should we promote such a transition? The answer to the latter question depends on the distributional side, not on the contributional

side. That is, we must ask whether we should transfer national political decisions to an international level.

For the issue of taxation/contribution, the level that is actually reached is decisive. The principle which applies is this: the more the transition from level 1 to level 2 and further on to level 3 has taken place, the greater becomes the need to apply the normative justice principles of taxation discussed in the previous sections to international taxation.

References

Aristotle. 1984. *Nichomachean Ethics. The Complete Works of Aristotle*. Vol. 1 + 2, (ed. Jonathan Barnes). Oxford: Oxford University Press.

Black, Carola. 2010. *Eigentumsfreiheit und Besteuerung aus liberaler Perspektive. Eine Untersuchung der Steuerpolitik auf Grundlage der Eigentumstheorie von Locke und Kant*. Berlin: Lit.

Frank, Robert. 1999. *Luxury fever: Why money fails to satisfy in an era of excess*. New York: Free Press.

Frank, Robert. 2007. *Falling behind: How rising inequality harms the middle class*. Berkeley: Univ. of California Press

Frank, Robert. 2008. Should public policy respond to positional externalities? *Journal of Public Economics* 92:1777–1786.

Frank, Robert. 2011. *The Darwin economy: Liberty, competition, and the common good*. Princeton: Princeton University Press.

Gaisbauer, Helmut P., Otto Neumaier, Gottfried Schweiger, and Clemens Sedmak eds. 2013. *Erbschaftssteuer im Kontext*. Wiesbaden: Springer VS.

Kirchhof, Paul. 2013. *Einkommensteuergesetz. Kommentar*. Köln: Verlag Dr. Otto Schmidt.

Koller, Peter. 2013. Plädoyer für progressive Erbschaftssteuern. In *Erbschaftssteuer im Kontext*, ed. Helmut P. Gaisbauer, Otto Neumaier, Gottfried Schweiger and Clemens Sedmak, 59–79. Wiesbaden: Springer VS.

Locke, John. 1991. *Two treatises of Government* (Ed. by Peter Laslett). Cambridge: Cambridge University Press.

Marx, Karl. 1974. *Kritik des Gothaer Programms, MEW 19*. Berlin: Dietz-Verlag.

Murphy, Liam, and Thomas Nagel. 2002. *The myth of ownership. Taxes and justice*. Oxford: Oxford University Press.

Nozick, Robert. 1974. *Anarchy, state and Utopia*. New York: Basic Books.

Plato. *Eutyphro*. 1990a. Werke 1. Darmstadt: Wissenschaftliche Buchgesellschaft.

Plato. *Gorgias*. 1990b. Werke 2. Darmstadt: Wissenschaftliche Buchgesellschaft.

Plato. *Charmides*. 1990c. Werke 1. Darmstadt: Wissenschaftliche Buchgesellschaft.

Plato. *Politeia*. 1990d. Werke 4. Darmstadt: Wissenschaftliche Buchgesellschaft.

Plato. *Alcibiades*. 1990e. Werke 1, Darmstadt: Wissenschaftliche Buchgesellschaft.

Rawls, John. 1973. *A theory of justice*. Oxford: Oxford University Press.

Smith, Adam. 1776. *An inquiry into the nature and causes of the wealth of nations*. Chicago: The University of Chicago Press.

Tan, Kok-Chor. 2012. *Justice, institutions, and luck: the site, ground, and scope of equality*. Oxford: Oxford University Press.

Thomas, Aquinas. 1987. *Recht und Gerechtigkeit/Summa theologiae II-II*. Bonn: IfG Verlagsgesellschaft.

Thomas, Aquinas. 1993. *Commentary on Aristotle's Nicomachean Ethics*. Transl C. I. Litzinger. Indiana: Dumb Ox Books.

Thoreau, Henry David. 1993. Civil disobedience. In id. *Civil disobedience and other essays*. New York: Dover Publications.
von der Pfordten, Dietmar. 2006. Ist staatliche Folter als fernwirkende Nothilfe ethisch erlaubt? In *Darf der Staat ausnahmsweise foltern?*, ed. Wolfgang Lenzen, 149–172. Paderborn: Mentis.
von der Pfordten, Dietmar. 2008. On the structures of justice and its application to global justice. In *Political practices and international order*, ed. Hans G. Ulrich and Stefan Heuser, 168–183. Münster: LIT-Verlag.
von der Pfordten, Dietmar. 2010. *Normative Ethik*. Berlin: de Gruyter.
von der Pfordten, Dietmar. 2012. Five elements of normative ethics, a general theory of normative individualism. *Ethical Theory and Moral Practice* 15:449–471.
Weston, Stephen F. 1903. *Principles of justice in taxation*. New York: The Columbia University Press.
Wingert, Lutz. 2012. Mit Steuern steuern? Steuern zwischen Effizienz und Gerechtigkeit. In *Steuern und Umverteilen. Effizienz versus Gerechtigkeit?*, ed. Gisela Hürlimann, 83–104. Zürich: vdf Hochschulverlag an der ETH Zürich.

Chapter 5
'You did not Build that Road'—Reciprocity, Benefits, Opportunities and Taxing the Extremely Rich

Bruno Verbeek

Il faut prendre l'argent là où il se trouve, c'est-à-dire chez les pauvres. Bon d'accord, ils n'ont pas beaucoup d'argent, mais il y a beaucoup de pauvres.

Alphonse Allais

Abstract In this chapter I examine a typical strategy that is used to argue for increases in the marginal tax burden for the extremely rich by stating that they amassed their wealth by taking advantage of economic opportunities that they had not created themselves. I show, first, that these arguments commit what could be called a 'fallacy of composition'. They assume that, since an entrepreneur's efforts would be in vain had those public goods and services not been provided, all economic gain therefore is attributable to these goods and services—a conclusion that does not follow. Secondly, I argue that this type of 'Warren argument' appeals to a principle according to which taxation is the price a citizen pays for the enjoyment of the benefits the state provides. Third, I want to show that such a principle not only undercuts the 'Warren argument', but also that it mandates a completely flat tax rate with no marginal rates at all. In the final part of this chapter, I will discuss an argument for taxing the extremely rich that does not appeal to a benefit principle. This argument proceeds from the idea that justice demands that taxation is levied according to the ability to pay. Social-democrats and left liberals who are concerned about extremely high incomes at the top end of the income distribution are better advised to adopt such a strategy.

In writing this chapter, I have benefitted from conversations with Govert den Hartogh, Cecilia Nalagon, and the members of the Thin Reed e-mail list. A special thanks for Govert den Hartogh for sharing his brilliant critical review of Murphy and Nagel's The Myth of Ownership (Den Hartogh 2011). A lot of what I claim in this chapter, is in one form or other already present in that manuscript.

B. Verbeek (✉)
Institute for Philosophy, University of Leiden, Reuvensplaats 3–4, 2311 Leiden, The Netherlands
e-mail: b.verbeek@phil.leidenuniv.nl

H. P. Gaisbauer et al. (eds.), *Philosophical Explorations of Justice and Taxation*,
Ius Gentium: Comparative Perspectives on Law and Justice 40,
DOI 10.1007/978-3-319-13458-1_5

5.1 Introduction

Since the onset of the financial crisis in 2008, many states in the Western world have struggled with declining public revenues and rising expenditures. Throughout the Eurozone and beyond, 'austerity measures' are being introduced in an effort to combat the crisis. Included in these are fiscal measures. The crisis has also emboldened critics of various stripes to point out that over the last decades there has been a growing income inequality between the very rich and the very poor. Though real income in almost all Western states at all income levels has grown since 1970, the very rich, so these critics claim, have benefitted disproportionately. This is definitely the case in the USA where the top 1 % of income earners now earn more than 17 % of the total income compared to 7 % in 1973. While this trend is less strong in Europe, it remains the case that in general income inequality is increasing.[1] Thomas Piketty has recently argued that this rise in income inequality is accompanied by an increase in the returns on investments that are higher than the average growth of the economy, resulting in an ever-increasing concentration of wealth in the hands of a small number of people (Piketty 2014).

These income differences are enhanced by the way tax schedules are set up. Most Western countries aim at a progressive rate by taxing income on several scales. In practice, however, the rate of progression slows down so much that for the extremely rich the rate for the top incomes is virtually flat. For example, in the Netherlands—my home country—roughly the first € 20,000 of one's income is taxed at a rate of 6 %; the next € 13,000 (so, up to € 33,000) at 11 %; the next € 23,000 at 42 %; and all income beyond € 56,000 is taxed at 52 %. This means that somebody who earns € 33,000 (the median income in the Netherlands) has an effective tax rate of 14,5 %; a person earning € 66,000 has an effective rate of 29,5 %—so almost double; and somebody who earns € 330,000, ten times the median, faces an effective tax rate of 44 %—only three times as high as the median wage earner (Tarieven—Belastingtarieven—Rijksoverheid.nl 2012).[2] If we add to this, first, the absence of a wealth tax, the fact that all personal wealth is taxed at the same (low) flat rate, and the fact that several forms of legally permitted tax evasion are feasible (and worth the effort) for those with high incomes and large wealth, the effective fiscal burdens for the extremely rich are considerably less than that 44 %, thus 'flattening' the rate of progression.

This lack of progressivity in the tax burden at the top end of the income distribution is widely regarded as yet another example of how the (extremely) rich have

[1] In the USA, the top 1 % income earners have earned an increasing share of the total earned income: from 7.7 % in 1973 to 17.4 % in 2011. In the UK, the figures are similar: from 7 % in 1973 to 13.9 % in 2009. In Germany, with its robust welfare state, the rise is minimal: from 10.1 % in 1974 to 10.9 % in 1998 and in France, the share of total earned income is virtually constant. If we look at the change in the Pareto-Lorenz coefficients of these countries since 1970, we see that in all these countries inequality is rising (Saez et al. 2013).

[2] These numbers are slightly misleading as they include the mandatory premiums for collective arrangements like social security and pensions. Without these, the effective tax rate is very progressive up to twice the average income and virtually flat after that.

benefitted disproportionately (see Robeyns 2013). This has led in many countries to a plea for higher taxes for the extremely rich, the so-called "one percent". From the "Buffet rule" in the USA, to François Hollande's (failed) attempt to introduce a 75% tax on incomes above 1 million €, all over the Western world the call to tax the 1% is heard. The additional funds thus captured might help alleviate public debt and it would do something to redress the disproportionate benefits the 1% receive.

These proposals have met with a lot of criticism, especially from the 1% and their sympathizers. There are those who dispute the fact that income inequality is growing. Others claim that higher taxes would be inefficient and drive high-income earners away or provide an incentive to be less productive. Yet others dispute the idea that the current income inequality is unjust since such income differences surely reflect differences in effort and desert (Mankiw 2013).

This last objection is often answered with a specific type of argument and it is this argument that will keep us occupied for much of this chapter. The argument says that the extreme rich have amassed their wealth by taking advantage of economic opportunities that they did not create themselves. Other members of society created those opportunities and reciprocity therefore demands that the extremely rich 'pay' for these opportunities they have enjoyed.

A well known, if somewhat imprecise, version of that argument was formulated by Elizabeth Warren, senator for Massachusetts, who defended hefty increases in taxes for the extremely rich in a speech that went 'viral' on the internet as follows:

> You built a factory out there? Good for you. But I want to be clear: you moved your goods to market on the roads the rest of us paid for; you hired workers the rest of us paid to educate; you were safe in your factory because of police forces and fire forces that the rest of us paid for. You didn't have to worry that marauding bands would come and seize everything at your factory, and hire someone to protect against this, because of the work the rest of us did. (Warren 2012)

Warren is not alone in making this kind of argument, nor is she the first.[3] Similar claims have been made by Barack Obama in the 2012 campaign and by politicians in Europe. However, it is not just politicians who like this argument, political philosophers often help themselves to it as well. Murphy and Nagel (2002) use an argument that is remarkably similar to this one.[4]

In this chapter I will argue, first, that arguments like that of Elizabeth Warren fail. They do not justify a marginally higher tax burden on the extremely rich. Secondly, I argue that this type of 'Warren argument' appeals to a principle according to which taxation is the price a citizen pays for the enjoyment of the benefits the state provides. Third, I will show not only that such a principle undercuts the 'Warren argument', but also that it mandates a completely flat tax rate if not a lump-sum tax.

---

[3] Apparently, the exact wording of the argument comes from (Lakoff 2004).

[4] There is no market without government and no government without taxes; and what type of market there is depends on laws and policy decisions that government must make. In the absence of a legal system supported by taxes, there couldn't be money, banks, corporations, stock exchanges, patents, or a modern market economy—none of the institutions that make possible the existence of almost all contemporary forms of income and wealth. It is therefore logically impossible that people should have any kind of entitlement to all their pretax income. (Murphy and Nagel 2002, p. 31)

It is, therefore, a genuinely argumentative poison pill for those who wish to defend high taxes for the 1 %.

In the final part of the chapter, I suggest an argument for taxing the extremely rich that does not appeal to a benefit principle. This argument proceeds from the idea that justice demands that taxation is levied according to the ability to pay. I will defend this principle against objections formulated against it by Liam Murphy and Thomas Nagel in *The Myth of Ownership* and show how it justifies setting high marginal rates for the extremely rich (Murphy and Nagel 2002). Social-democrats and left-wing liberals who are concerned about extremely high incomes at the top end of the income distribution are better advised to adopt such a strategy, rather than sticking to Warren-like arguments.

Before I proceed with the argument, I should include a caveat. I take it as my task in this chapter to strengthen the claim against the 1 % in a way that echoes the sentiments of the Warren argument, in such a way that it does not fall victim to the same pitfalls as the Warren argument. However, I am not convinced by that argument either—nor am I convinced that the 1 % should pay a much higher effective marginal rate than median income earners. These doubts and qualifications will have to wait for another opportunity.

5.2 A Fallacy of Composition?

Consider Senator Warren's argument again. We can reconstruct its main features in a couple of steps.[5]

1. A person's income is the result of her efforts and the goods and services provided by the state.
2. Without these goods and services this person would not have any income.
3. Therefore, all the benefits that this person receives are due to the goods and services supplied by the state.
4. Extremely high incomes have benefitted disproportionately from the goods and services provided by the state.
5. You should pay taxes proportionate to the benefits that you received.
6. Therefore, extremely high incomes should pay extremely high income taxes.

Two claims stand out in this argument. First, there is the claim (4) that the extremely rich have benefitted disproportionately from the goods and services provided by

[5] Admittedly, there is more going on in Senator Warren's argument. She refers to a social contract and the opportunities for 'the next kid who comes along', i.e., future generations. In what follows, I will largely ignore these complications. Not because they are unimportant—far from it, taxation as one's performance of an implicit social contract with future generations is an important idea that merits careful consideration—but because I am concerned with the first part of Warren's argument, to wit, that without the state's goods and services one could not achieve any income, let alone an extremely high income.

the state. Secondly, the claim (5) that taxes should be levied according to benefits received. In this section and the next, I will be concerned with the first claim (4).

One benefits from something if one is better off than one would have been without that thing. A benefit, therefore, is a comparative notion. So in order to demonstrate that someone has benefitted, let alone benefitted disproportionately, one needs to establish a basis for comparison. The 'Warren argument' does just that. It identifies as the proper baseline for comparison the total absence of any tax-funded state institutions and activities. It explicitly states that all benefits a person receives are due to the goods and services provided by the state. However, it is questionable whether that is the proper baseline for comparison. Several libertarian commentators have argued that rather than a world where these institutions and activities are absent, one should compare to a world where such institutions, goods and services are produced and provided based on voluntary market transactions (e.g., Gordon 2002). Yet others argue that rather than making comparisons with such a state-less, non-institutionalized world, other states with other (laxer) tax regimes are the proper baseline for comparison. If either of these baselines is correct, it may turn out that the state is not benefitting us at all—it may very well be harming us. In other words, the choice of baseline is already a normative choice and the choice that Senator Warren and her sympathizers make, needs defending.

What is more, any attempt to defend this runs into the following problem. Suppose that we can identify a no-state, Hobbesian world as the proper baseline for comparison. Is there any plausibility to the claim in (4) that the extremely rich owe their excessively high incomes to the state and its activities? Take steps 1–2. These are extremely plausible. Consider what is needed for a modern market economy to produce the levels of wealth and income that we witness today. You need a well-functioning infrastructure to transport goods and raw materials to where they are needed. You need elaborate systems of education to train workers and entrepreneurs alike. You need institutions and rules, like contract law, arbitration, as well as the enforcement of these rules. In the absence of a legal system, you would not have money, stocks, or patents, let alone markets at which these can change hands. Without any of these, none of us would be able to seek out an existence beyond minimal subsistence farming. The required institutions, legal and otherwise, and the infrastructure needed to run a market economy organized along the principles of labour specialization, are typically financed through taxes paid by us all. So in a sense, one's actual income is made possible by all members of the community of taxpayers.

However, from this one cannot infer (3) that, therefore, one's income is due entirely to the goods and services provided by the state and paid for by one's fellow citizens. Here is an analogy. It is true that without fertile soil, one's efforts in tilling the soil will not result in a good harvest. However, no matter how fertile the soil, if you don't put in any effort, you will not have any harvest either. Similarly with the goods and services provided by the state, without these you will not be able to realize any income, although, that does not mean that effort and initiative are unimportant and that all your income is entirely due to the state. Moreover, just because the presence of one factor is necessary in realizing the result, it does not follow that, therefore, the entire result is due to that factor. Claiming that it does commits something akin to the fallacy of composition. Therefore, from the fact that without the state, its institutions and the goods and services it produces paid for by all through taxes, one's income would be approaching zero, it cannot be concluded that one's entire pre-tax income equals the amount one has benefitted from the state's activities. Hence, excessively high incomes are not sufficient proof that one has benefitted disproportionately.

5.3 The Nature of Benefits

The previous section dealt with the question 'benefitting in comparison to what?' and we saw that the Warren argument moves too quickly in identifying the baseline of comparison at a really low level of benefit. Suppose, however, that Warren is right and that the proper baseline of comparison is a non-state world in which all the governments goods, services and activities are absent and not provided in alternative, anarchic ways. Then it is still an open question whether the extremely rich benefit disproportionately. To see this, we have to discuss some aspects of the question 'how much does one benefit from state activity?' That is, even if we could identify a suitable baseline for comparison, we would need to find the right metric to determine whether the extremely rich have benefitted disproportionately relative to that baseline in comparison to others.

It might be suggested at this point that there is a perfectly neutral and theoretically simple measure to determine how much one benefits: simply look at someone's utility index and compare this with the non-state world (or any other base-line of comparison) and then you know how much somebody has benefitted from the state. Since we have no direct access to somebody's utility, taking someone's pre-tax income would then be a reliable approximation of the extent of somebody's benefit.[6] However, this again makes the mistake identified in the previous section in that it ignores the contribution that a person's own efforts have made towards his or her pre-tax income. We would need a way to tease apart from other factors the contribution that the state's activities make to one's income.

At this point it becomes necessary to look into the nature of the benefits that state institutions, activities, goods and services provide to citizens. How is it exactly that an efficient infrastructure, a legal system, an education system, the market, etc., benefit the extremely rich? Or, for that matter, how is it that any of us benefits from the state?

We should distinguish between those goods and services that benefit all and those that benefit only some. For example, a public pension plan, like social security benefits all, whereas, say, subsidy for the opera benefits only a few. Another useful distinction is between benefits that are provided directly through the state

[6] This assumes, of course, that a person's utility is proportionate to her income—a highly dubious assumption at best.

and those that the state provides indirectly. An example of the former would be income subsidies for the unemployed; an example of the latter is the legal institution of marriage. The benefits of marriage—recognition for children, the power to inherit from your spouse, etc.—are made accessible by the institution of marriage. That is, they come in the form of *opportunities* for benefitting, rather than direct benefitting. Obviously, these distinctions are not strict. Rather, they are something like the extreme ends of continuous scales. Accordingly, benefits from state activity vary as to who they benefit and vary in whether their benefits are more direct than indirect. Also, the activities, goods and services of the state may present both an opportunity to some and a direct benefit to others.

With these relatively vague distinctions in the back of our minds, let us think about how the 1 % benefits from the state's activities. Elizabeth Warren lists these admirably: the extremely rich in her example benefit from the fact that there are educated workers, that there is a well maintained road, that there is a working legal system that protects property and makes property ownership possible in the first place. In other words, these benefits are overwhelmingly of the indirect kind: the activities of the state provide opportunities for benefitting to the 1 %.

The obvious rejoinder, then, of those who wish to defend the 1 % is that these opportunities are there for many, if not all, citizens.[7] Everybody has access to these well-maintained roads; anybody who wishes to employ educated workers can do so. In other words, if we think of the way in which citizens typically (but, admittedly, not always) benefit from the state, these benefits are spread out relatively equally. This observation is made stronger when we consider that most of the goods and services that the state provides have the characteristic of a public good: once it is there, it is impossible to exclude anyone from consumption. The same holds true for the type of opportunities the 1 % exploits: their presence does not crowd out others.[8] So if 1 % benefit from the state primarily through such opportunities, the extremely rich benefit as much as the extremely poor. What is more, one could argue like Mill, and claim that the poorest members of society typically benefit more from our kind of welfare state since, in addition to the opportunities that the institutions of the state offer, they qualify as recipient of all kinds of direct income subsidies.[9]

Therefore, the Warren argument looks like a poison pill for those defending high average tax rates for the extremely rich. If we assume that one owes taxes relative to the a mount one has benefitted and if it is correct that the majority of the benefits that the 1 % receive from the state come in the form of opportunities open to all, then there is no reason to tax the extremely rich at a higher rate. The just rate will be

[7] E.g., (Mankiw 2013) makes exactly this point.

[8] It could be the case that the use one person makes of such opportunities lessens the opportunities of others, but this holds for anybody making use of such publicly provided opportunities.

[9] "If we wanted to estimate the degrees of benefit which different persons derive from the protection of government, we should have to consider who would suffer most if that protection were withdrawn: to which question, if any answer could be made, it must be, that those would suffer most who were weakest in mind or body, either by nature or by position." (Mill 1848, Chap. 5, Sect. 2). Mill uses this argument to provide a reduction of the idea that taxes should be levied proportionate to how much one benefits from state activity.

a flat rate. What is more, if we take taxation to be a citizen's reciprocal obligation in return for benefits received, then, since these benefits are the same for all of us, we should introduce a lump-sum tax.

This may be too fast. It is perfectly possible that the state's activities do not provide equal opportunities to all. This can happen in two ways. First, it could be that the state's activities only provide opportunities to some and not to others. For example, the absence of good infrastructure in a remote sparsely populated area of a country will stifle the economic opportunities of those residing there. This particular example may be answered by pointing out that in most countries citizens are free to relocate so as to take advantage of the opportunities offered elsewhere, but the general point remains.

The other way in which opportunities might not be equally distributed in a society has to do with the nature of the opportunities themselves. A free-spirited artist, for example, will not appreciate the economic opportunities that good infrastructure offers as much as, say, a zealous capitalist entrepreneur.[10] It is then misleading to suggest that since both the artist and the entrepreneur had the same opportunities, they therefore were treated equally from the point of view of the goods and services provided by the state.

This points to an objection against the defender of the 1 %. Even if we take opportunities to be the correct measure for determining the size of one's benefit, it need not be the case that these are equally divided and, therefore, it still is a real possibility that the extremely rich benefit disproportionately from the state's activities. Secondly, and more to the point, focusing on opportunities as the measure for determining benefit may obscure objectionable inequalities in the treatment by the state of its citizens.

Unfortunately, this answer to the sympathizers of the 1 % shows that the Warren argument and the rejoinder argument are both hostage to empirical fortune: simply the presence of extreme income inequality is not enough to conclude that some are benefitting disproportionately. Close inspection of each individual's ambitions, preferences, utility curves, or what have you, are required to ensure that there is equality of treatment.

We can conclude that the Warren argument leaves a lot to be desired in its defence of the first claim: that the rich are benefitting disproportionately from the state's activities, goods, and services. First, because the baseline of comparison seems arbitrarily determined. Secondly, because the height of one's pre-tax income is not indicative of the degree to which one benefitted from the state, as effort, ambition, and labour are also relevant factors. What is more, a Warren-style argument could easily be made to show that the extremely rich receive the same opportunities for benefit from the state as the extremely poor. Combined with the second assumption in the Warren argument—that taxation is owed proportionate to how much one

[10] This is the same objection that the late Ronald Dworkin offered in (Dworkin 1981) when he objected to the idea that if one divides equally all plover's eggs of his imaginary island, all would be equally well off, as this discriminates against those that do not care at all for plover's eggs.

benefits—leads to the conclusion that the extremely rich should not pay more than the extremely poor: a lump-sum tax.

5.4 The Benefit Principle in Taxation

It is time we looked into the second major assumption in the Warren argument, that taxes ought to be paid to the degree one has benefitted from the activities, goods, and services provided by the state. Without this assumption the question about if and if so, how much, the 1 % have benefitted from the state is moot for determining the proper rate.

The assumption is known in the tax literature as the *benefit principle* (Musgrave 1959). It has a reputable intellectual history going from Adam Smith to the classical continental authors on taxation like Wicksell and Lindahl (Smith 1979, bk. V.ii.b; Lindahl 1919). Nowadays, the benefit principle is in its most plausible interpretation best seen as a principle of efficient taxation, according to which one's taxes ought to be set at such a level that the marginal utility (benefit) of public spending equals that of the individual's private spending.[11]

The attraction of the benefit principle for those who wish to justify high marginal average rates for the extremely rich is clear for two reasons. First, here is a principle that justifies different tax burdens for different people. Secondly, this principle should (and does) appeal to defenders of the market who usually reject high marginal taxes for the extremely rich. The benefit principle demands a form of reciprocity in that it treats taxes as shadow-prices for the goods and services citizens receive from the state. It mimics market outcomes (if there were markets for public goods). So if it can be established that the extremely rich benefit disproportionately, defenders of free markets should feel compelled to accept higher taxes for the 1 %.

The argumentative disadvantages of accepting the benefit principle are also clear. First, if the argument of the previous two sections is correct, the benefit principle cannot give any recommendation about the just rate as there is no neutral, 'natural' baseline of comparison or 'measure' of benefit.

Secondly, the benefit principle has plausibility as a principle for efficient taxation. However, the question about taxing the 1 % is not whether doing so would be efficient, but whether this would be just. As a principle of justice in taxation, the benefit principle is problematic. In order for the result of the application of this principle to be just, the pre-tax distribution of benefit (e.g., measured in terms of income, or, indeed, opportunities) needs to be just as well. If the initial distribution of benefits is unjust, taxing people according to the benefits they received will not result in a just distribution of the burdens.

[11] This is the proposal of (Lindahl 1919). Though many contemporary authors reject it as a principle of justice in taxation, it has wide-spread support as a principle of efficient taxation, e.g., (Murphy and Nagel 2002, p. 82).

Murphy and Nagel develop this criticism further (Murphy and Nagel 2002). Not only does application of the benefit principle to distribute burdens underdetermine the justice of the result, the very idea of the pre-tax income distribution as a morally relevant point of departure is incoherent in their opinion. They give two reasons for this. First, using the pre-tax income distribution as the relevant point of departure fails to take into account the many ways in which the institutions of the state influence the justice of the distribution of goods, benefits, and income among the citizens. This ignores what is done with the revenues of taxation. For example, it makes a big difference if one is taxed and then receives a large subsidy rather than the situation where one is taxed and does not receive such a subsidy. Therefore, it makes more sense to look at the total distribution of benefits and burdens, rather than focusing on the distribution of the burdens alone.[12] This is not a very strong objection to the benefit principle, as this principle explicitly relates one's share of the burden to one's share of the benefits.

However, this leads them to formulate their second reason as to why the pre-tax income distribution is morally irrelevant. In a very fundamental way, the state makes the total distribution of benefits and burdens possible. For example, the state makes it possible for there to be a labour market in the first place. Since the labour market is the place where incomes are determined, focusing on the pre-tax income distribution arbitrarily takes some state activities as given, while assessing the justice of others. This, so Murphy and Nagel claim, is incoherent (Murphy and Nagel 2002, pp. 14–15).[13]

Murphy and Nagel go on to argue that one cannot discuss the justice of taxation in the abstract without considering the overall distribution of income in a society. Taxation, therefore, is just one of the means to bring about a just distribution.[14]

We can conclude then, that accepting the benefit principle as one of the premises in the Warren argument does not compel one to accept the idea that the 1 % should be taxed at a higher effective average rate than others. What is more, if Murphy and Nagel are right, it is an incoherent principle in the first place.

For all these reasons, the Warren argument fails, or is at best inconclusive. It certainly does not justify the introduction of extremely progressive tax rates for the extremely rich.

---

[12] This is what (Murphy and Nagel 2002) call 'myopia'.

[13] Below, I discuss some reasons why one need not accept their opinions on this matter.

[14] They are not the only ones to do this. The general trend in thinking about distributive justice and public finance is to focus on overall distribution of income. The result of this focus is a rampant instrumentalism in taxation that has led to increasingly complicated tax legislation and declining tax morale and compliance (Togler et al. 2008). Murphy and Nagel go on to claim that the very notion of a claim to one's pre-tax income ('everyday libertarianism') is incoherent, since what counts as someone's property is conventionally determined by the state. In what follows I ignore this stronger claim, as it is not necessary to make the point about the moral irrelevance of the pre-tax income distribution.

5.5 An Alternative Argument

Does this mean there is no way to defend taxing the 1 % at high effective average rates? I think better arguments can be made. Many authors, when defending going after the 1 %, take an instrumentalist approach to taxation. What matters, according to these authors, is how the whole of the distribution looks, not whether the distribution of burdens satisfies some principle. Most of the time, the emphasis is on the distribution of net benefits (income, opportunities, wellbeing, or primary goods). Rawlsians and prioritarians, for example, defend taxing the extremely rich if this raises the relative position of the least well off. Utilitarians would defend such taxes if this meant that the gain in utility at the lower rungs of the income ladder offsets the loss for the 1 %. Luck egalitarians may defend such taxes if it can be shown that the pre-tax income distribution reflects all kinds of brute luck for which individuals cannot claim responsibility. Lockean libertarians might favour taxing the 1 % if it can be shown that their excessive positions are the result of exploitative arrangements or 'rents'.[15] What all these approaches have in common is that there is no specific concern for the justice of taxation. Although I agree that a fair distribution of the burdens of state activity should also take into consideration its benefits, I think it a mistake to consider taxation as merely one of the buttons one can push to bring about favoured distributive results.

In what follows, I will not defend my claim that this is mistaken. Instead, I will try to sketch an argument that proceeds from a specific concern for the justice of taxation. In a nutshell, the argument proceeds as follows.

1. Taxes should be levied according to the ability of citizens to carry the burden of taxation.
2. Extremely rich people can carry an extremely large burden.
3. Therefore, extremely rich people should be taxed extremely.

To make good this argument, I should now defend and refine 1 and 2 in such a way that they are acceptable.

Above, I argued that acceptance of the benefit principle in an argument aimed at taxing the 1 %, compels one to argue, first, that the baseline of comparison is relatively low—preferably a Hobbesian non-state world. We saw that there is no neutral argument for setting the baseline at a particular level. Secondly, one has to argue that the measure of benefit is such that it warrants higher average effective rates for the 1 %. We saw that the most plausible interpretations of the measure of benefit are such that a lump-sum tax or at best a proportionate, flat tax are justified. I also rejected, without argument, instrumentalist approaches to taxation. Survey of the literature, suggests that the only alternative is the family of ability to pay principles.

---

[15] I say 'might' because if there are rents in an economic system (e.g., due to import restrictions that favour local entrepreneurs), the first-best solution is to get rid of such arrangements. Taxation to tax away the rents received is a second-best solution. See, for example, (Van Parijs 1995; Van Donselaar 2009) for proposals how a theory of distributive justice should deal with rents.

The principle of ability to pay is accepted in most existing tax codes, in the sense that it is typically invoked as the moral principle underlying taxation.[16] However, what it exactly entails is far from clear. As far as I can see, three different interpretations are offered as to what the ability to pay entails. First, taxation according to ability to pay is sometimes explained as taxation on one's (income earning) endowment, that is, the talents one has for securing income (Bradford 1986, Chap. 8). This interpretation has obvious difficulties. It is difficult to determine a person's maximum income earning potential.[17] More importantly, such endowment taxation seems to open the door for questionable interference with people's freedom and autonomy, as it makes room for 'slavery of the talented'. People with exceptional income earning talents will be forced to accept careers where they can earn these high incomes so as to pay their tax bill.[18]

The second way the ability to pay principle has been understood is as requiring tax payers to make an equal proportional sacrifice (Musgrave 1959, Chap. 4). The idea is that a just tax scheme will discriminate among tax payers according to their pre-tax income since the more income one has, the more one can afford because the marginal utility of money for such people is less than it is for poor people. This interpretation is hostage to empirical fortune as well, as it is an open question whether extremely rich people do have lower marginal utilities for money. Very often, their choice of life style is such that they get locked into expensive activities without deriving noticeably higher utility than people with 'cheap tastes'. The third way the principle has been understood is as requiring an equal absolute sacrifice (Musgrave 1959, Chap. 4). Here the idea is that equality requires sharing the burden of government in equal real terms. Again, the relevant measure of the burden is in terms of utility, so the principle that requires equal absolute sacrifices do not *ipso facto* result in higher tax burdens for the 1 %.

Instead, I propose to interpret the ability to pay principle as it was originally understood.[19] In the eighteenth and nineteenth century, one's ability to pay taxes depended crucially on one's "faculty"—one's properties and wealth. In our times, property and wealth are still crucial for one's ability to pay tax, but jobs—especially, permanent jobs—are added to the mixture.[20] If we concentrate on people's

---

[16] It has constitutional status in Germany, Italy and Spain.

[17] Most recently, there has been renewed interest in so-called 'tagging' to establish one's income earning potential (Mankiw and Weinzierl 2009; Weinzierl 2012).

[18] This is precisely the reason that utilitarians and welfare economists play with the idea of endowment taxation as this is a tax that does not have any substitution effects, but instead, is an incentive for citizens to be as productive as they can (Murphy and Nagel 2002, pp. 20–21).

[19] See (Kiesling 1992, pp. 37–40) for a short historical overview of this interpretation of the ability to pay principle.

[20] In other words, if one accepts that one's ability to pay is determined by one's faculty, thus understood, the question about what to tax is also determined. For example, a discussion about whether it is fair to tax savings in addition to income would be moot.

"faculty", it appears that the 1 % have a very large "faculty" compared to median income earners.

Is the ability to pay principle, thus understood, acceptable? I think its *prima facie* plausibility comes from the fact that it expresses some core intuitions about fairness in the distribution of burdens. The ability to pay principle, thus understood, (unlike the benefit principle) can explain why people with low incomes and little possessions should be exempted from tax (all tax systems that I am familiar with exempt an initial amount of income from taxation): one cannot demand that somebody participates in carrying the burdens of maintaining the state—i.e., pay taxes—if that person lacks the ability to shoulder the burdens of his own existence.[21]

There are other aspects that make the ability to pay principle, which takes people's "faculty" as point of departure, attractive for those who wish to defend high effective marginal rates for the 1 %. For example, principled application of the principle will have egalitarian effects on the distribution of wealth, savings, capital and income, for we can more or less deduce a progressive rate structure from the principle.[22]

5.6 Myopia Reconsidered

However, there remains a major objection to the ability to pay principle, thus interpreted. The objection is the same as was brought up against the benefit principle: the distribution of people's ability to pay taxes (i.e., their wealth and income) may reflect injustices already. Application of the ability to pay principle will not correct those injustices—it will merely reflect these. More germane, just like the benefit principle, the ability to pay principle suffers from 'myopia' in that it takes the pre-tax income distribution as presumptively just. Which need not be the case (Murphy and Nagel 2002, p. 25).

However, this is too fast. Consider, again, the argument as to why the pre-tax income distribution is supposed to be morally irrelevant. One can only avoid 'myopia', it was claimed, if one also takes into consideration what is done with the revenues of taxation. The pre-tax income distribution is therefore, at best, a temporary one. Only if all one's obligations towards the state and fellow citizens are met, can one truly speak of a property right to one's income, but it is one's after-tax income.

This argument shares an assumption with those authors who claim that taxation is on a par with theft or even coerced labour. Robert Nozick (Nozick 1974), for ex-

[21] In the words of Cohen-Stuart, a classical author in the Dutch tradition, "... you should not burden a bridge until it can carry its own weight...". Cohen-Stuart was trained as a civil engineer, before he turned his attention to taxation (Cohen-Stuart 1890) translated and reprinted in (Musgrave and Peacock 1958).

[22] More or less, because there are still enormous degrees of liberty ranging from progressive to proportional rates. What is ruled out, however, are degressive rate structures.

ample, has argued that if one cannot dispose of one's income as one sees fit because the state still has claims on this income, it means that the income is not really yours, but the state's. Nozick balks at this idea and concludes that this means that we are the state's indentured labourers. On the other hand, those on the left of the political spectrum who claim that only your after-tax income is really yours assume the same thing: as long as the state has legitimate claims on your income it is not really yours.

This is an implausible assumption.[23] Compare the following situation. Suppose that I lend you € 100. You now owe me € 100. Does this mean that you do not own that money that you borrowed? Are you now forbidden to spend it on nice philosophy books? Are you not entitled to any protection of it? Can I come and remove the € 100 from your wallet as I see fit? Of course not! So even if there are positive claims (for example, by the state) on your pre-tax income, it does not mean that this pre-tax income is not in any relevant sense 'yours'. You are still entitled to all the protections that come with having a property claim.

In other words, the idea that the pre-tax income distribution is morally irrelevant and arbitrary is incorrect. The critique that defenders of the ability to pay principle are guilty of an objectionable form of 'myopia' is an exaggeration. This is not to say that one can regard questions of fiscal justice in total isolation from all the other state activities. All this means is that the pre-tax distribution of wealth, capital and income is an appropriate point of departure to assess our fiscal obligations.

Those who wish to defend higher tax burdens than we see now for the 1 % need not worry then. For what the alternative argument that I sketched in the previous section entails is that the burden of proof will be on the 1 % and their sympathizers: they need to show why we should not adopt high effective rates for the extremely rich.

5.7 Conclusion

Defenders of high average effective tax rates for the extremely rich do better if they appeal to the ability to pay principle than a version of the benefit principle. There is, furthermore, no need to assume that doing so involves objectionable 'myopia'. Therefore, a discussion about the level of the distribution of the burdens of living in the state can proceed from the prevailing pre-tax income distribution, even when it reflects injustices.

This means that the discussion about taxing the 1 % is conducted at the level at which it should be held in order to be convincing to opponents. Not at the level of the total net distribution of burdens and benefits without any specific concern for the fairness of the distribution of the burdens in particular, but at the level of how much of one's income should be ceded to the state in taxation.

[23] This part of the argument, I owe to (Den Hartogh 2011).

References

Bradford, D. F. 1986. *Untangling the income tax*. Cambridge: Harvard University Press.

Cohen-Stuart, A. J. 1890. Belasting Naar Draagkracht. *De Economist* 39 (1): 274–283.

Den Hartogh, Govert. 2011. The reality of ownership. Unpublished manuscript. Amsterdam.

Dworkin, Ronald. 1981. What is equality, part 2: Equality of resources. *Philosophy and Public Affairs* 10 (4): 283–345.

Gordon, David. 2002. Property: Convention or right? *The Mises Review*. http://mises.org/misesreview_detail.aspx?control=208. Accessed 26 June 2013.

Kiesling, H. J. 1992. *Taxation and public goods: A welfare-economic critique of tax policy analysis*. Ann Arbor: University of Michigan Press.

Lakoff, George. 2004. *Don't think of an elephant: Know you values and frame the debate. The essential guide for progressives*. White River Junction: Chelsea Green Publishing.

Lindahl, Erik. 1919. *Die Gerechtigkeit Der Besteuerung : Eine Analyse Der Steuerprinzipien Auf Grundlage Der Grenznutzentheorie*. Lund: Lund University.

Mankiw, N. Gregory. 2013. Defending the one percent. *Journal of Economic Perspectives* 27 (3): 21–34.

Mankiw, N. Gregory, and Matthew Weinzierl. 2009. *The optimal taxation of height: A case study of utilitarian income redistribution*. 14976. NBER working paper. Cambridge: National Bureau of Economic Research.

Mill, John Stuart. 1848. *Principles of political economy with some of their applications to social philosophy*. London: Standard Library Co.

Murphy, Liam B., and Thomas Nagel. 2002. *The myth of ownership: Taxes and justice*. Oxford: Oxford University Press.

Musgrave, Richard Abel. 1959. *The theory of public finance: A study in public economy*. 1st ed. New York: McGraw-Hill.

Musgrave, Richard Abel, and Alan T. Peacock. 1958. *Classics in the theory of public finance*. London: MacMillan.

Nozick, Robert. 1974. *Anarchy, state and Utopia*. New York: Basic Books.

Piketty, Thomas. 2014. *Capital in the twenty-first century*. Translated by Arthur Goldhammer. Cambridge: Harvard University Press.

Robeyns, Ingrid. 2013. Moeten We Een Sterbelasting Invoeren? *Spongia: Philosophy Blog EUR*. http://philospongia.wordpress.com/2011/09/21/moeten-we-een-sterbelasting-invoeren/. Accessed 21 June 2013.

Saez, Emanuel, Thomas Piketty, Facundo Alvaredo, and Tony Atkinson. 2013. The world top incomes database. http://topincomes.parisschoolofeconomics.eu/. Accessed 18 June 2013.

Smith, Adam. 1979. *An inquiry in the nature and causes of the wealth of nations. The glasgow ediiton of the works and correspondence of Adam Smith*. Oxford: Oxford University Press.

Tarieven—Belastingtarieven—Rijksoverheid.nl. 2012. Onderwerp. http://www.rijksoverheid.nl/onderwerpen/belastingtarieven/inkomstenbelasting/tarieven. Accessed 19 June 2013.

Togler, Benno, Ihsan C. Demir, Alison MacIntyre, and Markus Schaffner. 2008. Causes and consequences of tax morale: An empirical investigation. *Economic Analysis & Policy* 38 (2): 313–339.

Van Donselaar, Gijs. 2009. *The right to exploit: Parasitism, scarcity, and basic income*. New York: Oxford University Press.

Van Parijs, Philippe. 1995. *Real freedom for all: What (if anything) can justify captitalism*. Oxford: Oxford University Press.

Warren, Elizabeth. 2012. You didn't build that *YouTube*. http://www.youtube.com/watch?v=i-P-CoSNYaI&feature=youtube_gdata_player. Accessed 20 June 2013.

Weinzierl, Matthew. 2012. *Why do we redistribute so much but tag so little? The principle of equal sacrifice and optimal taxation*. 18045. NBER Working Paper. Cambridge: National Bureau of Economic Research.

Chapter 6
The Challenge of Tax Avoidance for Social Justice in Taxation

Benjamin Alarie

Abstract The Occupy Wall Street (OWS) movement has been criticized for not having a tax policy agenda. Critics contend that it has "no message," "no goals," and "no leaders." This contribution accounts for this policy agenda deficit. Various tax policy prescriptions that address social resource inequality, including a wealth tax proposed by Pikkety and Goldhammer (Capital in the twenty-first century, 2014), suffer from serious weaknesses. More specifically, I explain why the most salient of the income tax policy ideas (increasing rates) is not, on its own, a solution. To see why, consider the US. The US has high corporate income tax rates; nevertheless, large American corporations such as Apple, GE, Starbucks and Google have been able to reduce their effective corporate income tax rate liability below statutory rates, often close to zero. The crux of the problem is that increasing income tax rates leaves those confronting such rates with greater incentive to engage in various activities in order to avoid those taxes. It also increases the return from lobbying for tax changes that make avoiding that burden more possible. Therefore, increasing income tax rates is not the clear-cut effective policy prescription one might think it should be. The example of the Bush tax cuts for individuals, and certain kinds of capital income, illustrates that cutting income tax rates is also not the right approach. In many countries, claims that cutting taxes will increase tax revenues (i.e., that we "are on the wrong side of the Laffer curve") are incorrect. Thus, if income tax rates are increased, it is not necessarily the wealthiest that will bear the greatest burden, and if tax rates are cut, it is not certain—or even particularly likely—that it will be the least well off who will benefit. OWS ought therefore not to be criticized for not articulating a message with respect to income tax policy. Recent developments show that popular political pressure on leaders has led the G20 to the right—albeit difficult—track. The best income tax reform is one of base broadening and increasing international tax cooperation, perhaps coupled with making a transition from reliance on income tax to a greater reliance on coordinated wealth taxes. Responding intelligently to demands for a more progressive tax system that promotes the realization of social justice will require us to confront difficult practical and political challenges. These tax policies are available only if the political will can be found to sustain their introduction and implementation.

B. Alarie (✉)
Facutly of Law, University of Toronto, 84 Queen's Park, Toronto, ON M5S 2C5, Canada
e-mail: ben.alarie@utoronto.ca

H. P. Gaisbauer et al. (eds.), *Philosophical Explorations of Justice and Taxation*,
Ius Gentium: Comparative Perspectives on Law and Justice 40,
DOI 10.1007/978-3-319-13458-1_6

6.1 Introduction

The Occupy Wall Street (OWS) movement seized headlines in September 2011 with the occupation of Liberty Square in Manhattan by hundreds of protestors. At the time, mainstream media featured interviews with OWS participants, many of whom aired different sets of grievances. External commentators were critical of the protest, not least because it was unclear what was being protested about and because there was no clarity as to what, moreover, would constitute success. One could plausibly put all this down to the difficulty of finding a sound bite that neatly captured the protest's origins and its goals. However, there may be an underlying reason why the impetus for the OWS movement could not adequately be expressed in sound bite form. In this contribution, I focus on the social justice dimension of tax policy in positive terms and provide an account of the challenges faced by the OWS movement in articulating tax policy goals. More specifically, I identify and describe a form of screening or second-degree price discrimination that is at the core of domestic and international income tax systems, and argue that this mechanism complicates measures that would seemingly address the economic inequalities that motivate the OWS movement. A similar mechanism would also impair the effectiveness of a wealth tax along the lines now suggested by Piketty and Goldhammer (2014), though less seriously.

What is it that provides fuel for the OWS movement in the tax policy context? One view is that it is a sense that the wealthiest are not paying their fair share of taxes. The feeling is linked to the perception that wealthy individuals and large corporations often have the motive and opportunity to influence the design of tax rules so as to minimize their tax burdens and, where the rules are ambiguous, engage in tax planning that ranges from run-of-the-mill compliance to aggressive tax avoidance (not to mention evasion). The irritation exhibited by the OWS movement with this perceived rigging of the tax law is understandable given that many of the most effective anti-avoidance tools, such as retroactive specific anti-avoidance rules, lie unused much of the time. Even when governments use such tools, they are usually deployed with a significant time lag after new tax avoidance strategies have come to light. Moreover, most of the time, tax law changes are effective only prospectively. This allows tax avoiders to retain their transitory tax savings. Thus, the popular discontent with tax avoidance evidenced by the OWS movement is in tension with governments choosing to countenance ongoing and significant forgone tax revenues. Some in the OWS movement resolve this tension by assuming that there are imbalances in the social, political and economic structure. Indeed, one gets the sense that some OWS protestors believe in something that amounts to an elite conspiracy. In my view, these suspicions are too extreme to be credible. I argue in this contribution that, although there is no elite conspiracy, there is an identifiable socio-political-economic dynamic that accounts for the perceived unfairness motivating the OWS movement. Unfortunately, responsibility for this dynamic is diffuse. No one party in particular is to blame, and the appropriate policy responses will be difficult to coordinate and sustain. The contribution here is to argue that once we correctly diagnose the underlying conditions, it will be possible to have a clearer view of how best to address the resulting consequences in a socially just and desirable way.

Two recent developments addressing tax avoidance are on the right track. The first is a report from the OECD (2013a) entitled “Addressing Base Erosion and Profit Shifting” (BEPS). The report advocates collective action by all OECD member governments to create similar, if not uniform tax rules to prevent corporations from shifting profits from higher tax to lower tax jurisdictions. The second recent development is the coordinated announcement on July 19, 2013 by the finance ministers of the G20 of an “action plan on BEPS” that essentially adopts the OECD’s recommendation of a fundamental rethink of international tax rules. While the report focuses primarily on profit shifting, a number of the corrective measures proposed could be extended to other forms of tax avoidance. The action plan (OECD 2013b) includes 15 different areas where tax rules need to be improved in order to mitigate tax avoidance and contemplates concerted action in these areas within 24 months. How likely is serious reform?

It is predictable that governments will tolerate tax avoidance until it becomes sufficiently visible to motivate political opposition or sufficiently widespread so as to significantly reduce tax revenues. If the BEPS action plan does yield tangible change—as seems possible—it will be a sign that the pendulum has swung too far in favour of tax avoidance. However, if the action plan does not yield aggressive anti-tax avoidance in an internationally coordinated way, it is likely that two accounts will be offered to justify its failure: justice and political economy. The first of these accounts, justice, invokes the rule of law to make the case that many of the most effective anti-avoidance strategies, such as retroactive legislation, are inherently antithetical to the principles and aspirations of modern legal systems and are, for that reason, off the table (except perhaps in the most exigent circumstances). The second account takes seriously the political economy hurdles militating against vigilance in enforcing tax laws. It may, for example, be extremely difficult to tackle aggressive tax avoidance because of the political clout of the economic interests favoured by inaction, or the practical difficultly of mobilizing tax authorities to revisit earlier tax assessments.

In what follows, the prospect for effective responses to concerns surrounding inequality is assessed against the backdrop of the political and economic realities of taxation. The result is an outline of the challenges for social justice in taxation. Part II provides a review of the literature on anti-avoidance. Part III elaborates on the rule of law and political economy accounts that provide an explanatory basis for anti-avoidance activity on the part of governments. Part IV describes the mechanism by which domestic and international income tax systems at their core depend (perhaps unintentionally) on screening and second-degree price discrimination, and explores the implications of this insight for the BEPS action plan, tax policy and administration more generally and, ultimately, for social justice in taxation. Part V concludes.

6.2 Literature Review

The legal and economic literatures discuss how tax avoidance strategies are identified by taxpayers, why they are tolerated, and how governments ought to respond to them. In a recent contribution, Leo Katz (2010) argues that the tax system embodies the result of multi-dimensional decision-making where the government decides what to tax based on a number of different underlying legal and economic criteria, each of which is susceptible to some degree of manipulation by taxpayers. The key idea is that some of the criteria made legally relevant for assessing tax liability by the government are substantially irrelevant from the point of view of the potential taxpayer. As a result, the taxpayer can structure her affairs by adjusting the criteria that are most relied on by the government in assessing tax liability, but least harmful to her economic or personal objectives in the light of the reduction in tax liability that these adjustments will occasion. Katz's argument can be shown in a simple example. Suppose the government decides that dividend income from equity should be taxed, but interest payments on debt should not be. Assume that the criterion that this decision is based on is some non-tax benefit associated with the equity. An avoidance strategy forms as soon as there is a person who is indifferent to the benefit of the equity, as that person will simply choose the tax-free debt. This can be seen as a form of agenda manipulation because the inclusion of the irrelevant criteria leads the person to choose the non-tax route, i.e. the avoidance strategy.

In discussing the economic impact of government responses to various kinds of tax avoidance strategies, David Weisbach (2002, p. 90) explains that anti-avoidance is simply a form of expanding the tax base. The consequences of tax avoidance can be viewed as false negatives—those who should be paying tax are not. In his view (99), the goal of anti-avoidance doctrines is to reduce the ability of taxpayers to substitute into non-taxed activities, thereby forcing them into compliance—making their actions true positives rather than false negatives. However, in many cases, anti-avoidance rules may shift taxpayers into less efficient tax avoidance schemes rather than into compliance; that is, instead of becoming true positives, taxpayers may simply go to even greater lengths to remain false negatives. This results in a loss of utility for the taxpayer with no offsetting benefit for the government. The logical response to this would be to increase the scope of the anti-avoidance doctrine to preclude the new form of avoidance. However, Weisbach (116) warns that this could then make the anti-avoidance rule too inclusive, and accidentally penalize people who are engaging in legitimate business transactions through the generation of an inefficient rate of false positives. Furthermore, the cost of creating and enforcing anti-avoidance doctrines is often high. In essence, Weisbach's argument is that due to uncertain taxpayer responses, it is often unclear whether the benefits of an anti-avoidance measure will outweigh its costs of enforcement.

Leigh Osofsky (2013, p. 1058) raises a similar argument to Weisbach regarding the structure of avoidance rules. She notes that, ideally, avoidance rules should create frictions that make it more costly for tax avoiders to avoid taxes, which forces them to comply. However, poorly constructed avoidance regimes might also lead to a deadweight loss for non-planners, or result in the planners finding a more costly method of avoidance. Thus, the existing literature suggests that there are some circumstances in which full enforcement of tax laws is not desirable.

The account that I develop here shows that the problems of full enforcement are linked to a form of screening mechanism that is similar to second-degree price discrimination. A number of contributions by Alex Raskolnikov implicitly recognize aspects of this kind of screening function. Raskolnikov (2009, p. 695) suggests that there are two kinds of taxpayers: gamers, and non-gamers. Gamers are the neo-classically "rational" taxpayers, who avoid taxes as long as the cost of avoidance is less than the cost of compliance. Non-gamers generally comply with taxation, even if it can be avoided at a cost less than paying tax. Raskolnikov (691) argues that the American tax system adopts a one size fits all approach to tax law enforcement, resulting in the inefficient treatment of both gamers and non-gamers. In its place, Raskolnikov suggests a system that causes taxpayers to self-select in an incentive-compatible way into a particular enforcement regime, with the result that gamers and non-gamers self-identify. The government would then offer two parallel systems, one that is best for gamers, and one that is best for compliers. Take for example a simplified version of Raskolnikov's regime. The government would offer a system similar to the current deterrence approach, as well as an alternative filing option with lower penalties. The low-penalty option would presume that the government is correct in the event of a tax dispute. Those who comply do not mind this presumption since they do not expect a dispute, and therefore elect to take advantage of the lower penalties. Gamers, on the other hand, expect a dispute to be more likely, and do not choose the alternative option. Thus, as a consequence of this self-selection, the government would be able to introduce tailored and efficient enforcement policies for each taxpayer type.

Raskolnikov (2006, p. 590) also argues that current deterrence regimes are ineffective because the available penalties do not vary with probability of detection. As such, the expected penalty of avoidance methods that are difficult to detect is quite low, since the magnitude of the penalty is no larger than most other avoidance methods. These flaws make enforcement strategies less effective at catching or deterring tax avoiders. Extending Raskolnikov's work perhaps explains some of the tolerance towards tax avoidance, as the ineffectiveness of anti-avoidance rules could be a reason why they are not used more often. Raskolnikov's assumption that taxpayers exhibit differing levels of responsiveness to tax liability has empirical support. Empirical work has found that effective tax liability does track the morale of taxpayers with respect to taxation. For example, Doerrenberg et al. (2012, p. 1) found that governments are likely to tax citizens based on levels of "tax morale" (a taxpayer's "intrinsic motivation to honestly pay taxes"). They also suggest that tax morale is a suitable proxy for proclivity for tax avoidance. The result of these two ideas is that governments are likely to tax those who are least likely to take measures to avoid taxation at the highest rates—an implicit recognition of the screening function at the core of domestic and international income tax systems.

This finding is also consistent with theoretical work done by Hettich and Winer (1999, p. 46) who present a model of a democratic government with a governing party that wishes only to be re-elected. Voters have different valuations of government services, which lead them to support the government, and different reactions to taxes, which make them likely to oppose the government. The optimal solution makes the "marginal political cost"—which is understood as the reduction in expected votes of raising an additional dollar in revenue—the same for all taxpayers. As a result, under this system, the financing of beneficial government services will largely be borne by those taxpayers whose political preferences are the least likely to be affected by increases in their tax burden. This maximizes the probability of the government being re-elected. While this model does not explicitly discuss tax avoidance, it can easily be extended to do so. The model assumes that the government has perfect information and can tax individuals at their exact marginal political cost. However, information asymmetries exist in the real world. Tolerating tax avoidance is therefore one way that a government could encourage taxation at a level close to the marginal political cost for each taxpayer, as the more tax averse will end up with lower taxes. Under the extension of this model, the government can be seen to tolerate tax avoidance in the government's own self-interest.

Brennan and Buchanan's *The Power to Tax* is a precursor to these more recent works. Brennan (2000, p. xiii) states that the object of the book was to fill the gap between the only two available normative tax theories at the time, the public choice model and the public finance model. The result is a Leviathan model, which features a government that seeks only to maximize its revenue, and is subject to few constraints. This work is important not only because it showed that taxation could be examined outside of the constraints of the original models, but also because the Leviathan model itself has current implications. For example, while Hettich and Winer reject the Leviathan model, they implicitly adopt the underlying logic of taxing based on price discrimination, which the Leviathan model uses to maximize revenue. The Leviathan model is closely related to the story of second-degree price discrimination that I use to assess the BEPS action plan below.

6.3 Anti-Avoidance: Justice and Political Economy

There are at least two accounts of why governments do not do more to counter tax avoidance. The first account highlights the rule of law as a disciplining mechanism on the kind of aggressive responses that might be necessary to stem tax avoidance in a system with high tax rates. The second account highlights the political environment that might render an otherwise effective response to tax avoidance politically or economically inadvisable.

Friedrich August Hayek (2007, p. 112) articulated the concept of the rule of law as follows, "stripped of all technicalities this means that government in all its actions is bound by rules fixed and announced beforehand—rules which make it possible to foresee with fair certainty how the authority will use its coercive powers in given circumstances, and to plan one's individual affairs on the basis of this knowledge." More recently, credit for popularizing the concept of the rule of law is often given to British jurist Albert Venn Dicey. Dicey described three distinct meanings for the phrase "the rule of law." Only the first of these meanings is directly relevant to taxation. The primary meaning Dicey (1897, p. 197) gave to the rule of law is that, "no man is punishable or can be made to suffer in body or goods except for a distinct breach of law established in the ordinary legal manner before the ordinary courts of the land."[1] Rawls built on Dicey's account, and subsequently identified five requirements of the rule of law: (1) compliance must be possible; (2) there must be regularity; (3) there must be publicity; (4) there should be generality to law; and (5) there must be respect for due process (Solum 2009).[2]

Joseph Raz (1977) has also articulated an influential set of requirements of the rule of law.[3] Others, including Lon Fuller (1969), have also attempted similar lists.

While there has been some writing in the academic tax literature on the rule of law, it is relatively limited. Geoffrey Loomer (2006) argued in an article in the British Tax Review that unwritten constitutional principles relating to the rule of law might well legitimately constrain the domain for Parliament to respond with retroactively effect tax legislation. In another recent publication, Thomas E. McDonnell (2006) argues that, in the taxation context, the rule of law can be regarded as entailing four specific consequences with respect to retroactive legislation: "(1) that curative amendments are always acceptable; (2) that a taxpayer who has reasonably relied on the state of the existing law has an interest worthy of consideration, depending on the degree of reasonable reliance involved; (3) that the concept of fairness should be understood as applying to all taxpayers generally and not just to members of a group adversely affected by a retroactive change; and (4) that fiscal considerations in and by themselves should never be relied on in support of a retroactive change."

The upshot of both the more general philosophical accounts of the demands of the rule of law and the writings that are more practical and focused on the taxation context is that retroactive legislation that violates the legitimate expectations of taxpayers is impermissible. This raises a number of questions, however, surrounding just what precisely constitutes the legitimate expectations of taxpayers when taxpayers are engaged in tax avoidance, and whether the described impermissibility is absolute or only cautionary. It is enough, however, to emphasize that retroactive laws are generally inconsistent with demands that the law be knowable *ex ante* so that it can reliably guide taxpayer behaviour.

The political economy perspective can be ably summarized by an aphorism attributed to Jean-Baptiste Colbert: "the art of taxation consists in so plucking the goose as to obtain the largest amount of feathers with the least amount of hissing" (Yablon 2006, p. 123).[4] There are several ways in which the political economy

[1] For a discussion of Dicey's contributions to the popularization of the idea of the rule of law, see (Cosgrove 1980).

[2] For a brief but instructive elaboration on these five elements, see (Solum 2009).

[3] Among these general principles for Raz (1977, are that "all laws should be prospective, open and clear" and that "laws should be relatively stable."

[4] This is an old French maxim, often attributed to Jean-Baptiste Colbert (1619–1683).

environment affects the timing of government responses to tax avoidance.[5] The most significant is likely to be the collective action problem that arises as a consequence of the fact that the loss to the public purse from tax avoidance is normally felt diffusely and usually remotely in time, whereas the gain to the taxpayer from tax avoidance is immediate, direct and often personal.[6] Overcoming this collective action problem, however, involves confronting numerous obstacles from an administrative standpoint. For example, whereas each taxpayer is ideally situated to know the information that affects his or her tax situation, it is considerably more difficult for the government to monitor the information that pertains to each taxpayer's liability. Moreover, unlike a purely rational taxpayer, who would be willing to pay up to the amount of their tax liability in avoidance costs, governments are generally willing to expend lesser resources on auditing and enforcing income tax laws. Thus, there are three asymmetries that contribute to the phenomenon of tax avoidance: (1) an asymmetry in the concentration of stakes (diffuse for government versus concentrated for taxpayers); (2) an asymmetry in information (typically less for governments versus more for taxpayers); and (3) an asymmetry in the resources devoted by governments in enforcement and taxpayers in avoidance (less on enforcement by governments and more by taxpayers in avoidance).

These three asymmetries play out in a number of ways. Consider that for any individual employee of the tax administration, it will naturally be the case that the taxpayers that they interact with will be more keen to avoid additional tax liability than the employee will be to enforce the tax law to its full extent (though they may well be eager to do so, they will be less so than they would if they were personally allowed to keep in full whatever is recovered from the taxpayer in tax, interest, and penalties). While most tax administrators are honest and dutiful servants, this difference in incentives can reasonably be expected to manifest itself in suboptimal exertion on investigation and enforcement of the tax law. It is easiest to imagine this suboptimal enforcement in the context of a negotiated settlement to a dispute regarding an alleged underpayment of tax. In these circumstances, the prediction is that the settlement will, tend all other things being equal, to favour the taxpayer (relative to what the outcome would on average be in judicial proceedings).

Moving from tax administration to tax legislation, governments are likely to be slower than taxpayers in the tax avoidance context. When creative tax planners devise a new unanticipated scheme that manages to avoid tax under plausible interpretations of current income tax law, it is reasonable to expect these innovations to spread relatively quickly within the tax planning community (most obviously often within the same law firm or accounting firm). This contributes to the growth of tax avoidance and, if governments are not responding with counter-measures that are carefully calibrated to match threats, the resulting equilibrium will favour sophisticated taxpayers who will constantly be innovating in the tax avoidance con-

[5] For a book length treatment addressing a number of these issues, see (Aaron and Slemrod 2004).

[6] In an influential contribution, political scientist Terry M. Moe (1989, p. 273) wrote that, "American public bureaucracy is not designed to be effective. The bureaucracy arises out of politics, and its design reflects the interests, strategies, and compromises of those who exercise political power."

text in order to respond to competitive pressures in product and capital markets. It will only be when governments act collectively and effectively with respect to both domestic and international tax rules that the resulting equilibrium will be socially satisfactory.

6.4 Screening, Tax Avoidance and Social Justice

Adopting a screening account of tax avoidance generates considerable new insight into the dynamic which complicates the development of a more progressive tax system. In order to explain the operation of this price discrimination mechanism in the context of income taxation, this part begins by describing the three principal types of price discrimination that have been identified by economists. The argument proceeds to examine the main modifications that must be made to the usual producer-consumer paradigm of price discrimination models in order to apply the screening implications to the domestic and international income tax setting. With the screening / price discrimination argument in place, this part concludes with the implications for social justice in taxation.

A leading economics text on industrial organization states that, "It is hard to come up with a satisfactory definition of price discrimination. Roughly, it can be said that the producer price-discriminates when two units of the same physical good are sold at different prices, either to the same consumer or to different consumers" (Tirole 1988, p. 133). First-degree or "perfect" price discrimination occurs when a producer is able to precisely identify each consumer's willingness to pay for the goods or service and can prevent the resale of the goods or the service in a secondary market. In these circumstances, a profit-maximizing producer will choose to charge each consumer a price equal to their maximum willingness to pay. In doing so, the producer will supply the entire market in a manner that will ensure economic efficiency and extract all available consumer surplus from the purchasers of the goods or service. To be operational, perfect price discrimination requires that strong assumptions be made. Specifically, the producer of the goods or supplier of the relevant service must have complete information about the willingness of consumers to pay and it must be possible to prevent arbitrage in the secondary market for the goods or service. Perfect price discrimination is, for that reason, largely regarded as being of theoretical interest rather than an empirically realistic phenomenon.

Second-degree price discrimination occurs when the producer has incomplete information about the preferences of particular consumers and cannot reliably target individuals or groups of consumers for particular pricing strategies. The producer will, in general however, have information about the mix of consumer preferences in the population. Therefore, unlike perfect price discrimination, where the producer knows precisely the willingness to pay of each consumer, in second-degree price discrimination the producer is aware only of the distribution of willingness to pay among consumers. In these circumstances, the goal of the producer is to induce consumers with different willingness to pay to choose different price-quantity bundles from a menu of options offered by the producer. If the producer is successful in setting a menu of price-quantity bundles that causes consumers with different willingness to pay to choose different bundles, then the producer will secure a greater share of the consumer surplus than uniform pricing would facilitate. Naturally, inducing the separation of consumers into different consumption bundles requires incentive-compatibility between the bundles on offer and the willingness to pay of each consumer. An example of second-degree price discrimination is a coupon that entitles the bearer of the coupon to a discount. It will systematically tend to be the case that more price sensitive consumers will make use of the coupon.

Third-degree price discrimination relies on an exogenous attribute of consumers that can be observed by the producer that is correlated with the consumers' willingness to pay. Unlike second-degree price discrimination, where the distribution of willingness to pay among consumers is known, but nothing is known about the willingness to pay of any particular consumer, in third-degree price discrimination, the producer is able to observe certain attributes of consumers that are linked to higher or lower willingness to pay for the goods or service. An example of third-degree price discrimination would be discounts that are made available only to seniors or students. If seniors or students have systematically lower willingness to pay for a particular good or service, and yet are still willing to pay enough to cover the marginal cost to the producer of the goods or service, it will be profitable for the producer to service the customers by allowing them to self-identify as members of the relatively low willingness to pay group.

It is possible to translate these three types of market-based price discrimination into versions that correspond with the task facing governments in setting the various structural features of domestic and international income tax law. For the purposes of the screening account, the translation requires the government to take on the role of the producer. The central challenge is that, unlike a private producer who can be assumed to be seeking to maximize profit, it is not at all obvious that the government's objective function corresponds to maximizing its tax revenues. Because of this, there must be an assumption made about how much revenue the government desires to raise through the income tax system. The simplest approach, which will be the one adopted here for the purposes of exposition, is to assume that the expenditure determination is independent and exogenously given. This assumption, while artificial, yields the reasonable result that the government's objective in structuring income tax is to collect a certain set amount of tax revenue in the "best" way possible. For a price discriminator, the "best" way involves charging consumers in a tailored fashion according to their willingness to pay, thereby capturing the maximum amount of surplus from consumers. While a government using price discrimination taxation may not be seeking to maximize its tax revenue, it will still tax based on the willingness to pay of taxpayers. In doing so, the government will capture the specified amount of revenue in the most efficient manner possible. The price discriminator, therefore, will charge more to consumers or taxpayers who place a higher value on the product or on compliance. As a result, those with higher tax morale and greater inclination to comply will pay more tax. This is an empirical as well as a theoretical outcome, and is supported by work by Doerrenberg.

On the taxpayer's side, there is also a significant modification that must be made to the conventional price discrimination account. Here the issue is that taxpayer preferences do not yield a demand function of the kind typically associated with price discrimination models. In most models of price discrimination, consumers are assumed to exhibit declining willingness to pay for each additional unit of the goods or service provided by the producer. Because there is no explicit *quid pro quo* in income taxation, it is not possible to derive this kind of demand function directly on the taxpayer side. It is, however, possible to substitute a measure of taxpayer responsiveness for the more conventional demand function. By responsiveness I mean to refer to the extent to which taxpayers, either directly or, more commonly, by proxy through a tax adviser, respond in various ways to mitigate their effective tax obligations. Responsiveness is composed of three factors: the economic fundamentals of the taxpayer and the taxed activity, the willingness to comply, and the ability to use the tax system to avoid taxation.

Economic fundamentals matter because the nature of a taxpayer's economic activities will affect the ability of that individual or corporation to manipulate their legal relationships to mitigate their effective tax obligations. In particular, not only is it easier for taxpayers to respond to taxes on some sources of income than it is on others, the ability of taxpayers to respond to a tax on a particular source of income is also affected by the nature of their economic activities. For example, for some taxpayers, especially those with operations that span multiple jurisdictions, the most natural way to respond to changes in their tax liability will be to relocate their income-earning operations to another jurisdiction, either directly or indirectly. However, many taxpayers who wish to take advantage of such a response may be unable to do so if their operations are contractually simple or limited to one jurisdiction. Moreover, while taxpayers can undoubtedly mitigate their effective tax obligations purely by adjusting the economic substance of their taxable activities, for example, by electing to work less, doing so without any corresponding change in the legal nature of their economic arrangements will occasion an economic distortion and result in a loss of utility for the taxpayer. As a result, taxpayers will vary in their ability or willingness to increase or decrease the amount they work in response to taxation. To the extent that taxpayers are motivated to actually reduce their exposure to income tax through various behavioural channels, including shifting income to other jurisdictions, engaging in various tax avoidance transactions and, perhaps most worryingly from a social welfare perspective, simply deciding to be less productive by substituting leisure for labour, they are being responsive in the sense intended by the word. For many taxpayers, however, the economic fundamentals of their situation grant them little scope for rearranging their income-earning activities so as to mitigate an enhanced tax liability.

Personal values are a key component of taxpayer responsiveness. The perfectly rational and self-interested taxpayer is willing to spend up to a dollar avoiding each dollar of tax. However, taxpayers are not always rational in this way, and routinely pay more than would be expected by neoclassical economists.[7] Less responsive

[7] The work of Erich Kirchler in economic psychology demonstrates this in the taxation setting.

taxpayers may stray from the economic definition of rationality due to their social identity, attitude towards government, or an expected sense of shame if they are caught avoiding taxes. While most of the literature and empirical evidence suggests that individuals avoid taxes to a lesser extent than would be expected pursuant to rational self-interest, it is also possible that someone could avoid more than the rational amount of tax. As an extreme example, a libertarian might be willing to pay more in avoidance costs than would be saved in taxes. The most radical legal response is exiting the tax system altogether, such as by leaving the jurisdiction or ceasing to work entirely. The idea that one's personal values can cause a decision to deviate from the economically rational choice is not new. Albert Hirschmann (1970) noted forty years ago that many consumers have an attachment or loyalty to brands that prevents them from exiting as a consumer of that brand even when it declines in quality relative to identical competitors. The same reasoning extends to taxation. Taxpayers who have a high degree of loyalty to their country of residence will be more willing to pay taxes and less likely to exit the jurisdiction and vice versa.

Responsiveness is also influenced by the skill or ability of taxpayers to employ methods of reducing taxation. In a sense, ability brings together the other components of responsiveness, allowing taxpayers to reduce their taxes to the desired extent by taking advantage of the economic fundamentals of their situations. Ability can either be either direct or by proxy, for example, by hiring a tax professional or purchasing tax software. Stylistically and for the purposes of exposition, one can imagine taxpayers falling into one of three groups: (1) sophisticated taxpayers; (2) taxpayers of ordinary sophistication; and (3) less sophisticated taxpayers. Although these categories are apt to be somewhat inexact, it is possible to differentiate among them as follows. The most sophisticated group of taxpayers understands that the income tax system is complicated and that this complexity comes with both opportunities and pitfalls. The hallmark of the most sophisticated group is, therefore, an ability to proactively manage and plan their income-earning activities in order to minimize their tax liabilities. In doing so, sophisticated taxpayers will typically retain elite tax professionals who assist them in developing plans to minimize their tax liabilities. The majority of taxpayers, of course, will not be highly sophisticated and, out of necessity, will tend to be reactive rather than proactive with respect to their tax obligations. Taxpayers in this group will not generally be forward-looking in managing and planning their income-earning activities, and will instead focus on complying *ex post* with their tax obligations each year. Most small and medium sized businesses and middle to high income taxpayers will properly be regarded as being of ordinary sophistication. When taxpayers of ordinary sophistication hire tax advisors or consult resources, they most often turn to non-elite tax sources of tax advice, such as tax preparation services, small accounting firms, or software programs. Another group of taxpayers is less sophisticated still. For these individuals, the demands of the income tax system are intimidating and sometimes overwhelming. These taxpayers are generally of more limited means, less well educated, and often have more significant challenges (or at least challenges that loom larger) than tax compliance. It should be clear from this account that taxpayers of ordinary and low sophistication are unlikely to be responsive to (or, realistically, to be much affected by) legislative changes addressing tax avoidance. Instead, taxpayer responsiveness to anti-avoidance measures is largely a phenomenon involving highly sophisticated taxpayers.

Put simply, the solution offered to the translation from consumer to taxpayer is to replace the usual measure of consumer preferences, the demand function, with a function representing the responsiveness of taxpayers to higher *prima facie* income tax burdens. The idea of taxing people differently based on their responsiveness to taxation is not novel. Hettich and Winer demonstrate how a government can tax individuals based on the probability that the tax level will cause them to vote for the opposing party in the next election. That model assumes perfect information, allowing the government to set a tax rate exactly equal to an individual's willingness to pay tax. While perfect information is a useful assumption for modelling purposes, it rarely exists in real life. One of the benefits of the price discrimination approach is that second-degree price discrimination allows the government to tax people in this manner without actually knowing each individual's responsiveness.

In order to analyse the application of ideas taken from the industrial organization literature relating to price discrimination in the income taxation context, it will be helpful first to set out how second-degree price discrimination can be translated into the income tax environment. To the extent that governments can anticipate a certain distribution of responsiveness to income taxation in a given group, but are unable to identify *exante* who among that group will be more or less responsive, there may be scope for second-degree price discrimination. As mentioned above, for second-degree price discrimination to be effective, there must be a common set of options that are available to all taxpayers such that taxpayers of different responsiveness respond predictably differently. One way that a government might achieve this outcome is by setting out a relatively high "advertised" tax rate that applies on a tax base that is common to all taxpayers. Because in the abstract all taxpayers will be governed by the same set of rules, one can regard this as an invitation to taxpayers to choose among the tax treatments permitted by the legislation. In such a case, highly responsive taxpayers will be able to proactively manage their income tax burden through innovative tax avoidance measures (shifting income to other jurisdictions, using sophisticated tax shelters, etc.) more easily than will low responsiveness taxpayers. As a result, highly responsive taxpayers will usually be able to help themselves to effective tax rates that are lower than the effective tax rates that will apply to low responsiveness taxpayers. There may be social welfare gains from this kind of system since this form of screening or price discrimination will tend to promote a better correspondence between the marginal welfare loss to each taxpayer from taxation and the marginal social gain in government expenditures than would be associated with an income tax system that did not permit this kind of screening. Moreover, this price discrimination mechanism is advantageous to the extent that it provides a variety of tailored options to taxpayers. A taxpayer without a viable avoidance strategy would have to choose between paying full taxes and engaging in an economically detrimental activity such as working less, or exiting the jurisdiction altogether. Adding price discrimination as an option makes exiting a relatively less attractive option to the taxpayer as she can remain in the jurisdiction and escape some taxation. Therefore, to the extent that it is realistic to believe that there will be a group of sophisticated taxpayers amongst whom it will be difficult for the government to discriminate explicitly, then there will be a case for price discrimination in income taxation.

Stylistically, there is a stark choice confronting domestic and international tax policymakers emerging from the foregoing account. The choice is between (1) a dynamic higher rate income tax system with an active yet flexible approach to tax avoidance; and (2) a less flexible lower rate income tax system with a relatively strict approach to tax avoidance. Because most tax systems have decided not to rely extensively on retroactive specific anti-avoidance rules or multiple alternative tax bases, I suggest that it is clear that most governments can be characterized as having embraced the first choice.

If the government's aim is to raise a certain targeted amount of revenue, in the long-run there is not likely to be a third option in which the tax system has both low tax rates and a flexible approach to tax avoidance. However, depending on the tax systems adopted by other jurisdictions, it is possible that such an option might be available in the short-run. For example, in the transfer pricing context, it is likely that the country with the lowest effective tax rate for business income will generate more revenue because of income-shifting into the jurisdiction from higher tax rate jurisdictions. Why will this not work in the long-run? Because the revenue gains will largely be transitory, even if they do happen to be repeated transitory gains in a race to the bottom. Indeed, if a jurisdiction becomes accustomed to such "income-shifting" tax revenue, it should not be surprised if it becomes a participant in a race to the bottom that will—if the strategy is not abandoned—lead to it becoming insolvent (or a tax haven).

Thus, from the international and collective perspective, the only real choice is to embrace the reality that relatively high rate income tax jurisdictions will need to work together to be more dynamic, flexible and responsive in exerting counter-acting pressure on taxpayers advised by leading accounting and law firms. While the appropriate policy responses, including expanding the tax base and increasing international tax cooperation, will not eliminate the deleterious effects of the price discrimination mechanism, there is no long-run alternative that will preserve social justice. It is only with constant partial enforcement of anti-avoidance measures that governments that are aware of the second-degree price discrimination mechanism at the core of their tax system can maintain their revenues. As such, governments must be constantly on guard against being too permissive or too draconian with respect to tax avoidance. In these circumstances, it is clear why governments might simultaneously complain about tax avoidance while not pursuing all measures legally available to combat it.

It is, incidentally, in the best interests of sophisticated taxpayers not to overplay their hands. The leading tax advisers in law and accounting firms recognize that it is appropriate to foster a tension between tax planning and the responses taken by governments domestically and internationally. An enlightened pragmatism suggests that it is better for both governments and sophisticated taxpayers to be mutually plucking geese with a minimum of squawking. To mix metaphors, the awkwardly effective tax strategies of GE, Google, Apple and others may take the plucking of feathers from the coffers of governments too far.

It will be interesting to see what comes of the BEPS action plan recently endorsed by the finance ministers of the G20. Popular discontent with the growing levels of income and wealth inequality in many countries suggests that there is an imbalance between the degree of tax avoidance now achieved by many sophisticated taxpayers and the tax collection by governments to support expenditures that are socially just and in the public interest. Neither governments nor taxpayers should be given an easy ride in avoiding tax or in imposing taxes.

6.5 Conclusions

It will be difficult to achieve social justice in taxation without recognizing that income tax systems act as a second-degree price discrimination mechanism through which the most sophisticated and responsive taxpayers self-select into lower effective income tax rates and less responsive taxpayers are left facing relatively higher income tax liability. Although some solutions would gain more traction than others were they to be adopted—the global wealth tax of Piketty (2014) is one such idea—in all likelihood a global tax on capital is, as Piketty acknowledges (515), a "utopian idea."

To minimize the deleterious effects of the self-selection and other avoidance mechanisms described in this chapter, governments must remain cognizant of the screening function and be ever vigilant in working together to sustain optimal anti-tax avoidance pressure. The OWS movement and BEPS initiative of the G20 thus face significant challenges, the most considerable of which is sustaining the political will necessary to tackle the difficulty associated with the price discrimination mechanism that lies at the heart of systems of domestic and international income taxation. In a world of scarcity, pragmatic taxpayers, governments and voters must work together respectfully in common cause to realize economic, political and social justice.

References

Aaron, Henry J, and Joel Slemrod, eds. 2004. The crisis in tax administration. Washington, D.C.: Brookings Institution Press.

Brennan, Geoffrey, and James M. Buchanan. 2000. *The power to tax: Analytical foundations of a fiscal constitution*. Indianapolis: Liberty Fund.

Cosgrove, Richard A. 1980. *The rule of law: Albert Venn Dicey, Victorian jurist*. London: Macmillan.

Dicey, A. V. 1897. *An introduction to the study of the law of the constitution*. 5th ed. London: Macmillan.

Doerrenberg, Phillip, Denvil Duncan, Clemens Fuest, and Andreas Peichl. 2012. Nice guys finish last: Are people with higher tax morale taxed more heavily? IZA Discussion Paper Series, No. 6275.

Fuller, Lon L. 1969. *The morality of law*. Rev ed. New Haven: Yale University Press.
Hayek, Friedrich A. 2007. *The road to serfdom: Text and documents, the definitive edition,* ed. Bruce Caldwell. Chicago: University of Chicago Press (Orig. pub. 1944).
Hettich, Walter, and Stanley L. Winer. 1999. *Democratic choice and taxation: A theoretical and empirical analysis*. Cambridge: Cambridge University Press.
Hirschman, Albert O. 1970. *Exit, voice, and loyalty: Responses to decline in firms, organizations, and states*. Cambridge: Harvard University Press.
Katz, Leo. 2010. A theory of loopholes. *Journal of Legal Studies* 39 (1): 1–31.
Loomer, Geoffrey. 2006. Taxing out of time: Parliamentary supremacy and retroactive tax legislation. *British Tax Review* 1:64–90.
McDonnell, Thomas E. 2006. Retroactivity: policy and practice. In Report of proceedings of the fifty-eighth tax conference, 2006 Conference Report, 2:1–33. Toronto: Canadian Tax Foundation.
Moe, Terry M. 1989. The politics of bureaucratic structure. In *Can the government govern?* eds. John E. Chubb and Paul E. Peterson, 273–329. Washington, D.C.: Brookings Institution Press.
OECD. 2013a. *Addressing base erosion and profit shifting*. OECD Publishing. http://dx.doi.org/10.1787/9789264192744-en. Accessed 4 Dec 2014.
OECD. 2013b. Action plan on base erosion and profit shifting, OECD Publishing. www.oecd.org/ctp/BEPSActionPlan.pdf. Accessed 4 Dec 2014.
Osofsky, Leigh. 2013. Who's naughty and who's nice? Frictions, screening, and tax law design. *Buffalo Law Review* 61 (5): 1057–1117.
Piketty, Thomas, and Arthur Goldhammer. 2014. *Capital in the tweenty-first century*. Cambridge: Harvard University Press.
Raskolnikov, Alex. 2006. Crime and punishment in taxation: Deceit, deterrence, and the self-adjusting penalty. *Columbia Law Review* 106 (3): 569–642.
Raskolnikov, Alex. 2009. Revealing choices: Using taxpayer choice to target enforcement. *Columbia Law Review* 109 (4): 689–754.
Raz, Joseph. 1977. The rule of law and its virtue. *Law Quarterly Review* 93 (2): 195–211.
Solum, Lawrence B. 2009. Legal theory lexicon: The rule of law. http://lsolum.typepad.com/legaltheory_lexicon/2004/01/legal_theory_le_3.html. Accessed 4 Dec 2014..
Tirole, Jean. 1988. *The theory of industrial organization*. Cambridge: MIT Press.
Weisbach, David. 2002. An economic analysis of anti-tax-avoidance doctrines. *American Law and Economics Review* 4 (1): 88–115.
Yablon, Jeffery L, comp. 2006. Certain as death—Quotations about taxes 110 tax notes 103.

Part II
Justifying different Types of Taxation

Chapter 7
Why Taxing Consumption?

Justifications, Objections and Social Cooperation

Xavier Landes

I am thankful to Bruno Verbeek and Daniel Halliday for their comments and inputs as well as to the participants to the conference on Justice, Taxation and Social Policy organized by the Center for Ethics and Poverty Research at University of Salzburg.

Abstract Robert Frank is famous for proposing an incremental tax on consumption. His proposition is motivated by the control of positional externalities, i.e. the costs that individuals impose on each other when they consume goods for securing or acquiring social status. A close analysis of Frank's proposition identifies three justifications for a tax on consumption: efficiency, paternalism and equality. This chapter has two purposes. Firstly, it reviews these justifications, highlighting some objections and possible replies. As such, it suggests that reasons based on equality or paternalism are controversial while the invocation of efficiency is actually grounded in an underlying view of social cooperation. Secondly, this chapter advances the idea that an ultimate justification for the choice of specific tax base (consumption, income and wealth) expresses such an underlying view. In other words, the choice of a specific tax base is not totally instrumental, it has some intrinsic moral value too. In this respect, the chapter ends with a comparison between taxing income and taxing consumption. It is shown that a tax on consumption raises questions that should be answered by political philosophers.

7.1 Introduction

> Taxation is the price which we pay for civilization, for our social, civil and political institutions, for the security of life and property, and without which, we must resort to the law of force.
> Journal of the House of Representatives of the State of Vermont, October Session, 1851

X. Landes (✉)
Department of Media, Cognition and Communication, University of Copenhagen, Karen Blixens Vej 4, 2300 Copenhagen, Denmark
e-mail: xavier.landes@gmail.com

H. P. Gaisbauer et al. (eds.), *Philosophical Explorations of Justice and Taxation*,
Ius Gentium: Comparative Perspectives on Law and Justice 40,
DOI 10.1007/978-3-319-13458-1_7

Taxation is a key component of public policy by generating resources for public goods, social insurance and redistribution. Decisions about taxation may also affect political stability by nurturing social unrest and revolutions. Examples are abundant: the American Revolutionary War started with a tax controversy (the 1765 "Stamp Act"), like the French Revolution.[1] In United Kingdom, the introduction of a poll tax ("Community Charge") contributed to Thatcher's fall in 1990.

Despite the importance of the topic, it has attracted little interest in political philosophy. This is striking when compared to the refined analyses in distributive justice about the use of resources extracted from taxation. Various reasons can explain such neglect. One might argue that no matter how resources are collected, the only relevant question is what to do with them. There is also the view shared by many egalitarians that just contributions are contributions that mirror one's ability to pay or produce (e.g. talents in Rawls), which is supposed to end the discussion.

However, unless one controversially assumes that how public resources are collected does not matter at all, there is space for investigating the normative dimensions of taxation. It is difficult to consider that, for instance, the choice of taxing consumption instead of wealth or income, or to impose a progressive rate instead of a flat one is normatively indifferent. If this point is accepted, a normative theory of taxation has to articulate the following dimensions.

1. Why taxing? What reasons do public institutions have for collecting part of, what looks like at first sight, individuals' resources?
2. What taxing? What is the "right" tax base, consumption, income or wealth?
3. How taxing? Which rules should be followed when implementing citizens' tax duties?

I address here the second question through a discussion of Robert Frank's advocacy for a progressive tax on consumption (Frank 1999, 2007, 2008, 2011).[2] The methodology is to present Frank's position (first section) and to evaluate three reasons that might support a consumption tax: efficiency (second section), paternalism (third section) and equality (fourth section). When discussing these reasons, income or wealth taxes are not mentioned for the sake of a comparative analysis, but for highlighting the strengths and weaknesses of Frank's position. The contribution ends with a brief exposition of the core of the issue: the conception of social cooperation embodied in the choice of a tax base (fifth section). In the fifth section and the conclusion, I claim that political philosophers, especially those interested in distributive justice, need to be more concerned with taxation.

[1] The reader may refer to Nicolas Delalande's historical monograph for France (Delalande 2011) and Martin Daunton for United Kingdom (Daunton 2002).

[2] Frank and other authors (e.g. Thomas Hobbes, David Hume, John Stuart Mill, Irving Fisher, Milton Friedman) have advocated for a spending tax, sometimes to replace the current tax system.

7.2 Positional Consumption and Externalities

Inspired by Thorstein Veblen's seminal work on conspicuous consumption (Veblen 1994), Frank advocates for a steeply progressive tax on consumption. According to him, citizens should pay taxes at a marginal rate that is positively correlated to their amount of consumption: the more they consume, the higher the marginal rate should be.

His proposition is rooted in the observation that individuals are trapped in a positional arms race, which produces externalities (i.e. costs imposed on third parties to an original exchange). In the United States and elsewhere[3], individuals consume too much in general and too much of positional goods in particular, i.e. goods that are mostly demanded for their extrinsic qualities (i.e. for signalling one' status).[4]

Frank's central claim is that consumption is context-sensitive: other individuals' decisions matter in one's consumption. Individuals are influenced by social standards of spending, i.e. the rules about appropriate consumption. This context-sensitivity cannot be reduced to status-seeking alone as some suggest (Botton 2004) since someone's relative standing may deeply affect his ability to pursue his life projects and realize his conception of the good (Frank 1999, pp. 122–145). People care about their relative standing (determined by their relative spending) because it affects their opportunities in life and the opportunities of people for whom they care (e.g. children, spouse, dependants).

The origin of the problem lies in the positional dynamics that have been accentuated by the dramatic increase of top-incomes since the 1970's whereas low and middle incomes have stagnated or only slightly increased (Frank 2007, pp. 7–16).[5] The crux of the argument is that top-earners strongly influence social standards on appropriate spending in relation to home, clothes, travel, and so forth. 'Expenditure cascades' (Frank 2011, p. 61) explain how these patterns spread throughout society: top-earners' habits are imitated on a smaller scale by the income group who is below, whose consumption is imitated by the income group just below, and so forth.

By their spending habits individuals create *positional externalities* for others: for decades, standards for a "decent" home, gifts, clothes, vacation, cars, electronic appliances, and other goods and services have been rising. For instance, according to the National Association of Home Builders, the average size of US houses had almost doubled between 1970 and 2009. So, individuals have been using more resources for keeping up with criteria of socially adequate spending. Individuals

[3] Positional consumption is present in developing countries too (Solnick et al. 2007; Van Kempen 2009).

[4] Positional goods are 'goods, services, work positions, and other social relationships that are either (1) scarce in some absolute or socially imposed sense or (2) subject to congestion or crowding through more extensive use (Hirsch 1976, p. 27)'.

[5] Various authors highlight such dynamics, especially in the American context. For instance, Juliet Schor identifies a 'new consumerism' in the 'national culture of upscale spending' (Schor 1998, p. 4) while Oliver James diagnoses an epidemic of 'affluenza' (James 2007).

might spend too much, to their own detriment. In addition, positional consumption creates prisoner dilemmas where agents are trapped in suboptimal situations.

These situations are suboptimal due to 'positional externalities': everyone's spending increases the pressure on everyone else to adopt the same strategy.[6] This pressure creates further damage: overwork, wasteful conspicuous spending, pressure to perform, psychological distress, etc. (Frank 1999). This damage results from 'positional arm-races' where most of participants try to outperform (outspend) their competitors. Frank sees these dynamics at work for housing, gifts, vacations, clothing, and so forth. As with the arms race between the Soviet Union and the United States during the Cold War (Brams 1985), the increased spending on housing or cars incurs an adjustment of the consumer's immediate surroundings (relatives, friends, colleagues), which propagates further spending.[7]

Frank's appeal to 'positional externalities' strengthens the case for public intervention, especially in relation to those who are reluctant to accept the state's interference in private matters (Frank 2008, 2011, pp. 194–215). Based on John Stuart Mill's *harm principle*[8], Frank argues that positional consumption generates a broad array of costs that justify public intervention because they are imposed on third parties. His argument is to add to the loss of welfare the constraints imposed by individuals on each other and the individuals' incapacity to independently scale down their expenses (Frank 2008 p. 1782), which results in the impossibility of reducing the production of externalities in a significant manner.

Frank identifies two levels of positional harms. Firstly, individuals ruin their psychological situation. They do not optimize the happiness potential that could be derived from their material resources.[9] They get less satisfaction or subjective well-being than they would get in at least one attainable alternative (i.e. Pareto improvement is possible).

Secondly, individuals ruin their material situation, both individually and collectively. Individually, expenditure cascades increase positional spending and activities whereas decreasing non-positional consumption and activities (e.g. time spent with friends and family). People save less and become more vulnerable to future adverse events (e.g. unemployment, illness). Less affluent individuals rely on bank

[6] One may argue that positional externalities and costs from lack of coordination are two different things since the latter are imposed on individuals who are part of an exchange that has the form of a prisoner's dilemma while the former are imposed on individuals who are not part of the exchange (external to the exchange). Such a distinction implies the ability to draw a sharp line between agents involved in an original exchange and outside agents who suffer from the consequences of this exchange. The problem is the impossibility of identifying an original exchange or to clearly distinguish between costs stemming from a lack of cooperation and externalities.

[7] Other illustrations of positional arms-race include sports in US Ivy League universities (Dixit and Nalebuff 1993, pp. 225–227), the 'publish-or-perish' dilemma in academia (Landes et al. 2013) or reproductive competition in some animal species (Frank 1999, pp. 148–152).

[8] '[T]he only purpose for which power can be rightfully exercised over any member of a civilized community, against his will, is to prevent harm to others. His own good, either physical or moral, is not a sufficient warrant' (Mill 2003, p. 80).

[9] Frank blends happiness with subjective well-being (constituted by positive and negative affects and life satisfaction) even if he is aware of their difference (Frank 2007, p. 18).

credit for keeping up (and counter-balancing the stagnation of their income). Socially, private and public investments are squeezed, jeopardizing public goods and growth. Also, the increased pressure to "keep up with the Joneses" partly explains the current resistance to accept taxation.

As a solution, Frank proposes a progressive tax on consumption that will not apply on specific positional goods (contrary to a luxury tax), but on individuals' volume of spending.[10] Such a tax will curb positional consumption in particular and consumption in general. If the rates are steep enough, it will cause a decline in top-earners' spending, but also in the spending of lower income classes in virtue of the expenditure cascades. Individuals will be forced to save more, which will be beneficial to private investments and enhance individuals' capacity to cope with adverse events. Finally, more resources will be levied for financing public goods, which will benefit everyone in the society.

Frank's argument is a mix of at least three different justifications, namely *efficiency*, *paternalism* and *equality*. The subsequent sections will present and discuss each of them.[11] Then I will argue that the core of the issue is how to envisage social cooperation. My suggestion is that the choice of a tax base expresses a particular conception of social cooperation.

7.3 Efficiency

Usually economists and philosophers share the view that efficiency is an *a-moral* concept since it would be silent on the good and the bad, the right and the wrong features of different actions or states of the world. Thus, the efficiency of a social arrangement would be a purely empirical matter. This view is rooted in a division of intellectual labour between economists, who would deal with factual issues, and philosophers, who would deal with evaluative ones.

This division might have some cogency, but it cannot be denied that the concept of efficiency is partly normative. In order to judge that a given arrangement is efficient, two normative "things" should be decided: (1) what needs to be efficient, i.e. the object of efficiency, and (2) which principles must ground this evaluation, i.e. the rules of efficiency.

1. The debate on whether Gross Domestic Product (GDP) offers a fair evaluation of socioeconomic performance illustrates the first point (van den Bergh 2010). No doubt the choice between GDP or alternative indicators such as UNDP's *Human Development Index* or *the Happy Planet Index* is to some extent influenced by practical considerations (e.g. the data's availability, the possibility to sum different aggregates or undertake international comparisons). But the choice is nor-

[10] Individual spending is calculated by deducting savings from income. The practical advantage of this proposal is to avoid the difficulty of defining and identifying positional goods.

[11] I discuss in details the different normative arguments for curbing positionality in another piece (Landes 2013b).

mative too since it expresses views about what should be collectively valued (economic growth, education, life expectancy, environment, etc.).

2. Choosing between different conceptions of efficiency is not axiologically neutral either. For instance, a choice between Pareto and Kaldor-Hicks efficiencies is a choice between a conception that excludes the improvement of the situation of an agent at the expense of another (the so-called "minority sacrifice")—Pareto's conception—and a conception that precisely allows a trade-off as long as compensation is *hypothetically* possible—Kaldor-Hicks' conception.

Efficiency is a normative concept that allows different interpretations (conceptions). Ultimately, the "what" of Frank's conception (i.e. what should be efficient) boils down to the conditions of social cooperation. In his writings, there are at least three aspects in which implementing a progressive tax on consumption would render social cooperation more efficient: the reduction of positional externalities' "leakage", the maximization of the social output (especially through private and public investments), and the improvement of individuals' satisfaction or happiness.

In that respect Frank is the heir of Welfare Economics that attributes to the state the responsibility of correcting 'market failures' (Baumol 1952, 1972), i.e. to enhance welfare. However his use of Mill's harm principle expresses the additional argument that public intervention is ultimately justified by the prevention or correction of harms imposed on others (Frank 2008). Since market failures imply *imposed* harms to others, the state ought to intervene.[12] Pigovian taxation is the classical tool. It consists of charging a tax on the emitters of the negative externalities (Landes 2013a). Frank's originality is to stretch the concept of externalities and Pigovian taxation for including *positional* dimensions.

However, Frank does not clearly define the concept of positional externalities in his writings. A plausible interpretation is that a positional externality consists of the negative variation of the status of a given individual that results from an initial interaction of which he has not been part (implying that he has not agreed to the terms of this interaction), inducing two kinds of costs: material ones (e.g. high consumption, low savings, or under-financing of public goods like roads, bridges, hospitals, etc.) and psychological ones (e.g. reduced well-being and happiness).

By contrast, efficient cooperation is characterized by limited "positional leakage", high private/public investments and high individual satisfaction/happiness. However, if the objective was to reduce or suppress positional externalities, why is a (incremental) tax on consumption more efficient than, say, a (incremental) tax on income or wealth?

It is one thing to justify the efficiency of a tax on consumption, it is another to justify its superior efficiency vis-à-vis a tax on income or wealth. Superior efficien-

[12] Like many, Frank oscillates between two uses of externalities. The first consists in weighting the current situation against an ideal for identifying the divergences, i.e. the famous "market failures". The main reproach against that view is that it succumbs to the 'Nirvana fallacy' (Demsetz 1969), which is to compare actual situations to hypothetical, non-feasible, alternatives. The second use is more pragmatic since it is only to identify actual harms and redress/prevent them on a case-by-case basis.

cy does not follow from efficiency. For instance, tax structures relating to income or wealth can become so quickly confiscatory that conspicuous consumption will be reduced in larger proportions than offered by any tax on consumption. Also, if the problem is positional externality, why not capping income and wealth through regulation? In short, why is taxing consumption is the preferable option?

In the literature, the principle of 'neutrality' or 'non-discrimination' between consumers and savers advocates for consumption as a more appropriate tax base than income.[13] According to Mill, taxing income leads to a double taxation of the savers (Mill 1848, V, I, 4): first, when they earn their income, even if part of it is invested, and, afterwards, on the return of this investment.[14] Beyond the 'unfairness' to agents in proper (Andrews 1974), i.e. the advantage given to some lifestyles over others, this absence of neutrality is detrimental to private and public savings and investment, i.e. efficiency.

The last point is the reason Frank emphasizes in support of substituting a tax on consumption in the current US tax system*: reducing positional externalities without dis-incentivizing economic activities*. If consumption is taxed at a steeply progressive rate, individuals will save more, which will positively affect investment and economic growth. Moreover, work will not be discouraged since the accumulation of wealth and investment will be rewarded.

Efficiency, then, justifies taxing consumption, instead of income, since it helps to tame positional externalities while not dis-incentivizing agents to engage in productive activities and, furthermore, incentivizing them to invest. However, Frank's conception of efficiency, as well as common defences of consumption tax, appears to include more than a consequentialist calculation. A "thicker" normative ideal seems to inspire the choice of consumption as the appropriate tax base arising from the idea that consumption is wasteful, especially in affluent societies. Furthermore, consumption is presented as being the source or vehicle of perverse social interactions implying signalling and counter-signalling, status-seeking, rat-races, etc. (James 2007; Schor 1998).

The taxation of consumption is, at least partly, driven by an underlying moral commitment to anti-consumerism or by an ascetic ideal according to which consumption should be directed towards the satisfaction of basic needs, the rest often being superfluous or harmful. This commitment would explain the heavy emphasis on non-positional goods such as family, social relations, environmental concerns, altruism and generosity. Such emphasis would not be fully explainable by efficiency alone, but by a deeper conception of what has value in life.[15]

---

[13] For a brief criticism of this idea, the reader could read the few pages written by Alvin Warren (Warren 1979–1980, pp. 1097–1101).

[14] Under non-idealistic conditions, income tax may be discriminatory between different types of savings, for instance if there is a realization requirement for savings for becoming tax liable as it is the case in the United States (McCaffery 2002, pp. 28–29).

[15] This is particularly visible in the literature on happiness and sustainability, ranging from voluntary simplicity to psychological studies on materialism (Kasser 2003). The point of interest is that literature is tangential to Frank's works, who regularly refers to it for backing up some of his points.

Without detailing further this idea, the conception of efficiency that underlies Frank's position could be summarized as follows: an efficient society is a society that keeps consumption under control to the benefit of more valuable economic activities, like saving and investing, and non-economic ones, like spending time with friends and family. In short, *efficient social cooperation is cooperation that maximizes the cooperative gains in both material and subjective, productive and non-productive terms.*

7.4 Paternalism

Human frailty is the source of a second justification for taxing consumption. Because individuals often fail to adequately perceive or pursue their own good, taxing consumption will be justified. To a certain degree, this argument elaborates on the psychological costs highlighted in the previous section. Nevertheless, it is paternalistic in the sense that public intervention is rooted in people's own good: individuals will be made better off by the imposition of a tax on consumption that 'would greatly enhance every citizen's opportunity to pursue independent visions of the good life' (Frank 1999, p. 224).

Two versions of the argument may be differentiated, each based on a different view of the dynamics at work in conspicuous consumption.

1. Individuals suffer from defects in their capacity to perceive their own good. Research on perceptive and cognitive biases supports this view (Ariely 2008; Kahneman 2011; Stanovich 2009). Biases lead individuals to commit evaluative mistakes and act upon them, which is detrimental to their well-being. For instance, they tend to under-save in provision for their future retirement. Therefore it is necessary to incentivize them to do so. Compulsory contributions to pensions constitute forced savings that one can justify for paternalistic reasons. Likewise, a consumption tax will force individuals to downscale their positional spending.

This view is nonetheless problematic. First of all, it conflicts with Mill's harm principle that justifies interfering only for preventing harms to others, not self-harms (as put by Mill: 'his own good, either physical or moral, is not a sufficient warrant'). As such, the first view subverts the externality rationale. In response, it may be argued that: first, individuals actually cause harms to each other, not only to themselves (the positional externalities), and, second, they cannot downscale their spending *without external help*.

A second objection is that the postulate of individuals suffering from biases may justify abusive interference in individual lives since, in the absence of further qualifications, the only condition is to single out self-inflicted harms of any sort. As for any slippery slope argument, it may be replied that the problem is not public intervention, but abusive public intervention, which can be fixed by establishing strict rules, in particular in regard to what should count as morally relevant self-inflicted harms. For being fully convincing, the second objection should demonstrate that taxing consumption represents an instance of abusive intervention *per se*.

Lastly, public intervention may handicap or even jeopardize ways of life that imply self-harm (e.g., extreme sports, unhealthy lifestyles), but which are freely chosen or endorsed by individuals. An additional argument is to claim that this kind of justification for public policy could easily become the vehicle for political perfectionism, i.e. the external imposition of a full-fledged comprehensive doctrine upon a given population. Against this, it may be replied that fully unconstrained lives are impossible: all individual decisions are bounded in one way or another by other people's choices and institutional regulation. So the relevant question is: how much constraint can be justified? Does a tax on consumption excessively burden some individuals or groups? In fact, the only agents who might object are high-spenders. Without going further, it should be noticed that Frank precisely shows how a consumption tax will be both individually (e.g. saving resources) and collectively (e.g. public goods) beneficial.

Nevertheless the main shortcoming of this version of the paternalistic justification is probably the assumption that individuals cannot, as a general rule, perceive their own good. Actually, all it takes is to demonstrate that individuals can perceive their own good in order to undermine the first version. In any case, Frank's case does not require such a stringent assumption.

2. The second view holds that individuals are capable of perceiving their good, but experience difficulties in pursuing it because of the structure of social interactions. Individuals would rather consume less (especially positional goods), work less, spend more time with their relatives and friends, but they simply cannot. They must adjust to social patterns of consumption, appear "adequate" in given situations (job interviews, professional meetings, social gatherings, community events, etc.), buy a home close to an excellent school, etc. The problem is that, by adjusting to social standards, each individual raises the bar for everyone else. Regulation is justified, not by self-inflicted harms, but by the individual's inability to cease the production of mutual harms conveyed by positional consumption.

Thus, the awareness of the existence of mutual harms does not guarantee that individuals will curb their positional spending. Individuals cannot stop spending because positional consumption is essential for securing important life opportunities (e.g. getting promoted, sending kids to excellent schools, networking with the 'right' people, etc.) and because they may think that, in the end, they could outperform their competitors on consumption grounds. An incremental tax on consumption is meant to solve this collective action problem by changing the rules of the game: increasing the price of positional consumption and reducing the relative price of alternatives (non-positional activities).

In summary, the second justification for taxing consumption is that *because individuals cannot opt out of positional dynamics (except at high cost), taxing consump-*

tion will make them better off on their own terms.[16] However, this second version of the paternalistic argument is not free of concern.

First of all, depending on how much individual spending is actually determined by social patterns, the incentive of a tax on consumption may be reduced or annihilated. If we take seriously the idea that positional consumption is led by relative concerns and social patterns from which it is extremely difficult to escape, imposing a (incremental) tax on consumption may further harm individuals, especially the most vulnerable, by imposing an additional burden (the tax amount).

Secondly, it may be claimed that positional consumption *qua* consumption is necessary for economic growth. Some aspects of consumption could be individually and collectively detrimental, but the global effect would still be positive: the economic stimulus arising from positional consumption would generate more individual and collective benefits than harms (e.g. created jobs, increased taxes). Economic theories like Keynesianism even consider that consumption is the engine of economic growth and development. Therefore, curbing consumption would harm the economy and individuals.

At the end of the day, paternalism is controversial when it comes to justifying a tax on consumption, as are most of the other reasons for taxing consumption. Before presenting the idea that the choice of a tax base expresses an underlying view of social cooperation, it is necessary to consider equality.

7.5 Equality

The third argument is that a consumption tax will help roll back inequalities, which have been rising in most industrialized countries since the 1970's. Frank is concerned with income and wealth inequalities (Frank 2007, pp. 7–16). For instance, he notes that between 1979 and 2000, the top 1% of households increased their income by 201% against 9% for the bottom 20, 13% for the second 20, 15% for the middle 20, 24% for the fourth 20%.[17] His 'point is not that the creation of these big fortunes is by itself a bad thing' (Frank 2007, p. 15), but that inequalities harm the middle class by increasing a variety of costs, jeopardizing heath, etc. More specifically, inequality also aggravates positional harms. Therefore, if one cares about positional externalities, one should care about inequalities. Equality has however no intrinsic value within Frank's framework. The perspective of egalitarian societies with high levels of positional spending would not be terribly attractive for Frank.

[16] *This* second justification generates additional difficulties regarding the potential consequences of the kind of policies that could be conducted. Since positional externalities are partly evaluated according to some subjective standards, tax on consumption may lead to the politics of envy.

[17] The most recent evidence shows that the trend has worsened in the United States (Stiglitz 2013). Furthermore, this spread between the very top-incomes and the rest of the income-earners is not unique to United States, but has become common in a lot of (if not all) industrialized countries (OECD 2011).

Positional competition in a context of rising inequalities generates harms or worsens existing ones (Frank 2007, pp. 92–102). Individuals work longer hours than they are willing to do in order to keep up with increased positional expenditures in a context of stagnation of real incomes. They also reduce their savings and increase their debts (e.g. by abusing credit card payments). Since it has been expensive to live in inner cities, they commute further and longer, which creates stress and sleep deprivation.

From the perspective of equality, a tax on consumption should nonetheless respond to a serious objection, especially if it is supposed to replace other taxes, on income or wealth: it will favour rich people since they will accumulate wealth at an exorbitant rate, in particular in a situation, as assumed by Frank, of rising income inequalities. By the way, the idea is generally acknowledged that large concentrations of wealth can undermine democracy and that one of the first functions of taxation is to tame this tendency (Avi-Yonah 2002; Rawls 2001, p. 279). If consumption alone is taxed, nothing prevents a handful of individuals of accumulating vast material resources that can be transformed into political power at the service of their own interests.[18]

Two answers are possible. The first is to say that accumulation of wealth is not equivalent to actual exercise of power. The second is to point out that a tax on consumption primarily aims at taming positional concerns and their deleterious effects, not at enforcing any kind of equality, especially of wealth, power or capacity to influence.

On the one hand, it is true that accumulation of wealth is not the same as actual use of wealth for exercising influence. Nevertheless, great wealth, if it does not automatically lead to concrete use of power, still represents what neo-republicanism labels as the *capacity to arbitrarily interfere* in citizens' life. Even if extremely wealthy individuals act virtuously, i.e. respect established laws and democratic rules (in regard, for instance, to the independence of elected representatives), they will still have the capacity to interfere (or they might be induced to do so by other agents who have an interest in their interference). Hence great accumulations of wealth are sources of domination (Pettit 1997), which threaten democratic institutions.

On the other hand, one may answer that a tax on consumption should be evaluated on its own grounds: the good that it promises to deliver. Since it does not promise to deliver equality of wealth, it is unfair to judge it on this criterion. The purpose of this tax being to curb positional externalities, it is then difficult to deny that consumption tax has some credential for this purpose.

However, part of the defence of a consumption tax as articulated by Frank is to interpret positional harms from the perspective of subjective well-being. It is then difficult to argue that a tax system that will limit conspicuous consumption, while leaving impressive accumulations of wealth, will fairly fulfil its *purpose on its own grounds*. Actually, the evidence mobilized by Frank demonstrates that

[18] This objection is not an argument against consumption tax, but against consumption as the unique tax base, which is different. A tax on consumption can be mixed with other tax bases, but by doing so, the originality of the defences of consumption tax, such as Frank's one, is lost.

people psychologically suffer from relative standing, including wealth disparities. Without even taking into account subjective well-being, it could be presumed that a society that will tolerate large wealth inequalities will nurture distrust among its members along with other social evils (Uslaner 2002; Wilkinson and Pickett 2010). This could impair social cooperation, which is at the core of Frank's conception of efficiency.

Finally, taxing consumption, especially at a steeply progressive rate, may have anti-egalitarian results, depending on the design of the tax. Individuals might actually have high levels of spending for reasons that are not positional and without producing positional externalities. For instance, people may suffer from chronic diseases, be handicapped or need to look after dependents, which implies higher levels of consumption. A tax will represent a sanction imposed on their unlucky condition.[19] People may accrue consumption for genuine reasons (again, handicap, sickness, dependents, etc.) by relying on credit. They will be harmed in several ways: the material cost, the psychological suffering (because of the initial handicap, sickness, etc., and of the material incapacity to cope with it), the incurred debts and the tax.[20]

These objections illustrate that a commitment to equality may be at odds with consumption as the appropriate (and unique) tax base. Despite the fact that Frank seems to worry about growing inequalities, his argument is rather instrumental than intrinsic: equality is not a good in itself, it is a source of concerns insofar that it exacerbates positional competition (which aggravates the situation of the worse-off and the middle-class). The force of appealing to equality as a reason for justifying a tax on consumption is limited. Furthermore, it is possible to consider that equality is an argument against taxing consumption (especially at a progressive rate) or, at least, against consumption as the only tax base since it may actually worsen some inequalities (material and political).

7.6 Two Conceptions of Social Cooperation

A tax on consumption raises various objections, especially if it should replace other tax bases as suggested by Frank and others (McCaffery 2002). These objections are useful because they offer opportunities for judging of the strength of different arguments for a tax on consumption. Equality provides a shaky ground since endorsing equality may lead to objections to the principle of a (unique) tax on consumption while a (unique) tax on consumption may still not be fully justified by equality. Pa-

[19] One might claim that this problem flows from the insensitivity of consumption tax to brute bad luck. The same person might argue that the principle of equality imposes not to worsen the situation of those who suffer from bad brute luck, i.e. who suffer from inequalities due to no reason of their own (Knight 2009).

[20] Depending on the design of the tax scheme, this shortcoming may be worsened by the steep progressivity proposed by Frank and others. There could also be correcting mechanisms external to the tax scheme, e.g. through hypothecation (see Daniel Halliday's contribution to this volume).

ternalism generates different objections, some stronger than others. Still, the global impact on individuals' well-being needs to be further assessed. Finally, the efficiency argument underlines the value of social cooperation for justifying a (progressive) tax on consumption.

Derived from the idea of the normative thickness of efficiency as an argument for justifying a tax on consumption, my final claim is that the choice between taxing consumption, income or wealth reflects a *parti pris* between different conceptions of social cooperation. The issue of taxation is not a purely material question about how to provide resources for public finances. Taxation enounces individuals' financial responsibilities vis-à-vis the political community, understood as a nexus of cooperative mechanisms. It spells out the "right" distribution of contributions among citizens according to a conception of the proper terms of cooperation. The fundamental choice of a tax base indicates how social cooperation is collectively understood and enforced.

The scarce works on taxation in political philosophy usually downplay this aspect. For instance, Liam Murphy and Thomas Nagel consider that the choice of a tax base is only instrumental for economic justice. They invoke the 'fair distribution of the burdens' (Murphy and Nagel 2002, p. 98) or 'just social outcomes' (Murphy and Nagel 2002, p. 99) as guiding principles for determining how to tax citizens. Taxation would be an instrument for reaching an ideal that is defined independently of what taxation is about.

There are several problems here. Firstly, a "fair distribution of the burdens" and "just social outcomes" are two different things and nothing guarantees that a fair distribution of the burdens advocates for the same tax arrangement as one that produces just social outcomes. Secondly, in themselves they are silent on what fairness and justice should be. Presumably, different conceptions will lead to significantly different tax designs. Thirdly, the view implicitly endorsed by the authors is that, at the end of the day, any tax base could be used for promoting any political ideal. Taxation would be a plastic, value-free, tool for pursuing political ideals.

Nevertheless, it may be argued that the choice of a tax base is *not only* a practical choice to be made in the light of a pre-existing conception of economic justice. It may be claimed that each of the three major tax bases—wealth, income and consumption[21]—tells a different story about how to conceive social cooperation, what our (material) responsibilities are and how we should relate to each other. Basically, a wealth tax is based on the idea that it is appropriate to tax individuals on what they own, an income tax on what they earn and a consumption tax on what they use for non-productive purposes.

This moral dimension appears in the discussions about the "common pool" metaphor, which is recurrent in the debates about taxation (Warren 1979–1980, pp. 1094–1095). Since society is a common pool of resources, individuals may be taxed according to their share of (wealth tax), contribution to (income) or use of (consumption) the common pool. The terms of the metaphor suggest that it is pref-

[21] We leave aside inheritance tax, which can be classified under other categories (e.g. wealth or income).

erable to tax people on how much they take out of the common pool instead of how much they put in (Kaldor 1955, p. 53; Rawls 1985, p. 278).

If we put aside its debatable cogency (Murphy and Nagel 2002, pp. 109–112), the metaphor has the merit to highlight the normative nature of the choice of a tax base. While many egalitarians take for granted that contributions to public resources should reflect one's ability to pay, only the wealth tax respects this principle. If we put wealth aside in order to contrast income and consumption taxes, it becomes clear that they represent different visions of social cooperation.

1. *Income tax* (i.e. revenues from labour and capital) bears on fluxes supposedly correlated with wealth creation. Individuals are presumed to receive an income reflecting their productivity. Their contribution to social cooperation through taxation should be calculated on this basis.

What the common pool argument gets right is that income tax expresses a financial liability that *partly* depends on individual contributions to the collective resources. But it only *partly* depends on individual contributions since it is reasonable to consider that a given individual's productivity has a spill-over effect on others' productivity. As a result, the distant resources (the positive externalities) that a given individual has contributed are not accounted for in her income (whereas her income also encapsulates others' distant contribution). However the fact that tax contributions are roughly correlated to the value one has contributed to create does not mean that one's taxes should be understood as being justified by (or bearing on) the value created by individuals. It is quite a different question.

Since society is a vast system where different cooperative mechanisms are intertwined, one's income (when based on productivity) reflects one's own work, but also one's use of cooperation, i.e. the work of other individuals. Taxing income can be understood not only as a tax levied on one's contribution to the common pool, but also as a tax levied on one's use of *cooperative mechanisms during the process of creating value*.[22] This reformulation expresses a conception of social cooperation where individuals' contributions to public goods, redistribution and public insurance are calculated by combining individuals' productive capacity and use of cooperative mechanisms.[23]

2. *Consumption tax* bears on someone's use of her income, i.e. her income minus savings. It relates to one's use of the created wealth. While an income tax defines someone's duties to contribute to public resources as depending on her ability to produce value and her use of cooperative mechanisms, consumption tax

[22] According to this view, the positive correlation between tax and income (under flat or progressive tax rates) could be justified by the fact that, presumably, the more individuals earn, the more they are likely to have benefited from social cooperation.

[23] Even if the contribution makes an analytical distinction between one's capacity to produce and one's use of cooperative mechanisms, it remains an open question whether the two can in fact be distinguished, whether individuals' productivity can be measured and, furthermore, if it makes sense to talk about "one's productivity" in most cooperative settings due to the intense division of labour that characterizes modern economies.

adjusts contributions to her actual use of the wealth that has been produced. A manner to flesh out this idea is to claim that since world resources are limited, it is legitimate to hold people liable for the resources they extract from the world, especially when these resources are scarce.

A tax on consumption links someone's contributions to her degree of use of the collectively produced wealth. Since this use depends on preferences, it is reasonable to postulate that consumption tax tells a story about social cooperation that emphasizes the legitimacy of individual contributions that match the goods and services that individuals decide to extract from social cooperation. Also, a tax on consumption does not make individuals liable for the wealth they put aside (i.e. savings) since it does not strain the common resources. In short, a tax on consumption tends to see individual choice about the use of common resources as the normatively relevant criterion for establishing one's tax duties.

7.7 Conclusion

The previous developments fuel more questions than responses. However, they unveil issues that are fundamental for the ethics of taxation. The main concern *is the moral significance* of the tax base: any solid defence of a given tax base needs to flesh out the underlying conception of social cooperation since it is where the moral force of the argument stands. In short, by taxing individuals on certain terms, the political community tells a particular story about our mutual duties. This illustrates the need for a fully-fledged normative analysis of the various models of social cooperation embodied in the different tax bases. The only ambition of this chapter was to introduce the relevance of such a project in political philosophy.

Without enumerating all the tasks encapsulated in this project, another challenge is to *clarify the moral status of individual preferences within the model of cooperation entailed by the choice of consumption as a tax base*. The rationale exposed above suggests that individuals are materially liable for their preferences since they determine their spending habits. However the preferences that determine one's contribution are what could be called realized preferences. Taxing consumption is taxing individuals on the preferences they are able to satisfy under constraints (e.g. budget, availability of alternatives and substitutes). It means that individuals are not taxed on their preferences, but on the overlap between them, their capacities and the options that are available at the time of the choice.

The *moral status of individual choice (and individual responsibility) in tax duties* is a major research theme for the ethics of taxation (as is already the case for distributive justice as epitomized by the debates around luck egalitarianism (Knight 2009)), especially because the strength of the case for a consumption tax is deeply indebted to the intuition that taxing people on their choice is the right thing to do: since people decide to spend their money on certain goods and services at a certain level (in doing so, they decide the kind and the intensity of the strain they impose on social resources), it is legitimate that their contribution accounts for that. But individual spending is actually determined by a mix of chosen and un-chosen preferences, a combination of choices and circumstances, which is difficult to disentangle. Individuals control only a part of their spending, the other part being affected by their needs. Thus, a defence of a consumption tax should address the following issue: *is it fair (or simply justified) to tune someone's contribution to social cooperation on factors that may be outside her control to a very large extent?*

References

Andrews, William D. 1974. A consumption-type or cash flow personal income tax. *Harvard Law Review* 87 (6):1113–1188.

Ariely, Dan. 2008. *Predictably irrational: The hidden forces that shape our decisions*. New York: HarperCollins.

Avi-Yonah, Reuven S. 2002. Why tax the rich? Efficiency, equity, and progressive taxation. *The Yale Law Journal* 111 (6): 1391–1416.

Baumol, William J. 1952. *Welfare economics and the theory of the state*. London: Longmans, Green and Co.

Baumol, William J. 1972. On taxation and the control of externalities. *The American Economic Review* 62 (3): 307–322.

Botton, Alain de. 2004. *Status anxiety*. New York: Vintage Books.

Brams, Steven J. 1985. *Superpower games: Applying game theory to superpower conflict*. New Haven: Yale University Press.

Daunton, Martin. 2002. *Just taxes: The politics of taxation in Britain, 1914–1979*. Cambridge: Cambridge University Press.

Delalande, Nicolas. 2011. *Les Batailles de l'impôt*. Éditions du Seuil.

Demsetz, Harold. 1969. Information and efficiency: Another viewpoint. *Journal of Law and Economics* 12 (1):1–22.

Dixit, Avinash, and Barry Nalebuff. 1993. *Thinking strategically: The competitive edge in business, politics, and everyday life*. New York: Norton.

Frank, Robert H. 1999. *Luxury fever: Why money fails to satisfy in an era of excess*. New York: Free Press.

Frank, Robert H. 2007. *Falling behind: How rising inequality harms the middle class*. Berkeley and Los Angeles: University of California Press.

Frank, Robert H. 2008. Should public policy respond to positional externalities? *Journal of Public Economics* 92 (8–9):1777–1786.

Frank, Robert H. 2011. *The darwin economy: Liberty, competition, and the common good*. Princeton: Princeton University Press.

Hirsch, Fred. 1976. *Social limits to growth*. New York: Routledge.

James, Oliver. 2007. *Affluenza*. London: Vermilion.

Kahneman, Daniel. 2011. *Thinking, fast and slow*. New York: Penguin.

Kaldor, Nicholas. 1955. *An expenditure tax*. London: Uwin University Books.

Kasser, Tim. 2003. *The high price of materialism*. Cambridge: MIT Press.

Knight, Carl. 2009. *Luck egalitarianism: Equality, responsibility, and justice*. Edinburgh: Edinburgh University Press.

Landes, Xavier. 2013a. Pigouvian taxation. In *Encyclopedia of corporate social responsibility*, eds. Samuel O. Idowu, Nicholas Capaldi, Liangrong Zu, and Ananda Das Gupta, 1846–1853. New York: Springer.

Landes, Xavier. 2013b. Positional concerns and institutions: Some arguments for regulation. *Central European Journal of Public Policy* 7 (2): 60–87.
Landes, Xavier, Martin Marchman, and Morten Nielsen. 2013. The academic rat race: Dilemmas and problems in the structure of academic competition. Learning and teaching: *The International Journal of Higher Education in the Social Sciences (LATISS)* 5 (2): 73–90.
McCaffery, Edward J. 2002. *Fair not flat: How to make the tax system better and simpler*. Chicago: Chicago Press.
Mill, John Stuart. 1848. *Principles of political economy: With some of their applications to social philosophy*. Boston: C.C. Little and J. Brown.
Mill, John Stuart. 2003. *On liberty*. New Haven: Yale University Press.
Murphy, Liam, and Thomas Nagel. 2002. *The myth of ownership: Taxes and justice*. New York: Oxford University Press.
OECD. 2011. *Divided we stand: Why inequality keeps rising*. OECD Publishing.
Pettit, Phillip. 1997. *Republicanism: A theory of freedom and government*. New York: Oxford University Press.
Rawls, John. 1985. Justice as fairness: Political not metaphysical. *Philosophy and Public Affairs* 14 (3): 223–251.
Rawls, John. 2001. *Justice as fairness: A restatement*. Cambridge: Belknap Press.
Schor, Juliet B. 1998. *The overspent American: Why we want what we don't need*. New York: Basic Books.
Solnick, Sara J., Li Hong, and David Hemenway. 2007. Positional goods in the United States and China. *The Journal of Socio-Economics* 36 (4): 537–545.
Stanovich, Keith E. 2009. *Decision making and rationality in the modern world*. New York: Oxford University Press.
Stiglitz, Joseph E. 2013. *The price of inequality: How today's divided society endangers our future*. New York: Norton.
Uslaner, Eric. 2002. *The moral foundations of trust*. Cambridge: Cambridge University Press.
van den Bergh, and Jeroen C. J. M. 2010. Externality or sustainability economics? *Ecological Economics* 69 (11):2047–2052.
Van Kempen, Luuk. 2009. *Status consumption and poverty in developing countries*. Saarbrücken: VDM.
Veblen, Thorstein. 1994. *The theory of the leisure class*. Mineola: Dover Publications.
Warren, Alvin. 1979–1980. Would a consumption tax be fairer than an income tax? *The Yale Law Journal* 89 (6): 1081–1124.
Wilkinson, Richard, and Kate Pickett. 2010. *The spirit level: Why equality is better for everyone*. London: Penguin.

Chapter 8
Egalitarianism and Consumption Tax

Daniel Halliday

Abstract Consumption taxes are often used to dissuade citizens from purchasing products that cause negative health outcomes, such as tobacco and alcohol. Such taxes are often criticized on the grounds that they discriminate against the poor: Consumption taxes are 'regressive', insofar as they require poor persons to pay a larger fraction of their income per consumed unit of good. After an attempt to spell out exactly what this objection asserts, this chapter attempts to respond to it. The apparently egalitarian complaint about regressive taxation can be countered by other egalitarian worries about the vulnerability of low-income groups to the harms resulting from the type of consumption being taxed. This calls for the redesign of consumption taxes rather than abolition. Further progress can be made by recognizing there are ways of taxing consumption other than the standard model of a sales tax that is typically assumed in these debates. One is to hypothecate the revenues from ways that aid the poor, mitigating the regressivity of the tax burden. Another is to replace sales taxes with licences or permits. Hypothecation and licensing can also be combined in ways that can eliminate regressivity altogether. This contribution attempts to develop these ideas in more detail.

8.1 Introduction

Consumption taxes are often used to discourage the consumption of products that cause harm. Familiar examples concern products that result in bad health outcomes for their users. These include sales taxes often attached to alcohol and tobacco products, which have been around for some time, as well as more recent attempts to tax food products linked with obesity. Other examples feature in proposals to extend the use of consumption taxes beyond the traditional focus on goods that harm their consumers. Taxing air travel, for example, might be defended in the name of reducing environmental harms that are absorbed by the global population (including persons yet to be born). There is also growing interest in the role that taxation might play

D. Halliday (✉)
School of Philosophical Studies, University of Melbourne, VIC 3010 Melbourne, Australia
e-mail: daniel.halliday@unimelb.edu.au

H. P. Gaisbauer et al. (eds.), *Philosophical Explorations of Justice and Taxation*,
Ius Gentium: Comparative Perspectives on Law and Justice 40,
DOI 10.1007/978-3-319-13458-1_8

in combating wasteful sorts of positional consumption. Examples of this phenomenon include the purchasing of suits for job interviews, and private tuition to help children prepare for important exams. Much of this consumption is competitive, as consumers are essentially trying to 'out-consume' each other. Although the moral case for taxation here is sometimes described in terms of preventing harm to others, such cases can perhaps be better distinguished by appealing to the way in which positional competition can instantiate a costly collective action problem.[1]

Differences between these cases[2] suggest that different moral justifications (or combinations thereof) might be at work in different cases. Often a justification for consumption tax might be straightforwardly paternalistic. Other times it might depend on principles for protecting third parties, and sometimes it might draw on the morality of using coercion to save people from conflict or coordination failure.[3] A proper separation and comparison of the force of each of these justifications, and of which justifications have which force in which cases, would take up a good deal of space. I don't have time to do this. What I want to address here is not really part of the positive case for attaching consumption taxes to harmful products, but part of the negative case against. Here's the problem in brief. Consumption taxes tend to be 'regressive' taxes. What it means for a tax to be regressive is for its real burden to be unevenly distributed across the persons who pay that tax, so that persons who are badly off pay a higher effective rate than persons who are better off. So the idea of a regressive tax, then, is the opposite of a progressive tax, where the effective rate goes up only when the person paying that tax is better off. Consumption taxes, when attached to particular products, have the tendency to be regressive insofar as they are insensitive to the circumstances of whoever's paying them. When the government imposes a tax on (say) a pack of cigarettes, this tax tends to stay the same irrespective of how rich or poor someone is when they buy this pack, and irrespective of how many packs they might have already bought. But poor people have smaller amounts of disposable income (or wealth) than wealthier people. So, a poor

[1] Taxing the consumption of some positional goods is recommended by Frank (2008). For more discussion, see the article by Xavier Landes in this volume.

[2] I should say, in passing, that I am not going to focus on the case for using consumption as a general tax base for raising revenue. This use of consumption tax does not aim to deter consumption of any specific product. At most, it is motivated by a concern to get consumers to spend less (and save more), largely irrespective of what kind of products they tend to spend their money on. Worries of the sort I discuss in this contribution can also be raised against views about consumption's suitability as a general base, but call for a rather different response that must draw on whatever the reason is for preferring consumption as a general base. Proponents of the use of consumption tax as a general base can handle the regressivity objection by allowing the idea that consumers don't pay any tax at all on a large initial portion of their annual consumption (this idea is analogous to the common practice of taxing income in ways that admit zero-percent bracket below a certain income floor). For discussion of this idea and defence of consumption as a general tax base, see McCaffery (2002). This proposal is of no help in the case of consumption taxes that aim to deter rather than raise revenue, since an exemption would simply remove whatever deterrent effect there is.

[3] The state's moral duty to address problems of collective action at least goes beyond traditional problems of providing security and law enforcement. On this point see Goodin (1995).

consumer who pays tax on a packet of cigarettes effectively pays more (understood as a fraction of their total financial resources) than a wealthier person. This is what it means to say that the higher the effective rate of such taxes is, the worse-off the person is who must pay it, and the poorer a person is, the higher the effective rate of any flat marginal-rate tax they must pay.

A bit of interpretive work is required to make sense of what this objection really says. An immediate problem is that regressivity is not strictly a moral concept. It is really just a mathematical one about one variable being inversely proportional to another—in this case, a person's effective tax burden being inversely proportional to their level of income or wealth. It is sometimes said that regressive taxation is unfair. Certainly, the moral force of objections to regressive taxation is often construed in this way. According to Liam Murphy and Thomas Nagel (2002, p. 13, 112), those who complain about the regressivity of consumption taxes are attempting to make a "vertical equity argument". Classically understood, vertical equity is just "what fairness requires in the tax treatment of people at different levels of income (or consumption, or whatever is the tax base)".[4] On this understanding of vertical equity, fairness might be something like a proportionality requirement whereby taxes should be extracted in ways proportionate to a taxpayer's ability to pay. Regressive taxation violates this sort of requirement. Insofar as it appeals to some idea of discrimination or unfair distribution, this way of formulating the concern about regressive taxation gives it an intuitively egalitarian air.

This simple appeal to fairness has some plausibility. After all, people often think that progressive taxation tends to be fairer taxation. Given this, it is tempting to think that regressive taxation is (therefore) unfair taxation. However, the relation between unfairness and regressive taxation is complicated in ways that reveal some reasons to resist this temptation. First of all, there is scope for questioning quite how easy it is to rely on appeals to vertical equity so long as these depend on more fundamental principles connecting fairness with ability to pay. A general problem here is that a person's ability to pay is, in large part, a consequence of tax policy rather than something that exists prior to it.[5] Possibly this concern has less force against highly localized elements of tax policy, such as the consumption of specific products. One might think that a person's income 'prior' to a tax on alcohol is more robust than the idea of their income 'prior' to the set of tax laws as a whole. These considerations suggest that more work needs to be done than to simply make a naïve appeal to vertical equity.

Second, it is not obvious whether views about the fairness of *progressive* income tax can be extended to support the *un*fairness of *regressive* consumption taxes very

[4] I should note that these authors are not arguing or claiming that regressive taxation is unfair, only that the opponents of regressive taxation are best understood as opposing it for this reason. The idea that a regressivity worries are grounded in fairness appears to be playing a role in McCaffery (2002) as well. Robert Goodin is careful to describe regressive consumption taxes as "undesirable" in ways that do not make an explicit commitment to their being unfair (1989, pp. 109–111).

[5] This is a general theme of Murphy and Nagel (2002).

easily. The most influential arguments connecting progressive income taxation with justice or fairness rest on detailed theories of distributive justice. These include ideas about one's income being an output of participation in some cooperative process, where one's talents (in the economic, salary-commanding sense) are largely a product of other persons' contributions to such cooperation. One other influential view is that the distribution of such talents is largely a matter of brute luck, whose effects should be reduced, if not wholly extinguished. These claims support the view that progressive income taxes represent a form of reciprocity between talented and not so talented co-operators, and/or some attempt to make distribution less sensitive to the effects of differential brute luck. But the morality of taxing harmful consumption is not obviously part of the morality of fair terms of cooperation or an application of any principle about eliminating a relation between social rewards/disadvantages and differential brute luck. As such, the justice of progressive income taxes does not entail the injustice of regressive consumption taxes. Third, paternalistic motivations for tax policies may even *support* the introduction of elements of regressivity into the tax policy, depending on which persons are deemed the most suitable candidates for paternalistic treatment. There is nothing incoherent in the idea (for example) that poor persons have more to gain from being deterred, and so can be fairly burdened by higher (effective) taxation. If the aim of a consumption tax is to prevent harm to others, or prevent coordination failure, then one might think that differential tax burdens are easier to defend if they are effective ways of realising these goals. I would like to stress that I am not defending these claims. But the fact that they are not obviously false suggests that the morality of taxation depends on all sorts of details regarding whatever bit of tax policy is under examination. So, we should hesitate before relying on very general claims about what makes for just or unjust taxation.[6] All of this suggests that the problem with regressive taxation is not so immediate that regressivity, in the cases being discussed, should be seen as constituting unfair treatment of poorer taxpayers.

The concern with regressivity is not that regressive taxation is, in itself, anti-egalitarian. Nevertheless, some sort of concern still exists. This emerges, I suggest, out of a more general concern that egalitarians have about the overall situation faced by the least advantaged members of society.[7] Regressive taxation can compound

[6] I have argued elsewhere for the more general claim that the morality of taxation is a rather fragmentary affair—see Halliday (2013).

[7] Some philosophers will interpret these remarks as indicative of a non-egalitarian concern, namely one focused only on the absolute levels of persons in ways that can be represented as a concern to give priority to the worse-off. I do not want to get drawn into the debate about exactly what is egalitarian and what is (merely?) prioritarian. Certainly, there is a robust formal distinction between methods of ranking material distributions according to the absolute value of the information about persons in them, and rankings that depend on relations between the information about such individual persons (e.g. inequality). This formal distinction is of some importance with respect to some pressing questions about distribution. But it is still possible to give an egalitarian motivation for using the first type of method even if the relevant welfare function is prioritarian. The short explanation is that welfare functions are formal tools that add precision to substantive informal claims about (say) the requirements of justice. Egalitarians have already made this claim elsewhere—see for example Cohen (2011, pp. 69–72).

existing patterns of disadvantage. What might bother us, about taxing the consumption of the poor is that, for example, poor consumers may forego important purchases in order to find the money to purchase the taxed product. To pay for tobacco, a poor person might forego purchasing food, or even food for their children. In short, the reason egalitarians should care about regressive consumption tax is that they should be seeking ways to relieve poor persons of unnecessarily burdensome aspects of their lives. Regressive consumption taxes tend to hit poor people harder because poor people are already vulnerable. This, I think, highlights a concern about taxing consumption of products that are consumed by poor people, even if it merely coincides with the way in which such taxes are formally regressive, and does not depend on any general moral concern with regressivity as such.

One (more general) way to spell this out is to say that regressive taxation coincides with situations in which the poor are burdened in an absolute sense, not just in the sense of being burdened more than their wealthier counterparts. It is worth noting that the regressivity objection only has substantial force when consumption taxes actually aim at deterring consumption among poorer members of society. Many other harmful products tend to be consumed in significant quantities, or in the most harmful ways, only by wealthier consumers. This is true of many forms of environmentally harmful consumption, such as air travel in first or business class.[8] This does not make taxation any less regressive in the formal sense, since the effective rate at which an air ticket is taxed will still vary with the financial circumstances of the consumer. However, these cases suggest that, the worry about regressivity has more force when applied to taxes on products like alcohol and tobacco than it does on some other sorts of consumption. It also has some force when applied to certain types of positional consumption, since competition for positional goods can often impose greatest costs on poorer competitors.[9]

As I shall explain (see the end of the next section), the concept of regressivity remains helpful as a way of describing proposals for addressing the problem as I am now describing it. However, the moral worry about taxing consumption is ultimately a worry about imposing non-trivial tax burdens on persons who are vulnerable due to their low absolute position.

[8] Paula Casal (2012) argues that higher consumption taxes should be paid by persons who use air travel on a frequent basis. Some countries, such as France and Great Britain, currently charge higher airport taxes for passengers departing in first or business class. (It is unclear to what extent these taxes are actually motivated by a goal of reducing environmental harm, since they are not levied on passengers who are merely entering or in transit.) For similar discussion see also Caney (2010).

[9] This observation was first made, I think, by Fred Hirsch (1977, p. 102). It is often true that collective action problems, when not properly addressed, do most damage to those already vulnerable. This is one reason to resist a misleadingly sharp separation between the requirements of egalitarian justice and those of 'mere' efficiency. These points are made in a compelling way by Iris Young (2011, Chaps. 2 and 6).

8.2 An Egalitarian Dilemma

Egalitarians should not respond to concerns about regressivity by abolishing consumption tax, at least not for the sorts of cases being discussed here. This is because, while there is some sense to the idea that egalitarians should dislike regressive taxation, the moral reasons for deterring harmful consumption can still be of an egalitarian sort. So, the problem posed by regressive taxation may be viewed, here, as one of how to resolve a conflict between competing egalitarian concerns. This suggests that egalitarians should at least hesitate before abandoning the taxation of certain products. Of course, there is much scope for suggesting ways in which the state might simply do more to combat whatever the antecedent causes are of inequality among consumers.[10] However, this is not the only way of responding to the problem. Solutions, or partial solutions, may yet be found that are internal to the practice of taxing consumption itself. Egalitarians should also seek proposals for redesigning consumption taxes so that their regressive tendencies might be reduced (or mitigated), in ways compatible with retaining their deterrent force. The rest of this chapter is largely an attempt to discuss ways in which progress might be made along these dimensions.

To make the dilemma a bit clearer, it is worth emphasising some ways in which the poor are especially vulnerable to the harms of certain sorts of consumption. To begin with, there is some general evidence that certain harmful products tend to be consumed in larger quantities by poorer consumers. Tobacco consumption is particularly high among those at lower income levels.[11] Obesity rates are most prevalent among the poor, particularly when they live in societies that contain rich people (Wilkinson and Pickett 2009, Chap. 7). In economically deprived urban areas, junk food outlets are often conspicuously more common than healthy food outlets. Of course, the facts vary for different kinds of goods. Alcoholism, for example, is certainly not absent at higher income levels. Nevertheless, evidence suggests that poorer people are more prone to excessive alcohol consumption, and that they are likely to begin alcohol consumption at an earlier age (Karriker-Jaffe et al. 2013).

I am not claiming that poor people are excessively harmed simply because they consume harmful products in larger quantities than wealthier people do. More significant is the fact that harmful products can compound pre-existing disadvantage. While it is true that alcohol and tobacco bring harms such as premature death, cancer, and other health outcomes that are bad for anyone, the range of harms widens for consumers occupying a low economic position. For example, workers at low income levels often benefit less from flexible working conditions or access to sick-leave. Often, poor people need to make a living from performing unskilled or manual labour that becomes impossible, or more burdensome, in cases of illness.

---

[10] This conclusion is drawn—with regard only to tobacco taxation in particular—by Goodin (1989, p. 110).

[11] For a report see "Tobacco and Poverty: A Vicious Circle" World Health Organization (2004), available at:http://www.who.int/tobacco/communications/events/wntd/2004/en/wntd2004_brochure_en.pdf (accessed 4/7/2013).

In some countries, poor persons do not even have access to healthcare, or can gain access only in ways that leave them with large financial debts. In contrast, wealthier persons might work in ways where performance is less dramatically impacted by becoming ill (for example, it may be possible to work from home). Disadvantaged persons may even be more likely to find themselves in situations where they are punished for having engaged in certain sorts of consumption.[12] Skilled workers are better placed with respect to health insurance, sick leave, and so on. Wealth can also subsidize time out of the labour market. These points bear importantly on how we should understand the problem posed by the egalitarian objection to consumption taxes. They underscore the way in which regressive taxation may not be problematic simply because of the way the tax burden is distributed, but due to the ways in which disadvantaged persons stand to be hit harder by it.

What this shows is that the egalitarian objection to consumption taxes should be construed, at least in certain cases of paternalistic taxation, as merely one half of a dilemma. Although the objection itself seems to occupy the egalitarian high ground, there are ways of responding to it that draw on, or at least are compatible with, egalitarian ideas about what society owes to the least advantaged. The remarks in the above paragraph are meant to give a sense of this, just by pointing out that, although consumption taxes are regressive, there are reasons for imposing them on poorer members of society in particular. Since some of the effects that harmful consumption can impose on poor people form part of systematic patterns of disadvantage, the desire to see these effects mitigated might be viewed as part of a general egalitarian view. Note that I am not trying to downplay the way in which harmful consumption can still harm wealthy people. The point is rather that physiological harms can exacerbate non-physiological harms linked to occupying a low socio-economic position. This fact should lead us to acknowledge a greater diversity of ways in which certain forms of consumption harm the poor.

To be clear, I am not claiming that their extra vulnerability shows that poor persons simply *ought* to be more burdened than wealthier persons by taxes on tobacco, alcohol, and other products. At most, I would only concede that the vulnerability of the poor makes it harder to establish that regressive consumption tax burdens indicate unfair treatment. The points I have made here are just meant to add support to the view that the use of consumption taxes poses a dilemma for egalitarians. There are egalitarian reasons to want to help poor people reduce their consumption of some products, partly because of the way in which the harms of such products

[12] Poor people often find themselves in certain institutional settings where they are monitored in ways that make the effects of harmful consumption harder to conceal and more likely to lead to costs. For example, a poor person's alcoholism is more likely to incur costs if that person is already being monitored by employment agencies who can withhold benefits. More generally, patterns of stereotyping often play a role in what sort of character attributions are made in response to fixed data. For example, alcoholism in poor persons is relatively likely to be explained in terms of weak will and ill-discipline, whereas alcoholism in a wealthier person might more likely be attributed to blameless stress at work. Of course, part of the right response to these factors is to seek the removal of the status hierarchies that compound the disadvantage of poor people. Nevertheless, these points are compatible with the urgency of saving the poor from harmful consumption.

are exacerbated by the vulnerable position of the poor. But, on the other hand, a heavy tax burden can still compound or increase the disadvantage that poor persons already face, perhaps just in other ways (for example, by causing other important purchases to be foregone). These points motivate an approach of trying to find ways to design consumption taxes that can mitigate their regressive nature, without decreasing their force as a deterrent against relevant forms of consumption. Calls to abolish the taxing of harmful products like alcohol and tobacco merely privilege one set of reasons over another set of reasons, and thereby overlook much that is important in motivating and guiding policies on consumption tax in the first place.

In spite of all these complications, use of the term 'regressivity' remains helpful as a way of understanding how consumption taxes might be redesigned. Given this, I will continue to talk of proposals that reduce or mitigate the regressive burden of consumption taxes, as they have been normally designed, on specific products. Nevertheless, while improvements will coincide with ways of making these taxes less regressive, the reasons for adopting the various changes I will discuss are not ultimately about the aim of reducing regressivity for its own sake, but draw more on concerns about disadvantage as described in this section.

8.3 Deterrence and Licensing

In principle, there are two ways of making a consumption tax less regressive. First, there are ways of making it actually better at deterring. Second, there are ways of making it impose a smaller or different (i.e. non-financial) burden without thereby undermining its degree to deter.

It should be emphasised, first, that the regressivity of a consumption tax depends on the idea that the tax has limited success at deterring the relevant consumption. In one sense, consumption taxes burden people only when the taxed exchange actually occurs.[13] Insofar as the purpose of a consumption tax is to discourage some form of purchase, total success at this would mean that the consumption tax did not get paid. This would prevent it from having a burden that was distributed disproportionately onto the poor. These considerations have led some authors to defend a more aggressive use of consumption taxes on harmful products, like tobacco (Chapman 2012; Halliday (forthcoming). Now, societies that tax tobacco and alcohol use sales taxes, rather than other modes of consumption tax. Sales taxes are applied to discrete exchanges, in proportion with how many units of the taxed good are actually exchanged. However, importantly, sales taxes do not exhaust the space of consump-

[13] There is, arguably, a sense in which one is burdened by being made to forego a purchase. Appeals to this sense of being burdened are less compelling to the extent that the foregone product is harmful. In addition, it is not obvious why the burden of foregoing a product must vary with the financial resources of whoever foregoes it, in the way that paying a consumption tax might be subject to such variation. It is often said that tobacco products provide a valuable resource for the poor on account of their role in relieving stress. This claim probably overlooks the likelihood that tobacco addiction raises base stress levels (see Halliday (forthcoming)).

tion taxes. This is because consumption does not need to be taxed at the precise moment of exchange. Another sort of consumption tax is represented by the idea of licences. Generally speaking, licences differ from sales taxes in that they require consumers to pay for some large number of units of consumption 'up front'.

Licences attempt to force consumers into making a harder decision than sales taxes do. Assuming a licence cannot be refunded, a consumer has to commit to a large amount of purchasing in order for a licence to purchase to seem rational. Many consumers will not want to do this, particularly consumers who are in the position of considering whether to start consuming for the first time, such as potential smokers. What is more, the fact that the cost of a licence has to be paid as a large lump sum may mean that the poorest consumers simply cannot afford it. In other words, licences contrast with sales taxes in requiring a higher level of commitment to purchasing the good to which they are attached, along with a higher level of cash flow. Both factors (especially the second) can be expected to suppress purchases made by persons at lower income levels. Insofar as a successful licence reduces the number of poor consumers (even if it also reduces the number of wealthy ones), it is to that extent less regressive than a sales tax might be.

A second advantage of licenses is that they can be made relatively difficult to obtain, but in ways other than financially. That is to say, getting a licence might simply be a considerable hassle. One might have to give up half a day to visit a government office in order to get one's application approved, or complete complicated paperwork simply in order to lodge an application. Whether or not poorer people find these obstacles harder to overcome than rich people is less straightforward than the absorption of financial burdens. Making people fill out paperwork and visit an office uses up time, but this is not necessarily a larger proportion of a poor person's time than a rich person's time.[14] A general point here is that there is a distinction between making a tax difficult to pay, and making it costly to pay.[15] Licences can be designed so that they are burdensome in a multi-dimensional way, which makes them difficult in addition to (or instead of being) costly. Sales taxes, on the other hand, are merely costly. This is a second way in which licences can be burdensome without being regressive. In principle, a state could develop licences that are extremely difficult to obtain but very cheap. Financially speaking, these licences would hardly burden consumers in a regressive fashion at all.

Licenses can have further advantages over sales taxes that do not really have anything to do with regressivity, but which deserve a mention. For one thing, they are more directly targeted at the good in question. More specifically, sales taxes sometimes fail to have their desired effect because sellers might simultaneously sell other goods that are not covered by the tax. The recent attempt to tax fatty foods in Denmark failed partly because supermarkets were able to keep prices low on taxed

[14] I should acknowledge that poor people often lack (e.g.) the transport options of wealthier people. So, it is possible that poor people are sometimes vulnerable to greater difficulties than rich people, as well as financial costs. However, insofar as this occurs, it is contingent in ways that the regressive distribution of a tax burden is not.

[15] This distinction is drawn by Cohen (2000, pp. 171–174).

items while marginally raising prices on untaxed items.[16] This is the sense in which the tax failed to accurately target the goods whose consumption it was meant to discourage. Smaller specialist businesses, like butchers and cheese makers, lacked this option due to the fact that the tax covered a much larger fraction of their product base. Had a licence been used, then supermarkets would have had less ability to effectively save the consumer from incurring a burden.[17]

To summarise, the general case for licensing depends, principally, on two ideas. First, licences may be more effective at suppressing consumption. Insofar as consumption taxes are regressive only when they are actually paid (i.e., when consumption actually occurs), licences are to that extent less objectionably regressive than sales taxes. Second, licences are unlike sales taxes in being able to burden consumers non-financially. None of this is to say that licences are without problems, or that they are always a better alternative to sales taxes. They are perhaps most defensible when used to suppress consumption that leads to addiction, and/or where the harms of consumption lag behind the act of consumption by a significant amount of time. As I have suggested, the strongest case for licences can be found with respect to the taxing of tobacco. It is less obvious whether a licence for alcohol or unhealthy food, let alone certain types of positional consumption, could be easily defended. However, the positive case for licences does not end here. It can, in fact, be integrated with another sort of proposal, which I will introduce next.

8.4 Hypothecation and Rebating

Usually, tax revenues go into a single pool. Governments then make their own decision as to how to allocate fractions of this pool to various areas of policy implementation. An alternative is to pre-assign particular revenues to particular policies. This is known as hypothecation. On the whole, hypothecated taxes are not very popular with governments. This may be largely because hypothecation lacks the flexibility of the pooling approach. Nevertheless, some instances of hypothecation do exist. One example is the sale of TV licences in the UK, the revenues from which are used as the sole source of funding for the BBC's television programmes. Hypothecation is the practice, then, of directing the revenue from some tax to the funding of some relatively narrow set of policies. While a consumption tax might impose a regressive tax burden in a very formal sense, use of hypothecation offers a way in which such taxes may become progressive in certain other respects. Overall, these approaches to consumption tax help to make it more tolerable from the point of view of egalitarian justice.

[16] "A Fat Chance", The Economist November 17th 2012: http://www.economist.com/news/europe/21566664-danish-government-rescinds-its-unwieldy-fat-tax-fat-chance (accessed Jan 12th 2013).

[17] Another method for dealing with supermarkets (which, in the UK, often sell alcohol as a 'loss leader') is to introduce a minimum pricing scheme (Ludbrook et al. (2012)).

Existing moral arguments for hypothecation invoke ideas about transparency and the value of empowering taxpayers (Le Grand 2003, Chap. 11). Roughly, these arguments exploit the idea that taxpayers ought to be informed as to where their taxes are going. Hypothecation can allow a citizen to opt out of funding a certain policy if they do not like it, since they can forego purchasing the good that is used to extract revenue for that policy. If British citizens are unwilling to fund the BBC, then they can opt out of purchasing a TV licence, so long as they agree not to use their television sets to receive BBC transmissions. Now, I am going to stay neutral as to whether hypothecation really empowers taxpayers in an interesting sense, and whether it is desirable for this sort of empowerment to be realised. Even if one is sceptical about the empowerment rationale, one might nevertheless be attracted to hypothecation for other reasons. What I want to argue for is that hypothecating a consumption tax is a way of making it less regressive.

As I have said, the idea of a regressive tax can be understood in terms of the distribution of its burden. Poor people pay a higher effective tax rate. However, tax does not just burden the people who pay it. Depending on how its revenues are spent, it also benefits people. This distinction is nothing new. It features in the old debate among tax theorists concerning the case for distributing a tax burden according to citizens' respective ability to pay, or according to some measure of how much benefit citizens respectively accrue from the state's policies. However, when it comes to defining tax regressivity, theorists tend to focus on burdens rather than benefits.

Now, I do not want to make any claims about whether a fair distribution of a tax burden is better captured by a benefit principle or an ability to pay principle, or any other principle. As I have said, these principles run into problems when subjected to proper scrutiny.[18] I just want to take the weaker view that a second sense of regressivity obtains with respect to the use of tax revenues. If tax revenues are used to fund state policies that primarily benefit the wealthy, then there is a sense in which the extraction of these revenues is regressive even if the tax burden is not regressive. A strongly regressive tax, then, would be regressive in both of these senses—one whose burden falls disproportionately on the poor, and whose revenues were used to disproportionately benefit the wealthy. If a tax were to burden the poor disproportionately, but have its revenues spent in ways that primarily at benefitted the poor, then this tax would, in a sense, be less regressive. It would do less to increase existing inequality that the first tax. It is in realising this second possibility that we might find a role for hypothecation.

With this in mind, we might consider the following sorts of possibilities. A consumption tax on junk food could be used to fund sporting facilities in areas where economically disadvantaged people live. A tax on tobacco could be used to fund provision of anti-addiction measures, such as nicotine patches.[19] I will not make any

[18] For an excellent discussion, see Olson (2010). The benefit principle and the ability to pay principle are also nicely distinguished in Slemrod and Bakija (2004), and Murphy and Nagel (2002, Chap. 2).

[19] Various policy ideas, including this one, are laid out in Voigt (2010) and Proctor (2011, Chap. 30).

precise claims about which instances of hypothecation would be most effective at benefitting the poor. Nevertheless, it is plausible to say that, insofar as such policies would be effective, consumption taxes would thereby be less regressive overall, even though they would not be any less regressive with respect to the distribution of the financial burden they impose. Hypothecation, then, should be regarded as a potentially useful way of at least mitigating an egalitarian concern about regressive tax burdens.

Like licensing, hypothecation has some limitations. Extensive hypothecation would likely lead to a mixture of overfunded and underfunded policies, and a government powerless to embark on sudden expensive projects. However, the proposal here is just that hypothecation should be used very locally, only with respect to consumption taxes on harmful goods. What is more, it is perfectly possible to combine hypothecation with licensing simultaneously (that is, direct licence revenues towards the sort of policies that benefit the poor). Here it is possible to make some further proposals that involve integrating the proposals made over the last two sections.

One advantage of licensing is that allows data to be gathered on the identity of consumers. When governments issue driving licences, they have a way of knowing which of their citizens drive cars. The same is true of any licence for any sort of product. There is no reason why the application for a licence cannot include its holder's income tax identity. If this is done, the state will be able to rebate the licence fee to the poorest fraction of consumers. This is a direct way of making a consumption tax less regressive.

The idea here is quite simple. Some subset of the population buy a licence, and the state collects data on the relative incomes of all licence holders. What the state then does is return some amount of the licence's cost to the poorest group of consumers. In this way, the poorer consumers end up with a tax burden that is more in proportion with their lower income. They may end up with no tax burden at all, short of the burden on their 'cash flow' accrued between the point of purchasing the licence and getting the rebate from the state.

There is a certain advantage to this proposal, which can be secured so long as the group entitled to a rebate is defined as relatively badly-off rather than absolutely badly-off. If consumers qualify for a rebate only if their income is low relative to that of other consumers, then consumers will struggle to be sure of whether they would qualify, when making the decision about whether to buy the licence. If a consumer would qualify for the rebate simply in virtue of having some pre-specified, absolutely low income, then consumers would be able to know in advance whether they would qualify. Preserving some ignorance among consumers as to whether they will get their money back is an important part of preserving the deterrent effect of a licence. No consumer can be assured of what the facts are about the incomes of other consumers at the time of purchasing a licence. Defining the qualifying set of consumers as a fraction of actual consumers means, apart from anything else, that the absolute level of income under which one qualifies will vary from year to year, as the information on actual consumers' incomes varies. In this way, the regressivity problem can be addressed in ways that need not undermine the role that the licence is actually meant to perform.

The simple way of describing the proposal above obscures some complexity as to how any rebating programme might be designed. There are at least two important dimensions along which the design of a rebate programme can vary. One is the size of the fraction of consumers who will qualify for a rebate. Generally speaking, a larger fraction makes it easier for consumers to predict that they might qualify. But the larger the fraction, the less regressive the distribution of financial burden may become. A second dimension is the size of the transfer itself. It is possible that the whole licence fee is rebated, or perhaps only half. It is also possible to vary both of these dimensions at once. For example, one can imagine a rebate scheme in which the full cost is returned to the poorest tenth of consumers, some lesser amount to the next tenth, and so on. It is also possible to imagine a programme in which the poorest consumers receive a payment that is larger than the original cost of the licence. This could be funded, perhaps, through revenues gained from the purchases of the wealthiest licence holders. Doing things this way would introduce an element of *progressivity* into the way the licence's financial burden is distributed, since funds would essentially be being transferred from the wealthiest to the poorest consumers.

It is important to note that even to the extent that consumers could (or would) predict that they would qualify for a rebate, the deterrent effect of licences would still remain. This is because, even if a rebate were guaranteed, consumers would still have to go through the process of actually paying for it and then of waiting a significant amount of time before the rebate gets processed. Even a guarantee of getting a rebate leaves a consumer exposed to the burdens related to cash-flow, and, the poorer one is, the more cash flow can matter. This is very often overlooked. For example, an unemployed person may turn down an offer of relatively lucrative temporary paid labour, simply because they lack confidence about how quickly their welfare payments will return once the period of labour ends. This can be a perfectly rational choice even if it is obvious that taking the labour will mean that more money is received overall. A failure to realise the importance of cash-flow is often a contributing factor to the practice of stereotyping poor people as irrational or simply lazy, when trying to account for their behaviour. Quite possibly a poor person will forego buying a tobacco licence on grounds of cash flow. This does not undermine the purpose of rebating poor consumers who actually do go ahead and make the purchase.

I have no precise suggestions to make as to which sort of rebating design would be optimal, with respect to the dimensions outlined above. Any stronger conclusions would presumably have to rely on some empirical findings about how the deterrent effect might be changed, and how to weigh any changes here against the value of making licences a less regressive form of consumption tax. The point I want to make is merely that, whatever other questions might arise, consumption taxes can genuinely be made less regressive. As I noted earlier on, the problem with consumption taxes (or, to be more precise, sales taxes) is that they tend to be insensitive to the circumstances of whoever pays them. The point I am trying to press here is that this insensitivity is ultimately a contingent rather than a necessary feature of taxing consumption, provided one is prepared to consider types of consumption tax other than the traditional sales tax.

8.5 Conclusions

The problem of regressive consumption taxes should be seen as a dilemma between two broadly egalitarian sorts of concern. On the one hand, there is something troubling about regressive taxation, albeit in ways less straightforward than first appearances might suggest. On the other hand, taxing the consumption of specific products can be motivated by a genuine concern to protect the least advantaged. I have not tried to propose any grand solutions in this chapter, but rather to make some modest suggestions about how this dilemma might be addressed by redesigning consumption taxes themselves, rather than relying solely on solutions outside of taxation. As with all policy problems that are of moral interest, we should sometimes be content with reaching conclusions about how we might improve on the status quo. The key observation to make about consumption taxes is that they are not regressive in principle, but only on some traditional and entrenched forms in which they are actually used. I have tried to suggest ways in which consumption taxes on specific products might be redesigned so as to make their use more morally defensible. Further and indeed better possibilities than those mentioned here may well exist.[20]

References

Caney, Simon. 2010. Climate change and the duties of the advantaged. *Critical Review of International Social and Political Philosophy* 13 (1): 203–228.

Casal, Paula. 2012. Progressive environmental taxation: A defence. *Political Studies* 60:419–433.

Chapman, Simon. 2012. The case for a Smoker's license. *PLOS Medicine* 9 (1): 1–5.

Cohen, Gerald A. 2000. *If you're and egalitarian, how come you're so rich?* Cambridge: Harvard University Press.

Cohen, Gerald A. 2011. In *On the currency of egalitarian justice, and other essays in political philosophy,* ed. M. Otsuka. Princeton: Princeton University Press.

Frank, Robert H. 2008. Should public policy respond to positional externalities? *Journal of Public Economics* 92:1777–1786

Goodin, Robert. 1989. *No smoking: The ethical issues*. Chicago: University of Chicago Press.

Goodin, Robert. 1995. *"The State as Moral Agent" reprinted in his Utilitarianism as a public philosophy*. New York: Cambridge University Press.

Halliday, Daniel. 2013. Justice and taxation. *Philosophy Compass* 8 (12): 1111–1122.

[20] I would like to thank participants at the conference on Justice, Taxation and Social Policy, held at Salzburg University in August 2013. I am especially grateful to Xavier Landes for sending detailed comments on a later draft. A subsequent version of this chapter was also presented to an audience at the Centre for Applied Policy and Public Ethics (CAPPE) at Charles Sturt University in early 2014, and I thank those present there, too.

Halliday, Daniel. forthcoming. The ethics of a smoking licence. *Journal of Medical Ethics*. http://jme.bmj.com/content/early/2013/12/11/medethics-2013-101347.extract
Hirsch, Fred. 1977. *Social limits to growth* London: Routledge.
Karriker-Jaffe, Katherine, Sarah C. M. Roberts, and Jason Bond. 2013. Income inequality, alcohol use, and alcohol-related problems. *American Journal of Public Health* 103 (4): 649–656.
Le Grand, Julian. 2003. *Motivation, agency, and public policy*. New York: Oxford University Press.
Ludbrook, Anne, Dennis Petrie, Lynda McKenzie, and Shelley Farrar. 2012. Tackling alcohol misuse: Purchasing patterns affected by minimum pricing for alcohol. *Applied Health Economics & Health Policy* 10 (1): 51–63.
McCaffery, Edward J. 2002. *Fair not flat: How to make the tax system better and simpler.* Chicago: University of Chicago Press.
Murphy, Liam, and Thomas Nagel. 2002. *The myth of ownership: Taxes and justice*. New York: Oxford University Press.
Olson, Kristi A. 2010. The endowment tax puzzle. *Philosophy & Public Affairs* 38 (3): 240–271.
Proctor, Robert. 2011. *Golden holocaust: Origins of the cigarette catastrophe and the case for abolition*. Berkeley: University of California Press.
Slemrod, Joel, and Jon Bakija. 2004. *Taxing ourselves: A citizen's guide to the debate over taxes*. Cambridge: Massachusetts Institute of Technology.
Voigt, Kristin. 2010. Smoking and social justice. *Public Health Ethics* 3 (2): 91–106.
Wilkinson, Robert, and Kate Pickett. 2009. *The spirit level: Why equality is better for everyone*. London: Penguin Books.
Young, Iris M. 2011. *Responsibility for justice*. New York: Oxford University Press.

Chapter 9
Ethical Taxation: Progressivity, Efficiency and Hourly Averaging

Douglas Bamford

Abstract This chapter argues that calculating taxation on an hourly average basis is an ethical requirement. In order to reach this conclusion it first presents an argument that tax policies should be guided by the requirements of distributive justice. The chapter takes an ecumenical position on distributive justice, merely showing that most prominent approaches to justice would support a taxation system with two broad features. The first is that the system would be progressive in nature and thereby provide transfers from the economically fortunate to the less fortunate. The second feature is that the system would retain economic incentives and thereby encourage an effective and efficient economy. These two requirements are commonly considered in opposition to one another, and so proposals that deliver both of these would be attractive in terms of all the approaches to distributive justice set out. A recently proposed form of tax calculation—hourly averaging—is presented and in the final two sections. This is shown to be attractive for its progressivity and for providing economic incentives.

9.1 Introduction

Tax policy has an important role to play in achieving distributive justice in society. Tax revenues have to pay for the affairs of state but also provide for the payments or services that will be supplied to those who should for reasons of justice be entitled to more than they would receive without state intervention. In this chapter I argue that most of the attractive theories of distributive justice favour two outcomes that push against one another. One is redistribution from the economically fortunate and the other is the desire for an efficient economy that will provide growth and a lot of the goods and services that people desire at the lowest possible prices.[1] Given this

[1] It is not controversial to claim that there is a trade-off between these two (Okun 1975).

D. Bamford (✉)
Department for Continuing Education,
University of Oxford, 1 Wellington Square,
Oxford OX1 2JA, UK
e-mail: dougbamford@hotmail.com

H. P. Gaisbauer et al. (eds.), *Philosophical Explorations of Justice and Taxation*,
Ius Gentium: Comparative Perspectives on Law and Justice 40,
DOI 10.1007/978-3-319-13458-1_9

conflict we need a tax system that will redistribute as much as possible given the constraints imposed by efficiency.

I will begin by briefly explaining that distributive justice is the correct lens through which to judge tax policies, and how several attractive theories of distributive justice accept that there is a trade-off between two important requirements; redistribution and efficiency. Each theory would resolve these trade-offs differently, but in this chapter I will not provide any attempt to adjudicate between them. I will instead present a form of tax calculation that would provide progressivity and efficiency to a greater degree than alternative approaches. This is my proposal for *lifetime hourly averaging*, and I will explain this in the third section of the chapter. In the final two sections I will outline how this form of tax calculation allows for greater progressivity and then how it should produce an efficient economic system.

9.2 Taxation and Distributive Justice

Taxation is an inherently normative issue since questions of policy ask what should, or alternatively what ought, to be the case. Since taxation plays a significant role in the distribution of resources within a society with a market economy, tax policies should be considered through the lens of distributive justice. Of course, the choice of tax policies needs to be properly informed by the best available economic theories and empirical information. Theories of distributive justice should also consider these factors, as all sensible ones do.

My claim in this section is of course relatively uncontroversial to political philosophers, and the need for distributive justice to be prominent has been well argued by John Rawls (1996, 1999, 2001) and Liam Murphy and Thomas Nagel (2002). However, I will express this common view in a slightly unusual manner, by highlighting how a properly conceived distributive justice approach to taxation takes appropriate cognizance of the wider context of taxation. Many approaches to taxation do not take appropriate account of the role of taxation within a society-wide notion of distributive justice. One common mistake is to focus on the justification of taxation with reference only to the taxpayer or producer.[2]

The above point is not intended to deny that taxation policies should be justified to taxpayers. The point is that we should not overlook the position that taxpayers have within society as a whole and the total impact of taxes on those various indi-

[2] This point covers many approaches used in discussions and analysis of taxation, such as the ability to pay principle, the contribution principle, and notions of horizontal and vertical equity. It also covers libertarian self-ownership rights-based approaches to distributive justice mentioned in the following section. All of these views fall foul of the problem that they utilise a free-market baseline for comparison which is unduly favourable to those who do well in a free market setting. This has been labelled by Nagel and Murphy as an unfortunate and unwarranted "everyday libertarianism" (Murphy and Nagel 2002, pp. 31–38). The distributive justice approach would include all distributive and policy options on the table and give no preliminary advantage to any one outcome over any others.

viduals. The outcome of all the relevant policies should be considered as a whole, and so we might say our approach to taxation should look at the role that any particular tax or proposed reform would play in making the entire system fairer. In the following section I will outline some of the prominent theories of distributive justice that imply a need for policies that achieve two aims; progressivity and economic efficiency.

The theories I will discuss apply a method to construct a notion of the just outcome. There is no room here to engage with theories that are based on entitlements arising from natural rights such as the various forms of libertarianism (Nozick 1974; Steiner 1994; Christman 1994). Neither will I engage with theories which argue that people should receive what they deserve in accordance with their moral character or their economic contributions (Dick 1975; Lamont 1994; Miller 1999). I will also avoid discussion of radical proposals that reject the possibility that market economies or capitalism can be morally acceptable.[3] Arguments could no doubt be made from some of these theoretical approaches in favour of the policies I suggest but they would be of a particular nature and there is no room to engage with these here. My argument in this chapter is ecumenical with regard to the correct approach to distributive justice, but space only allows me to be ecumenical to a certain extent.

9.3 Distributive Justice, Progressivity and Efficiency

In this section I will briefly describe several prominent approaches to distributive justice that would have strong reasons to desire a progressive taxation system and also an efficient and effective economy. The first approaches I will describe are liberal egalitarian, and it is not surprising that liberal egalitarians would be keen on a tax system that was economically efficient and progressive. I will also mention some other approaches to justice which would find these features of the tax system desirable. Those who consider egalitarian outcomes intrinsically valuable and those who wish to judge distributive justice on the amount of happiness in the world would also agree broadly on these aims.

I have said that liberal egalitarians would require progressive taxation as long as it would not be too inefficient and I will split this group into two broad camps. The first includes Rawls and his followers and the second we might call luck egalitarians. All of these thinkers believe in constructing justice in some sense from an egalitarian starting point. Rawls, for example, presents the original position in which everyone is imagined to be behind a veil of ignorance (Rawls 1974, 1999, 2001). In this position people would not know their particular features but must choose principles of justice. Luck egalitarians, by contrast, believe that inequalities arising as a result of bad luck are undesirable and should be rectified or at least be considered as reasons to provide compensation from the more fortunate.

[3] Such a view would be held by many followers of Marx as well as anarchist communists.

Rawls argues that from his original position people would choose two principles of justice. The first is that each person would have an equal right to the most extensive basic liberty compatible with a similar liberty for others. His second principle is that positions in society should be available to all and subject to fair equality of opportunity, and that "social and economic inequalities should be arranged so that they are both (a) to the greatest benefit of the least advantaged persons, and (b) attached to offices and positions open to all under conditions of equality of opportunity." (Rawls 2001, pp. 53) This means that inequalities are only justifiable to the extent that they maximise the position of the worst off, or that they maxi-minimise. This is Rawls' famous difference principle, which is generated on the assumption that people in the original position would want to be as well off as possible if they were among the economically worst-off in society. This means that they would allow inequalities that increased efficiency in ways that would make them better-off if they were in this group.

The difference principle implies the need for a highly redistributive tax system that will still provide people with incentives to work. This therefore fits in neatly with the broad principles of redistribution and efficiency I have outlined in this chapter. Rawls suggests the combination of a proportionate consumption tax and the imposition of a property-owning democracy in order to meet his principles (Rawls 2001, pp. 242–249).[4] For Rawls, progressivity would be provided by the taxation and redistribution of wealth in order to meet the broad distribution of the ownership of assets required for a property-owning democracy. This would presumably be best achieved by accession and wealth taxes. The proportionate consumption tax would provide some revenue which could be used for redistribution, but it would also encourage work and saving by not directly taxing these activities. This element would therefore promote economic efficiency. These policies are not the only means to achieve these aims, of course, and I will propose in a later section that the hourly averaging approach would better meet these aims. My point here is that Rawls and his followers, who may be alternatively described as *democratic egalitarians* (Anderson 1999) or *relational egalitarians,* would require redistributive taxation that would not be very damaging to economic efficiency.

Another very prominent liberal egalitarian approach to distributive justice is the one labelled *luck egalitarianism*. This view comes in a variety of flavours, disagreeing on the appropriate currency of justice[5] and on the appropriate level of compensation for bad luck.[6] Luck egalitarians will desire a tax system that would

[4] For more on Property owning democracy, and Rawls' views on taxation, see (Meade 1964; O'Neill and Williamson 2012; Fried 1999, 2002; Sugin 2004).

[5] One set of thinkers agrees with Rawls and his followers that justice should only look at resources (Dworkin 1981; Rakowski 1991; Bamford 2014). Others believe that welfare should be the focus, or a complex of resources and welfare (Arneson 1989; Cohen 1989). Further proposals that might that would reach similar broad conclusions about tax policy from a background of envy-free egalitarianism and economic analysis are those of Marc Fleurbaey (Fleurbaey 2008) and Serge Kolm (Kolm 2005). Another relevant work.

[6] The advantage of Dworkin's hypothetical insurance approach is that it fully specifies how much compensation people should receive—up to a maximum of returning the individual's resources to that of the other members of society. In many cases this level of compensation would be a poor

redistribute from the economically fortunate to the less fortunate. However, for the most part they would accept that there is no advantage in doing this where it would level down everyone to the position of the worst-off. Therefore, luck egalitarians can also be readily approved as members of the efficiency-with-progressivity club.

I would suggest that even egalitarians who are more radical and less liberal may be willing to temper their desire for a society in which people had equal income and wealth where this would increase efficiency. For example, G.A. Cohen in his *magnum opus* (Cohen 2008) seeks to defend the traditional notions of equality and justice as separate values that should not be used to construct a theory of the best overall outcome. Cohen instead would wish to insist that the desire for an equal and just outcome should ideally permeate all transactions and so there is no room to take account of economic efficiency when theorising about equality and justice. Nevertheless, even Cohen admits that equal outcomes are not the only things that matter, and that equality should not be imposed where it would seriously hamper human flourishing. This would legitimise tax policies designed to promote efficiency as well as equal outcomes (Cohen 2008, pp. 319). Cohen's is therefore a slightly more complicated case as he does not agree with the other theorists mentioned in this section that justice and equality should necessarily be the only drivers of tax policy. Nevertheless, I can include even Cohen in this argument as he believes both that justice should play the crucial role in determining tax policy and would allow for efficiency-promoting taxes.

I am providing a very broad sweep of theories about which many books and articles have been written. Due to the limitations of space this brevity is necessary and I will mention some further theories of distributive justice which would also be concerned to have progressive taxation that is economically efficient. One example is *republicanism*, which emphasises the need to have a society in which all play a role and in which people are free from domination (Pettit 1997). Richard Dagger, for example, has argued that republicanism requires highly redistributive yet freedom-preserving institutions such as those proposed by Rawls (Dagger 2006). A highly plausible and attractive theory with liberal, egalitarian, and republican influences is Stuart White's proposal for a civic minimum (White 2003). He proposes an egalitarian subsidy scheme, which would take account of the amount that people could contribute in taxation and charge people on a sliding scale with reference to their expected level contribution.[7] This theory also seeks to marry progressivity and

---

insurance choice and so people in the hypothetical insurance veil of ignorance would not choose this. As people are asked what insurance they would choose in a hypothetical pre-luck (or *ex ante*) position of equality the outcome after compensatory insurance payments from the fortunate to the less fortunate is both egalitarian and justified to all members of society. It is for this reason that I find Dworkin's resource egalitarian approach the most attractive approach to distributive justice.

[7] So, if someone is capable of earning a very high amount but earns the average wage they would pay more in tax than someone who earns the average wage that they would be expected to earn (see also White 1999). This is a form of endowment tax, which therefore differs from the proposal I will present in the next part of this chapter. I am sceptical of the equity of endowment taxes as they place higher demands on some people than others. Nevertheless, I include this as an example of a relevant theory here as it would be instantiated by the hourly averaging proposal if it were deemed practically or morally unacceptable to determine how capable everyone is in comparison to others.

economic efficiency by taxing people in proportion to their ability to contribute economically, and is therefore one that can also be included in the broad church of theories to which I am able to make reference.

Another theory that has had an influence in some circles, particularly international development, is Amartya Sen's *capability approach to justice* (Nussbaum and Sen 1993; Sen 1980, 2009). I am not aware of any specific suggestions about tax policy from this perspective, but it is very plausible to assume that state activity is necessary to improve capabilities and that those who with the most capabilities from their economic power would be the ideal source of government revenue in a capability-preserving manner. If economic efficiency were damaged this would also affect capabilities and so progressive taxation that encouraged efficiency would be attractive to capability theorists of all stripes. Another approach which emphasises the distributive position of individuals is sufficientarianism. This view holds that what matters is that people have enough resources to reach certain qualitative thresholds, such as to be able to live at all and then to live a reasonably good life (Frankfurt 1987; Shields 2012). Progressive taxation focused on the better off members of society would provide more resources to help those below any relevant thresholds. At the same time it would be less likely to allow those people to fall below any thresholds.

The above theories are primarily concerned with the way that individuals fare in society relative to others. Another prominent approach, utilitarianism (Bentham 1907; Mill 1993, chap. 5), has received criticism for ignoring the separateness of persons (Rawls 1999) and focusing instead on the total amount of good—usually taken to be welfare or utility—in the world. Despite this concern, utilitarianism remains influential in some circles and utilitarians also have strong reasons to prefer an efficient and progressive tax system. The utilitarian case for efficiency is obvious but the desire for progressivity is perhaps less so. The argument proceeds on the basis that there is a diminishing marginal return to utility, such that the most economically fortunate will gain less utility from additional money than the less fortunate. This gives utilitarians a strong reason to want progressive taxation up until the level is reached where the economic efficiency losses would begin to reduce total utility.[8]

I have indicated that utilitarianism is less popular than it once was among philosophers of distributive justice, but another proposal retains many of the features of utilitarianism while avoiding some of its less palatable features. This is the prioritarian view developed by Derek Parfit (Parfit 1997, 2000, 2012). This theory would

I therefore believe that the hourly averaging would be a good "second-best" institutionalisation of White's principles.

[8] One complication to this story arises where there are "utility monsters," people who always get more utility than others from resources (Nozick 1974). If such people exist and can be identified, then utilitarian tax policy would want to maximise the amount of resources to such people. I do not think this case is troubling to my argument as I do not believe it would be possible to reliably identify such utility monsters. Furthermore, I doubt whether the picture is plausible that there are people who can simply turn resources into utility as most people tend to have a wider range of concerns that would restrict their ability to simply make this conversion, including concern for how well people around them are doing.

take account of the total amount of utility in society, but give weighted priority to utility for those who have less utility. This view shares much with utilitarianism, but there is an even stronger case for progressive taxation since the revenues from this can be used to provide for the worst off. It is highly plausible to think—in the absence of any evidence on each individual person—that the most economically fortunate will be among the happiest and that those who have less income and wealth, as they do less well in the job marketplace, will be among the least happy. Taxing the former rather than the latter therefore fits very well with prioritarianism.

In this section I have presented—in a whirlwind fashion—how the majority of theories of distributive justice would advocate a tax system that was both progressive and efficient. They would trade-off these issues differently from one another, of course, but my point is that all of the theories would require a tax system that is able to provide highly progressive taxation while retaining economic incentives. In the remainder of this chapter I will explain a system which promises to do this.

9.4 Hourly Averaging

Hourly averaging is a proposal which utilises "hour credits" in order to calculate tax-rates (Bamford 2014b, Chap. 2). Each taxpayer's hour credits would be recorded on the tax authority systems and these would primarily be conferred when an employee spends time working for their employer. The employer would inform the tax authority how many hours have been worked and this, along with any compensatory or additional hour credits[9], would be used to calculate the tax rate for each individual. In this section I will explain how this works.

I have said that hourly averaging makes use of hour credits in order to calculate an individual's tax rate, and this would be done on a lifetime basis (Bamford 2002, Chap. 1). The approach is a lifetime one in that it makes use of lifetime totals of gross income and hour credits in order determine the tax rate for each taxpayer. It is referred to as hourly averaging since lifetime gross income and lifetime hour credits are used to generate a gross hourly average for each taxpayer. All taxpayers will have their tax-rate calculated on the basis of this average, so Jack, who has 100 hour credits and earned $ 1000 will have the same tax-rate as Jane, who has 10,000 credits and received $ 100,000. This is because both have a $ 10 lifetime hourly average.

Hour credits and income both increase as time goes on and so each taxpayer's lifetime tax-rate would also change. This is not a problem since the actual tax payment that a taxpayer is required to make will depend upon their lifetime totals. The total lifetime tax that a taxpayer should have paid up until the present is calculated by multiplying the hourly tax amount by the number of hour credits. At every pay-

[9] These might be provided for people who are disabled, have caring responsibilities, or are involuntarily unemployed and undertake whatever work or training is requested of them. They may also be given to students on registered education courses.

ment, this latest tax liability is determined by deducting lifetime past tax payments from the new lifetime tax calculation in order to determine current liability.[10]

I will now present an example. Let us assume for simplicity that those with a $ 10 hourly average have a zero tax rate, those who have a $ 20 average have a 30 % tax rate and those with a $ 50 average have a 60 % tax rate.[11] Jack in the next period obtains another 100 hour credits and earns $ 3000. His hourly average is now $ 20 and so his tax rate is 30 %. As he has not paid any tax previously the amount of tax he must pay at this point in time is $ 1200.[12]

Jack's career continues to take-off and for his next 100 hour credits he earns $ 11,000. This takes his lifetime gross income to $ 15,000 and his hourly average income to $ 50. His tax rate is now 60 % and so his tax liability at this point in time is $ 7800 ($ 9000–$ 1200). Unfortunately for Jack his career falters somewhat after this point and he finds it hard to sell his services. Before receiving his next payment he works long and hard and obtains 200 hour credits but only earns $ 2500. This takes his lifetime income to $ 17,500 and his hour credits to 500. The tax rate on a $ 35 average is 50 % and so Jack's new lifetime tax total is $ 8750. Jack has paid $ 9000 in the past, however, and so he receives a $ 250 rebate to top up his income.

The above example shows how hourly averaging smoothes out people's net income, in common with all averaging proposals. It means that when people have sudden economic fortune their tax payments will rise. However, they will not rise as quickly as they might for people who earn wildly different amounts in 1 year to the next as they would under an annual taxation system. If Jane had instead received the plaudits which led to Jack's meteoric rise then her tax rate would not have risen so quickly. Earning $ 11,000 would have increased Jane's lifetime totals to $ 111,000 and 10,100 hour credits. This only increases Jane's hourly average income to around $ 11, meaning that her tax rate would only rise a little. The sudden changes in tax rate experienced by Jack are actually very unlikely to occur as it requires a very large relative change in hour credits or in income. The former can only occur for someone in the first year or so of their account and so it is only when someone has a huge increase in income that they will face a sudden tax bill. If Jane was capable of continuing the success that Jack was not, then her tax rate will gradually rise over time edging slowly up to the 60 % that applied to Jack.

The introduction to the proposal is very brief, but hopefully it is sufficient to take the relevant points that people's net income would increase when they receive hour credits, when they receive gross income, and that it will increase the most when they receive both together. There are of course many practical concerns around this proposal, such as how the information would be transferred efficiently, the nature

[10] Alternatively, the taxpayer's net hourly average income could be multiplied by their hour credits in order to indicate the amount of net lifetime income that they should have received. This net amount could be compared to the net income they have received in order to calculate the amount of tax that is currently due.

[11] The best lifetime tax rate graph would be a smooth curve that rises steeply at first and then more and more gradually towards 99 % for those with huge hourly averages.

[12] Jack's tax rate on this single transaction might be considered to be 40 %, but this is only an indication that he had previously been paying a much lower tax rate (in fact, zero).

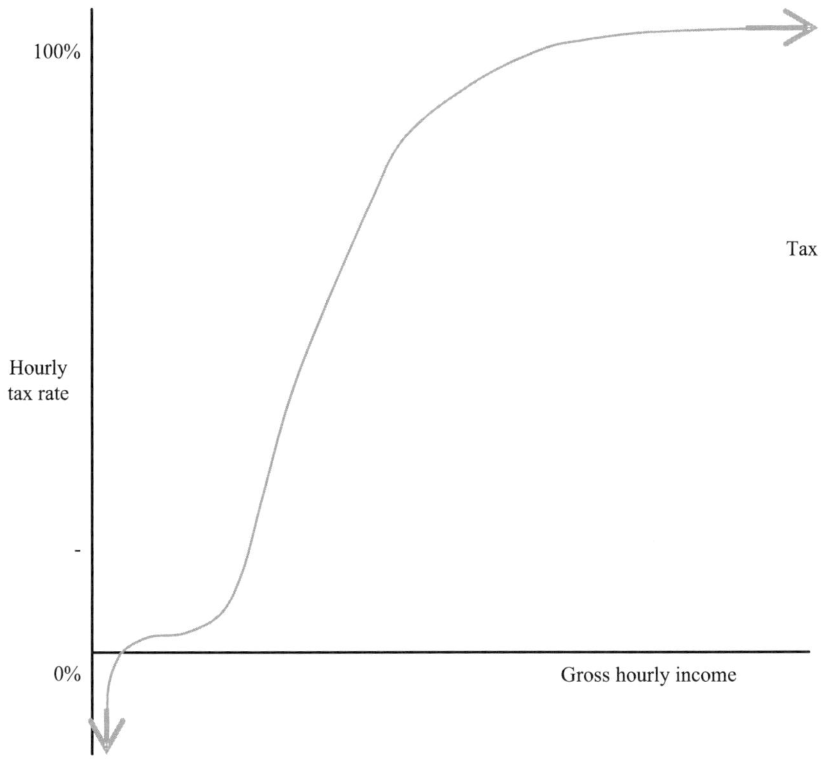

Fig. 9.1 Tax rate graph

of the transition to such a radically different system, the potential for a new form of tax fraud, and worries about the increased power that a government agency would have in such a system (Bamford 2014b). There are also worries about how a state with a highly progressive hourly averaging system would fare in a world of tax competition.[13]

9.5 Hourly Averaging and Progressivity

The examples provided in the previous section indicate that hourly averaging would impose much more steeply progressive tax-rates than any recent system has, or would be contemplated with any other tax proposal. The rates would rise relatively quickly, as shown in the proposed tax rate graph in Fig. 9.1. This graph shows that the tax system could provide an earnings subsidy to those who have a very low

[13] For proposals for international co-operation that would be compatible with lifetime averaging see (Bamford 2013, 2014a, 2014b, pp. 154–164).

hourly income. This would top-up the income of those who work very many hours for low pay for each additional hour that the individual works.[14]

The graph also shows that it would be possible to impose very high tax rates without and sudden jumps in tax rate. The point about smoothing can be further emphasised at this point. As people move along the graph their lifetime tax rate could change, but changes in a taxpayer's rate will often occur much more slowly than the change in gross income, since this will only gradually alter the hourly average. Furthermore, since past tax payments would be accounted for, even if someone's tax rate increased rapidly their gross income will always cover their tax bill and so people will not have to repay the tax authority.[15]

Another point to make is that the marginal tax rate someone will face will not work in the same way as it does with any other tax proposal. This is because multiple factors determine what proportion of someone's next payment they will pay in taxation. Someone with a low hourly tax rate could pay a large amount of their next chunk of income in tax if greatly increases relative to their total hour credits. This occurred in Jack's third period in the example above. Meanwhile, someone with a very high tax rate could receive a large additional payment from the tax authority on top of money that they receive. This is because they will have paid a large amount of tax in the past, and so if their average drops upon the receipt of additional hour credits this will release some of their previous tax payments to them. These smoothing features make it much more palatable to impose very high rates of taxation on consistently high earners. After all, those with temporary good fortune will not, over the course of their life, pay a very high rate of tax overall. This means that it is possible to tax the most economically fortunate at very high rates.

The general point I am making in this section is that lifetime hourly average is the best available observable indicator of economic fortune. This also applies to low earners as well, since those who work many hours but earn relatively little are likely to do so because they would like to earn as much as possible but struggle in the job market. The negative hourly subsidy provides the least economically fortunate with as high an economically sustainable income as can reasonably be expected (see also Bamford 2014b, pp. 57–65). Some people who are highly capable may of course earn a low income as they work in a job or sector they care passionately about. For this reason I suggest placing a higher minimum gross hourly income on certain sectors and job types which are also activities that people do as leisure activities or in order to support causes about which they are passionate (Bamford 2014b, pp. 28–29). This would put a limit on the amount of subsidy that people could obtain in order to pursue their personal interests. Aside from applying this policy, I do not see that the above issue is very problematic. There are strong reasons not to take account of the earning abilities that people have when calculating their tax

[14] The closest proposal to this of which I am aware is that presented by economist Edmund S. Phelps (Phelps 1997). Phelps' proposal, however, is restricted to full time workers only and is paid through employers rather than tax rebates to individuals.

[15] Assuming that income is withheld at source and that people do not have their hour credits reduced for any reason.

rate, such as the epistemic problems of reliably in determining this ability and the intrusiveness of attempts to place a monetary value on someone's ability. In contrast, assessing someone's actual market activity—as income taxes do—is entirely straightforward.

I have so far discussed hourly averaging as though it would be applied to earned income only. However, it could also be applied to all the gains that an individual receives irrespective of the source.[16] This would ensure that people with multiple forms of good luck would be taxed at as high a rate as possible while those who have one brief form of good economic fortune will have this taken into account with regard to their overall lifetime economic position.

9.6 Hourly Averaging, Incentives, and Economic Efficiency

As I have mentioned at several points above highly progressive taxation—including support to the less economically successful—is generally taken to be a strong drag on economic growth and efficiency. This is because it reduces the rewards of economic success and softens the fear of economic failure. While this may be worthwhile overall, there are usually assumed to be strong reasons not to have a highly progressive and redistributive tax system of the sort I have outlined in the previous two sections. In this section I will explain why these worries about disincentives and economic efficiency are less troubling for hourly averaging than other highly progressive proposals.

There is a general assumption that the unfettered market will generate the best economic returns. This may well be true, but the theories of justice outlined above would rule out the application of totally free market policies. This is because these policies would work poorly for a large subset of society and this group are entitled to equally as good treatment by their society as the economically fortunate. In this section I will ignore this ideal of the free market outcome and instead focus on what makes the free market outcome attractive; that it provides incentives for people to work and trade and that it generates the products that people need and want as cheaply as possible.

My claim is that the hourly averaging proposal would do a good job of incentivising people to work while taxing the economically fortunate as much as possible (Bamford 2014b, pp. 66–73). In the previous section I made some points that are also important to the argument in this section. The first is that the smoothing element of lifetime averaging means that higher tax rates will not be applied to all those who temporarily earn high amounts. This means that there is no disincentive for those who find themselves in a situation where they can make a decent amount of money in a short time period. The marginal tax rate will be nowhere near as high

[16] I have proposed a hybrid comprehensive income and consumption tax base, under the name of "Comprehensive Acquired Income" (Bamford 2014b, pp. 84–97).

as it would have been if the tax had been calculated over a shorter period. Furthermore, any income that someone receives will continue to be on their tax account for the remainder of their life and will continue to generate net income when they obtain more hour credits.

A further point relates to marginal taxation. As I said in the previous section, marginal tax rates are not as straightforward as they are with other tax systems. Since the marginal tax rate will depend upon many variables people will have a strong incentive to work and earn irrespective of what their headline or average rate happens to be at that point in time. An important factor in determining tax rate is the number of hour credits and these will impact upon marginal tax rates in a manner that will encourage people to work and earn more.

Since hour credits reduce tax rates at all points on the income scale there is always an economic incentive for people to work an extra hour when they can receive an hour credit for doing so.[17] One way to look at this is to say that hour credits will reduce someone's tax rate, certainly compared to what it would have been without that additional hour credit. As a result, people at all points on the hourly average tax graph would have an incentive to work for marginal tax rate reasons. This applies to people with a strongly negative tax rate whose tax rate could rise very quickly with increased gross income and also to those with tax rates of 90 % or more.

As well as marginal effective tax rates a similar point applies with regard to Participatory tax rates (Brewer, Saez and Shephard 2010; Saez 2002). This is the issue that someone does not only choose whether to work another hour, but can decide between working some hours or no hours at all. Other forms of progressive taxation and benefit payments[18] may encourage high earners to retire earlier and low earners to stop work altogether and utilise state support instead. Hourly averaging would strongly encourage participation on two counts. The first is that hour credits offer the chance to receive tax rebates where they reduce someone's average, and second that hour credits always create income for their recipient irrespective of their headline tax rate. If hourly averaging is combined with a comprehensive tax system, as I would suggest it should be, this would also mean that those who can obtain resources from their family or other sources would not be able to use this to avoid participation in the job market. Such people would need hour credits in order to release this unearned income and would therefore be more likely to work for hour credits than those without such economic fortune.[19]

I have said that hour credits will encourage workforce participation and that this will mean that more work is performed in society than it would be under rival

[17] Not all additional hours would lead to an additional hour credit. In order to reduce the scope for fraud, and to discourage over-working, I would propose a maximum number of hour credits that each taxpayer could receive in a given period (Bamford 2014b, pp. 44–45).

[18] The most obvious being the proposal for a basic income, which can also be referred to as a *negative income* tax among other names (Cunliffe and Erreygers 2004; Van Parijs 1995, 2006; Friedman 1962, pp. 191–192).

[19] We might put it that hourly averaging is a tax on excessive leisure. Leisure is an area that has been little discussed in political philosophy, but exceptions are Rawls (1996, 1988); and Rose (forthcoming).

progressive and redistributive proposals.[20] This should mean that prices are kept lower than they would otherwise be and most people would have greater disposable income as a result. This would be of benefit to all members of society whatever their level of economic fortune.

I have so far emphasised that hourly averaging would retain incentives to work that progressive systems may otherwise dampen. Some may worry that the high tax rates on some and negative tax rates for others would dampen market signals and thereby undermine the advantages of a free market economy.[21] I do not think that this is a serious worry, however. As I have said people still have incentives to do work that will increase their gross income. Furthermore, capitalism would still work in the same way. People would use their income to purchase what they desire and this will influence market prices and production decisions. Another point to emphasise is that a lot of the productivity of capitalism comes from the competition between firms and this would continue under the system I propose. The more efficient firms will thrive and those which fail to keep up will fail (or they will be taken over by their more profitable rivals).

In this section I have briefly presented the reasons we have to think that hourly averaging would create a very efficient economy. This fits into my argument as I would claim that hourly averaging can provide much greater progressivity. It does so by taxing people who are clearly very economically fortunate at very high rates and redistributing to the less economically fortunate while retaining economic incentives for all members of society. These economic incentives would lead to a more economically productive and efficient society than rival tax progressive systems could manage, and this therefore would be the most attractive institutional response to all of the approaches to distributive justice I outlined in the third section above.

9.7 Conclusions

In this chapter I have argued that tax policy should make use of hourly averaging. I began by arguing that since tax policy has such important distributive consequences this needs to be guided by the principles of distributive justice. I then took an ecumenical approach and presented a number of attractive theories of distributive jus-

[20] I would be less certain to say that more hours of work would be done than under *laissez faire* but it is possible that it would be.

[21] Another concern is that hourly averaging would greatly increase the amount of bureaucracy in society and that this will be a drag on productivity. I would accept that managers and firms would need to devote some of their time and resources to interacting with the tax authority, but I would contend that the amounts involved would be minimal. Using IT systems it should be readily possible to transfer the relevant information very efficiently from one computer system to another. After all, firms either expect their staff to work a significant number of hours in order to meet their responsibilities or they already monitor their staff closely and pay them only for the number of hours they have worked.

tice, which would all agree that the tax system should redistribute in a progressive manner when compared to a free market baseline. However, all of the proposals I described would also be concerned about the effects of the tax and benefit system on economic efficiency as the size of the economic pie would matter alongside the equality of its distribution.

I then presented a tax system proposal which promises to redistribute more than rival schemes and to incentivise economically beneficial behaviour. I have referred to this proposal as hourly averaging as it makes use of hour credits to determine the tax rate for each citizen. I explained why this proposal should be very effective at taxing the economically fortunate and assisting the economically unfortunate. I also explained that the proposal does this while ensuring that there are strong incentives for people to work. My argument is that if I am correct that the proposal combines these two features much more successfully than any rival systems then hourly averaging is required according to the requirements of distributive justice. As a consequence, we are ethically obliged to seek to implement the proposal. Of course, it would be necessary to further investigate the economic and empirical claims I have made in favour of hourly averaging, but this argument would show that such investigations are important ones to make in order that we can work out how to make the world a more just place in which to live.

References

Anderson, Elizabeth. 1999. What is the point of equality? *Ethics* 109 (2): 287–337.

Arneson, Richard J. 1989. Equality and equal opportunity for welfare. *Philosophical Studies* 56 (1): 158–194.

Bamford, Douglas. 2013. Comprehensive lifetime taxation of international citizens: A solution to tax avoidance, tax competition, and tax unfairness. In *Tax justice and the political economy of global capitalism*, eds. Jeremy Leaman and Attiya Waris. Oxford: Berghahn Books.

Bamford, Douglas. 2014a. Realising international justice: To constrain or to counter-incentivise? *Moral Philosophy and Politics* 1 (1): 127–146.

Bamford, Douglas. 2014b. Rethinking taxation: An introduction to hourly averaging. London: Searching Finance.

Bamford, Douglas. The holistic and policy focused interpretation of hypothetical insurance. *Moral Philosophy and Politics* (forthcoming).

Bentham, Jeremy. 1907/1780. *An Introduction to the Principles of Morals and Legislation*. Oxford: Clarendon.

Brewer, Mike, Emmanuel Saez, and Andrew Shephard. 2010. Means-testing and tax rates on earnings. In *Dimensions of tax design: The mirrlees review*, eds. Stuart Adam, Timothy Besley, Richard Blundell, Stephen Bond, Robert Chote, Malcolm Gammie, Paul Johnson, Gareth Myles, and James Poterba. Oxford: Oxford University Press.

Christman, John Philip. 1994. *The myth of property: Toward an egalitarian theory of ownership*. New York: Oxford University Press.

Cohen, G. A. 1989. On the currency of egalitarian justice. *Ethics* 99 (4): 906–944.

Cohen, G. A. 2008. *Rescuing justice and equality*. Cambridge: Harvard University Press.

Cunliffe, John, and Guido Erreygers. 2004. *The origins of universal grants: An anthology of historical writings on basic capital and basic income*. Basingstoke: Palgrave Macmillan.

Dagger, Richard. 2006. Neo-republicanism and the civic economy.*Politics, Philosophy & Economics* 5 (2): 151–173.
Dick, James C. 1975. How to justify a distribution of earnings. *Philosophy and Public Affairs* 4 (3): 248–272.
Dworkin, Ronald. 1981. What is equality? part 2: Equality of resources. *Philosophy & Public Affairs* 10 (4): 283–345.
Fleurbaey, Marc. 2008. *Fairness, responsibility and welfare*. Oxford: Oxford University Press.
Frankfurt, Harry. 1987. Equality as a moral ideal. *Ethics* 98 (1): 21–43.
Fried, Barbara H. 1999. The puzzling case for proportionate taxation. *Chapman Law Review* 2: 157–196.
Fried, Barbara H.. 2002. Why proportionate taxation? In *Tax justice: The ongoing debate,* eds. Joseph J. Thorndike and Dennis J. Jr. Ventry, 149–192. Washington D.C.: Urban Institute.
Friedman, Milton. 1962. *Capitalism and freedom*. Chicago: University of Chicago Press.
Kolm, Serge-Christophe. 2005. Macrojustice: the political economy of fairness. Cambridge: CUP.
Lamont, Julian. 1994. The concept of desert in distributive justice. *The Philosophical Quarterly* 44 (174): 45–64.
Meade, J. E. 1964. *Efficiency, equality, and the ownership of property*. London: G. Allen & Unwin.
Mill, John Stuart. 1993. *Utilirarianism, on liberty, considerations on representative government*. London: J. M. Dent.
Miller, David. 1999. *Principles of social justice*. Cambridge: Harvard University Press.
Murphy, Liam, and Thomas Nagel. 2002. *The myth of ownership: taxes and justice*. Oxford: Oxford University Press.
Nozick, Robert. 1974. *Anarchy, state, and utopia*. Oxford: Blackwell.
O'Neill, Martin, and Thad Williamson. 2012. *Property-owning democracy: Rawls and Beyond.* Malden: Wiley-Blackwell.
Okun, Arthur M. 1975. *Equality and efficiency, the big tradeoff.* Washington: Brookings Institution.
Parfit, Derek. 1997. Equality and priority. *Ratio* 10 (3): 202–221.
Parfit, Derek. 2000. Equality or priority? In *The ideal of equality,* eds. Matthew Clayton and Andrew Williams, 81–125. Basingstoke: MacMillan.
Parfit, Derek. 2012. Another defence of the priority view. *Utilitas* 24 (3): 399–440.
Pettit, Philip. 1997. *Republicanism a theory of freedom and government*. Oxford: Oxford University Press.
Phelps, Edmund S. 1997. *Rewarding work: How to restore participation and self-support to free enterprise*. Cambridge: Harvard University Press.
Rakowski, Eric. 1991. *Equal justice*. Oxford: Clarendon.
Rawls, John. 1974. Reply to alexander and musgrave. *The Quarterly Journal of Economics* 88 (4): 633–655.
Rawls, John. 1988. The priority of right and ideas of the good. *Philosophy and Public Affairs* 17 (4): 251–276.
Rawls, John. 1996. *Political liberalism*. New York: Columbia University Press.
Rawls, John. 1999. *A theory of justice: Revised edition.* Oxford: Oxford University Press.
Rawls, John. 2001. *Justice as fairness: A restatement*. Cambridge: Harvard University Press.
Rose, Julie L. (forthcoming) Money does not guarantee time: Discretionary time as a distinct object of distributive justice. *Journal of Political Philosophy*.
Saez, Emmanuel. 2002. Optimal income transfer programs: Intensive versus extensive labor supply responses. *The Quarterly Journal Of Economics* 117 (3): 1039–1073.
Sen, Amartya. 1980. Equality of what? In *The tanner lectures on human values,* ed. Sterling M. McMurrin, 197–220. Salt Lake City: University of Utah Press.
Sen, Amartya. 1993. Capability and well-being. In *The Quality of Life,* eds. Martha C. Nussbaum and Amartya Sen, 30–53. Oxford: Clarendon.
Sen, Amartya. 2009. *The idea of justice*. London: Allen Lane.
Shields, Liam. 2012. The prospects for sufficientarianism. *Utilitas* 24 (1): 101–117.
Steiner, Hillel. 1994. *An essay on rights*. Oxford: Blackwell.

Sugin, Linda. 2004. Theories of distributive justice and limitations on taxation: What rawls demands from tax systems. *Fordham Law Review* 72 (5): 1991–2014.
Van Parijs, Philippe. 1995. *Real freedom for all: What (if anything) can justify capitalism?* Oxford: Clarendon.
Van Parijs, Philippe. 2006. Basic income: A simple and powerful idea for the twenty-first century. In *Redesigning distribution: Basic income and stakeholder grants as alternative cornerstones for a more egalitarian capitalism* eds. Bruce A. Ackerman, Anne Alstott, Philippe van Parijs, and Erik Olin Wright. London: Verso.
White, Stuart. 1999. The egalitarian earnings subsidy scheme. *British Journal of Political Science* 29 (4): 601–622.
White, Stuart. 2003. *The civic minimum: On the rights and obligations of economic citizenship*. Oxford: Oxford University Press.

Chapter 10
Why Do the Public Oppose Inheritance Taxes?

Rajiv Prabhakar

Abstract Common wisdom supposes that inheritance taxes are very unpopular among the public. This public opposition seems puzzling as these taxes typically apply to a minority of estates. Usual explanations for this are that people are poorly informed about the extent of these taxes or that there is a lack of a compelling moral case for such taxes. This chapter argues that current approaches do not go far enough. It suggests public attitudes to inheritance taxes are better understood as a specific case of discontent with wider taxes. Addressing this means tackling a disconnection the public feel over the taxes they pay as well as exploring public reactions to different combinations of taxes. Greater public support for inheritance taxes is important for building public compliance with these taxes as well as improving the chances for policy reform.

10.1 Introduction

Common wisdom decrees that inheritance taxes are very unpopular among the public (Goodin 2003; Cremer 2010). These are taxes that are placed on transfers of wealth. These taxes can vary depending on whether the tax is imposed on the donor (estate tax), recipient (inheritance tax) or includes gifts as well as inheritances (capital receipts tax). For convenience, this chapter will usually refer to these taxes generally as inheritance taxes (unless referring to a specific tax in a particular country). Cremer writes that: 'Taxes are rarely popular, but wealth transfer taxes appear to be particularly and increasingly unpopular. A number of countries are already without an inheritance or an estate tax or, as in the case of France, have dramatically reduced its scope. Some others, including the United States, contemplate to phase it out' (Cremer 2010, p. 815). Bartels (2006) reports results from a 2002 National Election Study survey which asked 1,346 US respondents what they thought about repealing the estate tax. 67.6% of the sample favoured abolition versus 27.2% of participants opposed abolition. Majorities for repeal were recorded among those

---

R. Prabhakar (✉)
Faculty of Social Sciences, Open University, Walton Hall, Milton Keynes MK7 6AA, UK
e-mail: rajiv.prabhakar@open.ac.uk

H. P. Gaisbauer et al. (eds.), *Philosophical Explorations of Justice and Taxation*,
Ius Gentium: Comparative Perspectives on Law and Justice 40,
DOI 10.1007/978-3-319-13458-1_10

with family incomes of less than $ 50,000 (63.5 % in favour of repeal), those who wanted more government spending (66.3 %) and among those who were concerned about rising income inequality (65.5 %). Hammar et al. (2008) reports the results of a survey in 2004 of 1,774 Swedes aged between 15 and 85 of attitudes to 11 different taxes, including payroll tax, corporation tax and petrol duty. These researchers use an 'opinion balance' index (which measures the share of respondents who want to reduce or abolish a tax minus those who want to increase it) to explore attitudes to tax. The three most unpopular taxes were different taxes on wealth, in particular real estate tax, inheritance tax and gift tax with opinion balances of 70, 66 and 63. For the purposes of comparison, corporation tax scored the lowest opinion balance with a figure of eight. There was less hostility to a different wealth tax which imposed a 1.5 % levy on the net wealth of 160,000 € for single people and 215,000 € for couples. This wealth tax had an opinion balance of 24.

This public opposition to inheritance taxes seems surprising given what such taxes raise for the public purse (Beckert 2008; Boadway et al. 2010). Sir James Mirrlees chaired a recent review of taxation at the Institute for Fiscal Studies in the UK. A document from this review notes that: 'Most major economies raise relatively little from inheritance and gift taxes. None of the G7 economies has raised more than 1.0 % of national income in revenue from Estate, Inheritance, and Gift Taxes in any one year over the last forty years' (Boadway et al. 2010, p. 741). The public hostility also seems puzzling because inheritance taxes usually apply only to the wealthiest estates. One might expect majority opinion to oppose abolition because this raises the prospect that government will raise the taxes they pay to compensate for the scrapping of inheritance tax. Nevertheless, there seems to be popular support for abolition. In the US in 2001, a repeal of the estate tax was passed which meant that this tax was due to fall to zero in 2010. A sunset clause meant that the repeal had to be renewed. Although President Obama allowed the estate tax to return in 2011, he nevertheless weakened the tax over its pre-repeal level (Graetz and Shapiro 2005; Birney et al. 2006; Graetz 2011).

Studying public opinion is important for reasons of politics and policy. Within politics, taxation marks one of the most significant relationships between government and citizens (Commission on Taxation and Citizenship 2000; Murphy and Nagel 2002). In a representative democracy, politicians should ideally reflect preferences over taxation. Edlund comments: 'Ideally, in a representative democracy, the preferences of the population work as guidelines for political authorities that are supposed to translate these wishes into specific policies. Although the link between public opinion and political decision making in reality may be less than straightforward, democracy faces a huge problem if only the segment of the population can provide such guidelines' (Edlund 2003, p. 145).

Examining public attitudes is also significant for policy. One issue for any successful tax system is the degree to which citizens comply with its provisions. Research suggests that public morale is important for understanding whether people comply with taxes (Torgler and Schneider 2007). If people reject a tax, they may seek to avoid or evade paying these taxes. In certain circumstances, this public opposition can spill over into physical protests (Robinson 2003). This suggests the significance of attending to public opinion when designing a tax system. Indeed, public opposition to inheritance taxes is often cited as a key reason why politicians are reluctant to rely on such taxes. Goodin remarks: "Inheritance taxes have long been the 'third rail' of tax policy, touch them, and you are dead, politically" (Goodin 2003, p. 70). Exploring public opinion is also significant at the present time as governments across the world seek to rebalance tax and spending following the global financial crisis that started in the late 2000s. Politicians will find it useful to refer to public opinion when exploring options for reform. Hammar et al (2008) write: 'political difficulties in implementing the tax structure therefore call for optimal taxation theory to be complemented by analyses of tax attitudes' (Hammar et al 2008, p. 524).

Studying public opposition to inheritance tax in particular is significant because current research has difficulty explaining why a majority seems to oppose such taxes. There is a temptation to see this as a 'problem' with public opinion. McCaffery makes a judgement in the 1990s that seems to apply today: 'The most common answer to the puzzle of popular opposition to the estate tax is that people are making a factual mistake' (McCaffery 1994, p. 285). This chapter explores an alternative suggestion that the problem may lie more in how researchers understand public opinion. Rather than focusing on attitudes to inheritance tax in isolation from other taxes it is important to see inheritance tax as part of the wider tax system. This is important because the issue then is not so much providing more facts or more compelling moral arguments about inheritance tax. The issue instead is providing people with choices over different taxes.

This chapter is organised as follows. The first three sections outline three main ways that tax attitudes have been analysed, that is rational choice theory, framing and institutions. This part of the chapter suggests that existing approaches have difficulty in explaining why the majority of opinion seems to be against inheritance taxes. The fourth part suggests that the problem with existing research is that they tend to split off the study of inheritance tax from other taxes. However, it is important to see inheritance taxes as part of the wider tax system, and this helps understand the nature of public attitudes to inheritance taxes. The final section considers some implications for research.

10.2 Rational Choice Theory

Rational choice theory is used in standard economic analyses of tax attitudes (Gemmell et al. 2004; Slemrod 2006; Hammar et al. 2008). Rational choice theory assumes people are rational self-interested utility maximisers. Rational choice means that people satisfy axioms of consistent choice, such as not being swayed by irrelevant alternatives in the choices they make. Self-interest means that people satisfy their own preferences, although these preferences can be either selfish or altruistic. People also choose those actions that maximise their utility. However, they need the appropriate information to pick the actions that maximise their utility.

If this information is unavailable then people can make errors over the choices that maximise utility. Rational agents will make the maximising choices once the proper information becomes available (Sen 1990; Hammar et al. 2008). Rational choice theory also suggests that people consider benefits as well as costs when thinking about taxation. For example, people get benefits through tax-funded public services such as health and education and this should shape attitudes to taxation.

10.2.1 Public Opposition to Inheritance Tax

Rational choice theory provides several reasons why people might oppose inheritance taxes. First, people might object to it because of self-interest. The wealthy who are liable to inheritance taxes might be expected to oppose this tax on selfish grounds. Self-interest can also cover concern for others and a parent might be hostile to inheritance taxes because of worries of the taxes to be paid by their children.

Although the above helps explain some of the opposition to inheritance taxes, it fails to account for why public opposition seems so widespread. The main reason for this is that only a minority of estates are usually liable to estate or inheritance tax. For example, prior to its repeal, the estate tax in the US applied to about 2 % of estates (Graetz and Shapiro 2005). This means there is only a minority of wealthy estates who will be liable to the tax or a minority of parents whose children will be affected by the tax. Given this, the majority of people should not be either liable to inheritance tax or expect their offspring to have to pay inheritance tax. Only a minority should be opposed to inheritance taxes (Birney et al. 2006).

Second, people might oppose inheritance taxes because of poor information. Data exists which suggests that people have poor information about the extent of inheritance tax. Bartels (2006) notes that the 2003 survey by National Public Radio, Kaiser Foundation and Harvard Kennedy School found that half of respondents thought most families had to pay estate tax with a further 18 % saying they did not know. Bartels (2006) writes: 'Thus, two-thirds of the American public apparently failed to recognize the single most important fact about the estate tax: that it is paid only by very wealthy people' (Bartels 2006, p. 411). Rowlingson and McKay (2005) conducted a survey of 2,008 people in the UK on their attitudes to inheritance. This survey found people had a tendency to overestimate liabilities to inheritance tax. For example, only 6 % of respondents noted correctly that 6 % of estates in the UK paid inheritance tax, with 48 % thinking it was 25 % of estates or above.

This raises the possibility that providing more information about the incidence of inheritance taxes might reduce opposition to such taxes (Slemrod 2006). However, doubts can be cast on the likely impact of such a strategy. Bartels (2006) comments: 'Would correcting this misconception produce widespread public support for the estate tax? That is much less clear' (Bartels 2006, p. 411). Krupnikov et al. (2006) argue that surveys do not typically provide people with enough incentive to answer the questions correctly. They suggest that providing greater incentives can mean people spend more care answering questions and reveal greater knowledge of estate tax. The researchers tested this in a survey of 1,200 US residents done in 2004. Part of the sample was offered a $ 1 reward for each correct answer, with others receiving no reward. This experiment found that offering a modest cash incentive raised the chance of a correct answer by a third, with 36 % of those without the incentive getting the correct answer compared with 47 % who got the incentive.

Even where lack of information exists, people might filter extra information through their political biases and bend the information to suit their beliefs. Krupnikov et al (2006) say that their survey shows partisan differences in the way that people absorbed new information, with Democrat voters more likely to boost their acceptance of estate tax compared with Republican voters. Although more information might reduce some of the opposition it is likely, with societies with divided political opinion, to leave a substantial strand of opinion untouched.

A third possibility is that much of the public is simply being irrational when they oppose inheritance taxes. This is because most people are acting directly against their economic self-interest when they oppose inheritance taxes. On this view, providing more information about the incidence of inheritance taxes will have little effect because people are behaving irrationally about this. Such an argument suffers from several problems. First, it begs the question of why researchers, but not the wider public, are capable of examining inheritance taxes in a rational manner. A more plausible view would see less stark differences between researchers and the public. Second, it raises the question of why people should react irrationally on inheritance tax when it appears that rational choice helps understand behaviour in other areas. Third, this viewpoint overlooks the way that people might have reasons other than rational choice for opposing inheritance taxes. Rational choice is perhaps one of the influences on individual behaviour and that for inheritance taxes other factors trump considerations of self-interest. This leads into a possible role discussed below that moral arguments may play in shaping opinion towards these taxes.

10.3 Framing

A second approach to understanding public attitudes to taxation draws on themes from behavioural economics in understanding attitudes to taxation (McCaffery and Baron 2003, 2004; Löfgren and Nordblom 2009). Behavioural economics shares with the rational choice approach an emphasis upon self-interest. However, more attention is placed on the limits on rational choice. This has roots in earlier ideas such as bounded rationality. This literature highlights the importance of framing for understanding attitudes to taxation. This takes its cue from the point that people's choices over options can vary depending on how these options are presented or framed (Kahneman and Tversky 1979; Thaler and Sunstein 2008). Löfgren and Nordblom (2009) report that a study of economics students shows that support for environmental taxes tend to increase if it is referred to as a CO_2 tax rather than a gasoline tax. Lakoff (2004) argues that each person's mind contains a set of assumptions and values that forms a 'frame'. People are often unaware of their frames but use these to put their experiences in order. People can combine assumptions and values in varying ways and so yield different frames. Lakoff says that invoking a particular frame can help win public support for a policy. Language can nudge people to view policies in particular ways. For example, the term 'tax burden' tends to associate taxation with negative images, that is, being a burden to the individual that ideally should not exist. Moral stories or arguments are one way of trying to frame the debate. For instance, the term 'death tax' for inheritance tax is intended to invoke the idea that death comes to everyone as well the notion that government is interested in taxing people at a time of personal or family tragedy. This label then is intended to dispose people against accepting inheritance tax (Birney et al. 2006).

10.3.1 Will Reframing the Debate Reduce Opposition?

One possible explanation for the public opposition to inheritance taxes is that critics are better than supporters at framing the terms of the debate. Graetz and Shapiro (2005) argue that critics of the estate tax in the US relied mainly on developing stories with a clear and simple moral message. This covered emotive tales of how the estate tax destroyed the lives of hard-working Americans who were trying to provide for their children. Graetz and Shapiro (2005) say that supporters of the estate tax responded by citing statistics about the incidence of the tax. They continue that while the provision of some information has some uses, this 'scientific' strategy was not enough to convince public opinion. In situations where there are competing moral values and complexity, the role of simple stories proved to be a better guide than relying on statistics. They suggest the task for supporters of estate tax is to learn the lessons from their critics and develop simple moral messages in favour of the estate tax. They propose trying to reframe proposals to cut estate tax as a 'Paris Hilton benefit act' which promises a tax cut to the wealthy heiress (Graetz and Shapiro 2005; Birney et al. 2006).

If the problem with supporters of inheritance taxes is a failure to communicate their message effectively, then presumably this could be remedied through a better reframing of the debate. However, doubts can be raised over how far this is likely to shift public opinion. The main reason for this is that supporters of inheritance taxes have not relied only on science but have also tried moral persuasion when outlining their arguments. For example, in the mid-2000s various commentators in the US picked up on Graetz and Shapiro's (2005) suggestion and referred to the 'Paris Hilton benefit act' or 'Paris Hilton tax cut' when opposing cuts to the estate tax (Dionne 2005; Klein 2005; Levine 2006). It is unclear whether the public mood in the US has since swung in favour of the estate tax. Although such moral reframing might persuade some people, its overall impact on public opinion might be modest.

Fatemi, Hasseldine and Hite (2008) also report results that show that efforts to create positive frames for estate tax can have counter-productive results when people already have negative views of the estate tax. They highlight resistance theory which suggests that people can resist or oppose a 'primed' position. They conducted a telephone survey of 250 respondents in the US. They found that where people already have a negative attitude towards estate tax, efforts to create positive frames (looking at issues of equity, redistribution or ability to pay) in fact entrenched opposition to this tax.

Beckert (2008) argues that inheritance taxes provoke particular controversy among the public as this results in a series of conflicts over different principles. In particular, debate exposes tensions within and between values such as equal opportunity, family, justice and community. For example, a family principle might be critical of taxing transfers of wealth within a family as it undermines the formation of a stable family identity over time. However, an alternative view of the same principle might be concerned that a parent might use the threat of withdrawing a bequest to exert control over the decisions of their children. However, moral reasons face difficulty in explaining the public opposition to this tax. This is because moral arguments do not all point in the same direction. In fact, mainstream academic opinion suggests that the arguments in favour of inheritance tax are much stronger than the arguments against such taxes (McCaffery 1994; Cunliffe and Errygers 2012). McCaffery states that: 'Few matters in social and political philosophy seem as well-settled—as much the product of a broad right-thinking consensus—as the idea that a liberal state should have some form of wealth transfer tax' (McCaffery 1994, p. 281). One would expect therefore that moral arguments should mean that people are more supportive of inheritance tax, which seems contrary to public opinion.

10.4 Institutions

Rational choice models take preferences as fixed and do not usually explain how preferences are shaped in the first place. Research in sociology places more emphasis on the way that institutions or policies can help shape public attitudes (Edlund 2003; Torgler and Schneider 2007; Sachweh and Olafsdottir 2012). Edlund comments that the: 'institutional design of the state—the welfare state in particular—and the structure of organized interests can be expected to significantly influence the degree of political consciousness and knowledge in the citizenry' (Edlund 2003, p. 150).

One argument suggests that that existing tax institutions might help shape public opinion. Beckert (2007, 2008) examines traditions of taxing inheritance in the US, Germany and France. He says that different values shape institutions in each of these countries and this can be seen in varying rationales for inheritance law in these countries. These values can be traced back to the eighteenth century. He says that equal opportunity dominates in the US, a family idea in Germany and equality in France. If institutions mould public opinion, one would expect public acceptance of inheritance tax to be highest where government has taxed inheritances most heavily. However, Beckert (2007) notes that during the twentieth century the US had steeper taxes on inheritances than Germany or France: 'American estate tax had much steeper progression rates compared to the two European countries for much of the twentieth century. Between 1940 and 1981 the highest tax rate stood at 77 %. Even after the tax reforms which went into effect in the 1980s, the highest rate remained at 55 %, until the current phase-out of the estate tax went into effect' (Beckert 2007, p. 108). If institutions are a major influence on public opinion, then one would expect greater acceptance of estate tax in the US than other countries. However, the public backing for abolition of the estate tax in 2001 suggests important limits on how far institutional habits can shape public acceptance of inheritance taxes.

10.5 Optimal Taxation

This chapter now explores a different approach, namely that it is important to see all taxes as part of the wider tax system. This looks at how each tax fits alongside other taxes rather than treating taxes in isolation from each other. This stress on the tax system was one of the themes of the Mirrlees review of taxation. This discusses the 'crucial insight that the tax system needs to be seen as just that—a system. While we will often address the impact of each tax separately for simplicity of exposition, we focus throughout on the impact of the system as a whole—how taxes fit together and how the system as a whole achieves the government's goals' (Mirrlees et al. 2011, pp. 2–3). In fact, some of the contributors to the Mirrlees review argue that this came to be seen as increasingly important during the review (Johnson and Myles 2011). This approach has roots in a wider economic literature on optimal taxation (Mirrlees 1976; Slemrod 1990; Kaplow 2000, 2011). Optimal tax theory studies the most efficient way of raising a given amount of revenue. Kaplow (2011) argues this method is neutral about how revenue is spread through society and is a useful tool for analysing tax systems. Kaplow (2011) argues that this approach recasts moral debates about taxation. For example, Kaplow says that proposed rises in sales tax such as Value Added Tax are often seen as regressive. However, any such effect might be offset by changes elsewhere and so the overall effect of the tax system may be a progressive one. What matters from a moral standpoint is the overall effect rather than the specific changes brought by individual taxes.

This suggests that when examining public attitudes towards fair taxation, it is important to explore the opinion towards the overall nature of the tax system rather than focus on specific taxes. Asking people about their views on taxation as a whole might reinterpret existing findings on inheritance tax. Applying an optimal tax framework to studies of public opinion might allow people to engage in trade-offs between different taxes and reveal different responses from those made if people were asked about taxes on their own. People might voice different attitudes to inheritance tax if they were asked to balance this against other taxes such as income tax or sales tax. One possibility is that public opposition to inheritance tax will be reduced if people compare their reactions here with other taxes. Alternatively, even if people were still opposed to inheritance tax, one cannot read anything from this about their wider attitudes. People might support regressive reforms to inheritance tax but be committed to a progressive tax system.

The optimal tax literature also yields other practical insights for public attitudes to inheritance tax. Slemrod (1990) argues that optimal tax theory is incomplete without a discussion of the way government is able to collect taxes. In particular, government might lack the technology to stop tax avoidance or evasion. He says constraints facing tax collection means that a set of optimal taxes may not be a practical policy option. Slemrod proposes that policy-makers and researchers should focus on optimal tax systems which consider the capacity to collect taxes as part of an optimal set of taxes (Slemrod 1990).

The tax collection point is relevant for inheritance tax. Cremer and Pestieau (2010) argue that part of the reason why inheritance taxes raise relatively small amounts for the public purse is that they are often difficult for government to enforce. Globalisation and the increased mobility of capital create further opportunities for tax avoidance. Cremer and Pestieau suggest that tax avoidance by the very wealthy perhaps fuels some of the public disquiet over inheritance taxes: 'avoidance and evasion not only leads to poor tax yields but also leads to strong departures from both vertical and horizontal equality. This may explain at least in part, why wealth taxation is today so unpopular in some countries the political system is considering abolishing it' (Cremer and Pestieau 2010, p. 18).

Cremer and Pestieau (2010) argue that while it is important to acknowledge the constraints on collecting inheritance taxes, it is important not to overstate these difficulties. For example, international tax co-ordination might limit the scope for international tax avoidance (Cremer and Pestieau 2010). Taxes on certain types of wealth might also be less easily avoided than others. For example, property taxes are harder to avoid than taxes on financial wealth because property is less mobile and less easily disguised than financial wealth. One idea is for government to tax housing wealth more heavily than financial wealth. However, this might also help explain why taxes on wealth prompt public concerns in certain countries. For example, countries where there is a high degree of property ownership might be expected to display public antipathy to inheritance taxes. For example, part of public unhappiness with inheritance tax in the UK seems bound up with concerns that rising house prices will push people into paying inheritance tax. George Osborne, when he was shadow Chancellor, exploited such fears when he promised that a future Conservative government would raise the threshold of paying inheritance tax from £ 300,000 to £ 1 million. Osborne framed this as taking the family home out of inheritance tax (Osborne 2007).

Although the spread of property ownership might explain part of the public opposition to inheritance tax in the UK, this is less relevant in places with lower rates of home-ownership among the population. In the UK, the extent to which politicians pander to homeowners highlights the idea that different members of the public might exert varying levels of influence over politicians. The very wealthy often fund public campaigns against inheritance tax (Birney et al. 2006; Rowlingson 2008). While the opposition among the very wealthy might be expected because of self-interest, a similar calculation does not seem to apply for the rest of the public.

Politicians might try to mobilise the rest of the public opinion to counter opposition from the wealthy.

10.5.1 Beyond Optimal Taxation

Although optimal taxation offers valuable insights, studies of public opinion might usefully include but go beyond such a framework. The main reason for this is to consider the benefits as well as costs of taxation when studying public opinion. Using the rational choice approach, people balance the costs of taxation with benefits from tax-funded public spending on areas such as health and education. Moral arguments do not usually see taxation as an end it itself but rather a contribution to the creation of a good society. Fair taxation helps create a fair society. Popular support for such taxes exists where people see the benefits of taxation as outweighing the costs. However, if people feel disconnection between the taxes they pay and the benefits they receive, then they may question the point of taxation. The public might think that the government spends money wastefully or politicians are self-serving with public funds. If such disconnection exists, then people can be expected to oppose all taxes. People might tailor their criticisms to each tax under consideration, but they may be hostile to any tax. Large majorities of opposition might also occur if people are asked about fuel duty, income tax or sales tax instead of inheritance taxes.

Attention to the benefits as well as the costs of taxation in fact extends the analysis of the Mirrlees review. This review looked at the tax system as a whole rather than about how taxes mesh with spending. Kaplow (2011) writes:

> Tax by Design is typical in its focus on explicit income transfers to the exclusion of direct government spending on goods and services. Yet these expenditures, including in education and health care, contribute significantly, and perhaps disproportionately, to the well-being of individuals at the lower end of the income distribution. Moreover, like direct transfers, they affect labour supply. A more complete implementation of Tax by Design's systematic approach would integrate this dimension of fiscal activity as well. (Kaplow 2011, p. 433)

Doing this means that public attitudes to taxation should consider the benefits of taxation as well as asking people to consider taxes as part of the overall system.

10.6 Benefits of Taxation

There is limited evidence at present on the likely impact of an optimal tax framework on public opinion, in large part because public attitude studies on inheritance tax have usually considered this tax in isolation from other taxes. However, this chapter now suggests there are nevertheless signs in current data that suggest an optimal tax framework could help reinterpret the public opposition to inheritance tax. Evidence exists which suggests that examining the benefits of taxation can impact on how people view taxes. Torgler and Schneider (2007) examine why people comply with paying taxes. They suggest that the deterrents that governments use to stop tax evasion are insufficient to explain levels of tax compliance in different countries. They suggest that tax morale, the willingness to pay taxes, is important for compliance. Drawing on World Values Survey and European Values Survey data, they study tax compliance in Spain, Belgium and Switzerland. Their results show that trust in government has a significant positive impact on morale (Torgler and Schneider 2007). Edlund (2000) shows how attitudes to taxes can vary if people are asked to consider the benefits as well as costs of taxation. Edlund (2000) presents results from 6 national surveys in Sweden done between 1981 and 1997. One question asks people to comment on whether the general level of taxes is too high, about right or too low. Majorities were recorded in the different surveys saying that taxes were too high, ranging from 84 % of respondents in 1981 to 65 % of respondents in 1996. However, these figures dropped when people were asked to comment instead on whether taxes are not high considering the public benefits provided by the government. 57 % and 50 % of people agreed in 1981 and 1996 with the idea that taxes were not too high given the benefits from government.

10.6.1 Combinations of Taxes

Data on public attitudes towards different tax combinations as opposed to general levels of taxation is fairly sparse. Cole and Kincaid (2000) note that, until 1996, the US Advisory Commission on Intergovernmental Relations (ACIR) had an annual survey of attitudes to government spending and related tax questions, including what people thought was the worst tax, which is understood as meaning the least fair tax, from the following list: federal income tax, social security, state sales tax, state income tax and local property tax. Kincaid and Cole (2001) repeat the survey for 2001. Cole and Kincaid (2000) record that federal income tax has generally been seen as the worst tax: 'The federal income tax… has been most frequently rated the worst tax by the largest proportion of respondents, especially since 1977, while the local property tax has been less frequently rated the worst tax since the late 1970s' (Cole and Kincaid 2000, p. 195). Cole and Kincaid note that the average percentages citing the federal income tax as the worst tax was 28.9 % in the 1970s, 34.4 % in the 1980s and 32.7 % during the 1990s (until the survey ended in 1996). Local property tax was more unpopular in one decade but close behind in other decades, with figures for the successive decades of 32.1, 27.9 and 28.3 %. The state income tax was seen as the least worst tax with average numbers of 10.6, 10.1 and 11 %. These researchers say that there are demographic differences in the responses. Looking at the results for 1999, the federal income tax was more likely to be picked as the worst tax by white people (41.4 %) over black people (20.8 %) and Republicans (50 %) over Democrats (31.6 %). Kincaid and Cole (2001) say that in 2001 30 % of respondents thought the federal income tax was the worst with 22 % citing the local property tax. These results were roughly double those for the other taxes.

Hedges and Bromley (2001) provide the most comprehensive survey to date of public attitudes to taxation in the UK. Hedges and Bromley found that inheritance tax seemed to be particularly unpopular. The survey found that 51 % of respondents thought that inheritance tax should be abolished, while around 20 % thought that the threshold at which inheritance tax starts should be raised from its then level of £ 250,000 to at least £ 500,000. The remainder believed that the current level should be kept or reduced, with 2 % thinking that all inheritances should be taxed. Hedges and Bromley do not ask the same questions of other taxes as they do of inheritance tax. However, the survey did ask people to comment on whether they thought other taxes were too high, low or about right. The results suggest wider dissatisfaction with other taxes. They found that 58 % of respondents thought that income tax was too high or much too high; 76 % believed Value Added Tax was too high or much too high; and 75 % of people who felt that duties on cigarettes, alcohol and petrol were too high or much too high.

10.7 Discussion

The above studies suggest a more varied picture of public opinion than is obtained by concentrating on inheritance tax alone. Federal income tax is cited as the worst tax in the US and support for raising the inheritance tax threshold in the UK should be set against around three-quarters of people who thought Value Added Tax was too high or much too high. Seeing public opposition to inheritance taxes as part of wider concerns with all taxes carries at least two implications for how public attitudes to inheritance taxes should be addressed.

First, it is important to link taxation to government spending. Edlund (2000)'s results show that attitudes to taxation can vary if people are asked explicitly to consider the benefits as well as costs of taxation instead of looking only at taxes. Data from the European Social Survey challenges the idea that public trust across Europe in politicians is in decline (European Social Survey 2009). This means that spending decisions by politicians do not automatically have to be seen as being inherently self-serving or wasteful. Of course, setting out the benefits of taxation leads into ideology and disputes over the proper boundaries of the state, with neoliberals more critical of government spending than social democrats. Although libertarians support a minimal state, mainstream neoliberals allow for a more important, albeit limited, role for the state and so suggest some state spending is useful. Proposals for tackling a sense of possible disconnection between taxes and spending could be explored, for example earmarking certain taxes for particular spending programmes. This idea has been proposed for inheritance taxes, with a suggestion that a reformed inheritance tax might be used to pay for a capital grant that could be paid to all citizens upon maturity (Le Grand and Nissan 2000). Earmarking is a controversial idea as it reduces the flexibility of government to use tax revenues to meet shifting public spending challenges (Commission on Taxation and Citizenship 2000). However, the limited use of earmarking might be one way of addressing the disconnection that people feel over the taxes they pay.

Second, more attention should be paid to how taxes fit together as part of the overall system. Certain commentators have argued that it is important when designing tax systems to see how different taxes fit together and combine (Mirrlees et al. 2010). However, this attention to combinations of taxation should extend to the analysis of public opinion. People might be presented with choices over taxes to explore the trade-offs they make over taxes or the relative weight they place on different taxes. Presenting people with choices increases the complexity of decisions and might lead to conflicting responses. However, it also allows new areas of debate to develop and this might help stem public disquiet over inheritance taxes.

The public attitudes to inheritance taxes might be explored by asking people to compare reactions to wealth taxes versus other taxes. For instance, in the US people might be prepared to support rises in the estate tax as a way of cutting the federal income tax. Attitudes might also vary across different types of wealth tax. Taxes on wealth could mean taxes on the returns to wealth (such as duties on share dividends), taxes on holdings of wealth (such as land taxes) or taxes on transfers of wealth (which could be imposed on either the recipient or donor of the transfer). Hammar et al's (2008) results point to varying public attitudes to different types of taxes on wealth, with less opposition to a tax on the holdings of wealthy individuals or couples rather than real estate tax (a property tax), inheritance tax or gift tax. This suggests that it is important when exploring public attitudes to wealth taxes to distinguish between the tax under consideration. Even if people still react negatively to taxes on transfers of wealth, the Swedish data shows people may be more willing to support a tax on wealth. This raises the possibility for supporters of inheritance taxes that if even people remain opposed to these plans, they might nevertheless support other options for taxing wealth (Krupnikov et al. 2006).

The role of moral stories or information could be blended in at this point. One possible reason why taxing holdings of wealth may attract less opposition than transfers of wealth is that a simpler and more compelling moral case could be made for the latter over the former. This means that arguments about taxes in general, moral stories and information are not mutually exclusive and can be combined. However, the discussion of moral arguments here occurs within more general considerations of the tax system. Focusing on moral arguments or information on their own is unlikely to be enough to understand public opinion, and there is a need to go beyond this and understand the nature of public opinion in a different way.

10.8 Conclusion

Public opposition to inheritance taxes seems to be a puzzle. Large majorities of the public appear to oppose a tax that applies only to a minority of estates. Standard explanations of this suggest that people do this because they are misinformed of the extent of inheritance tax or supporters of such taxes do not present them in a compelling form. This public opposition would fall with the provision of more information or better moral stories.

This chapter suggests that the above strategies are likely to have a limited impact on public opinion. The problem is not that the public fails to respond properly to more information or better moral arguments but that researchers fail to understand the nature of public opinion. Opposition to inheritance taxes are part of concerns with all taxes and so discontent with inheritance tax is a local instance of wider unhappiness with all taxes. This means that the current approaches to address public opposition to inheritance taxes are too narrow and fail to address a disconnection people have with taxes. Seeing inheritance taxes in this perspective helps resolve the puzzle about inheritance taxes as well as suggest ways it should be reduced. The priority should be on seeing how taxes fit alongside each other as well as helping people tie the benefits of taxation with its costs. Unless this is done, the puzzle with inheritance taxes is likely to remain.

References

Bartels, Larry. 2006. A tale of two tax cuts, a wage squeeze, and a tax credit. *National Tax Journal* LIX (3): 403–422.

Beckert, Jens. 2007. The Longue Durée of inheritance law. Discourses and institutional development in France, Germany and the United States since 1800. *Archives Européenes de Sociologie* XLVIII (1): 79–120.

Beckert, Jens. 2008. Why is the estate tax so controversial? *Society* 45:521–528.

Birney, Mayling, Michael Graetz, and Ian Shapiro. 2006. Public opinion and the push to repeal the estate tax. *National Tax Journal* LIX (3): 439–461.

Boadway, Robin, Emma Chamberlain, and Carl Emmerson. 2010. Taxation of wealth and wealth transfers. http://www.ifs.org.uk/mirrleesreview/dimensions/ch8.pdf. Accessed 25 April 2014.

Cole, Richard, and John Kincaid. 2000. Public opinion and American Federalism: Perspectives on taxes, spending and trust—an ACIR update. *Publius: The Journal of Federalism* 30 (1–2): 189–201.

Commission on Taxation and Citizenship. 2000. *Paying for progress: A new politics of tax for public spending*. London: Fabian Society.

Cremer, Helmuth. 2010. Commentary. http://www.ifs.org.uk/mirrleesreview/dimensions/ch8.pdf. Accessed 25 April 2014.

Cremer, Helmuth, and Pierre Pestieau. 2010. Wealth and wealth transfer taxation: A survey. International studies program. Working paper 10–17. Atlanta: Georgia State University.

Cunliffe, John, and Guido Errygers, eds. 2012. *Inherited wealth, justice and equality*. London: Routledge .

Dionne, Eugine Joseph Jr. 2005. *The Paris Hilton tax cut. The Washington Post*, 12 April.

Edlund, Jonas. 2000. Public attitudes towards taxation: Sweden 1981–1997. *Scandinavian Political Studies* 23 (1): 37–65.

Edlund, Jonas. 2003. Attitudes towards taxation: Ignorant and incoherent? *Scandinavian Political Studies* 26 (2): 145–167.

European Social Survey. 2009. Exploring public attitudes, informing public policy. Selected findings from the first three rounds. http://www.europeansocialsurvey.org/docs/findings/ESS1-3_findings_booklet.pdf. Accessed 25 April 2014.

Fatemi, Darius, John Hasseldine, and Peggy Hite. 2008. Resisting framing effects: The importance of prior attitudes on estate tax preferences. *Journal of American Taxation Association* 30 (1): 101–121.

Gemmell, Norman, Oliver Morrissey, and Abuzer Pinar. 2004. Tax perceptions and preferences over tax structure in the United Kingdom. *Economic Journal* 117:F117–F138.

Goodin, Robert. 2003. Sneaking up on stakeholding. In *The ethics of stakeholding,* eds. Keith Dowding, Jurgen De Wispelaere, and Stuart White, 65–78. Basingstoke: Palgrave-Macmillan.

Graetz, Michael. 2011. The politics and policy of the estate tax- past, present, and future, yale law and economics research paper number 425. http://papers.ssrn.com/sol3/papers.cfm?abstract_id=1755161. Accessed 25 April 2014.

Graetz, Michael, and Ian Shapiro. 2005. Death by a thousand cuts. The fight over taxing inherited Wealth. New Jersey: Princeton University Press.

Hammar, Henrik, Sverker C. Jagers, and Katarina Nordblom. 2008. Attitudes towards tax levels: A multi-tax comparison. *Fiscal Studies* 29 (4): 523–543.

Hedges, Alan, and Catherine Bromley. 2001. Public attitudes towards taxation: The report of research conducted for the fabian commission on taxation and citizenship. London: The Fabian Society.

Johnson, Paul, and Gareth Myles. 2011. The Mirrlees review. *Fiscal Studies* 32 (3): 319–329.

Kahneman Daniel, and Amos Tversky. 1979. Prospect theory: An analysis of decision under risk. *Econometrica* XLVII (1979): 263–291.

Kaplow, Louis. 2000. A framework for assessing estate and gift taxation. National bureau of economic research, Working paper 7775.

Kaplow, Louis. 2011. An optimal tax system. *Fiscal Studies* 32 (3): 415–435.

Kincaid, John, and Richard Cole. 2001. Changing public attitudes on power and taxation in the American federal system. *Publius: the Journal of Federalism* 31 (3): 205–214.

Klein, Ezra. 2005. The Paris Hilton benefit act. *The American Prospect,* 12 April.

Krupnikov, Yanna, Adam. S. Levine, Arthur Lupia, and Markus Prior. 2006. Public ignorance and estate tax repeal: The effect of partisan differences and survey incentives. *National Tax Journal* LIX (3): 425–437.

Lakoff, George. 2004. *Don't think of an elephant! Know your values and frame the debate*. White River Junction: Chelsea Green Publishing.

Le Grand, Julian, and David Nissan. 2000. *A capital idea: Start-up grants for young people*. London: Fabian Society.

Levine, Art. 2006. The Paris Hilton tax cut: Call your senators now. http://www.huffingtonpost.com/art-levine/the-paris-hilton-tax-call_b_22453.html. Accessed 25 April 2014.

Löfgren, Åsa, and Katarina Nordblom. 2009. Puzzling tax attitudes and labels. *Applied Economic Letters* 16:1809–1812.

McCaffery, Edward. 1994. The political liberal case against the estate tax. *Philosophy and Public Affairs* 23 (4): 281–312

McCaffery, Edward, and Jonathan Baron. 2003. The Humpty Dumpty blues: Disaggregation bias in the evaluation of tax systems. *Organizational Behavior and Human Decision Processes* 91:230–242.

McCaffery, Edward, and Jonathan Baron. 2004. Framing and taxation: Evaluation of tax policies involving household composition. *Journal of Economic Psychology* 25:679–705.

Mirrlees, James. 1976. Optimal tax theory: A synthesis. *Journal of Public Economics* 6:327–358.

Mirrlees, James, Stuart Adam, Tim Besley, Richard Blundell, Stephen Bond, Robert Chote, Malcolm Gammie, Paul Johnson, Gareth Myles, and James Poterba. 2010. Tax by design: The Mirrlees review. Conclusions and recommendations for reform. http://www.ifs.org.uk/mirrleesreview/pamphlet.pdf. Accessed 25 April 2014.

Mirrlees, James, Stuart Adam, Tim Besley, Richard Blundell, Stephen Bond, Robert Chote, Malcolm Gammie, Paul Johnson, Gareth Myles, and James Poterba. 2011. Tax by design. http://www.ifs.org.uk/mirrleesreview/design/taxbydesign.pdf. Accessed 25 April 2014.

Murphy, Liam, and Thomas Nagel. 2002. *The myth of ownership. Taxes and justice*. Oxford: Oxford University Press.

Osborne, George. 2007. It's time for aspiration. Speech at Conservative party conference, 1 October. http://news.bbc.co.uk/1/hi/uk_politics/7022498.stm Accessed 25 April 2014.
Robinson, Nick. 2003. Fuel protests: Governing the ungovernable. *Parliamentary Affairs* 56 (3): 423–440.
Rowlingson, Karen. 2008. Is the death of inheritance tax inevitable? Lessons from America. *Political Quarterly* 79 (2): 153–161.
Rowlingson, Karen, and Stephen McKay. 2005. *Attitudes to inheritance in Britain*. Bristol: Policy Press.
Sachweh, Patrick and Sigrun Olafsdottir. 2012. The welfare state and equality? Stratification realities and aspirations in three welfare regimes. *European Sociological Review*. 28(2): 149–168.
Sen, Amartya. 1990. Rational fools: A critique of the behavioral foundations of economic theory. In *Beyond self-interest,* ed. Jane Mansbridge, 25–43. Chicago: Chicago University Press.
Slemrod, Joel. 1990. Optimal taxation and optimal tax systems. *Journal of Economic Perspectives* 4 (1): 157–178.
Slemrod, Joel. 2006. The role of misconceptions in support of regressive tax reform. *National Tax Journal* LIX (1): 57–75.
Thaler, Richard, and Cass Sunstein. 2008. *Nudge. Improving decisions about health, wealth and happiness*. New Haven: Yale University Press.
Torgler, Benno, and Friedrich Schneider. 2007. What shapes attitudes toward paying taxes? Evidence from multicultural European countries. *Social Science Quarterly* 88 (2): 443–470.

Chapter 11
The Role of Expressive Versus Instrumental Preferences in U.S. Attitudes Toward Taxation and Redistribution

Kirk J. Stark

Abstract Polling data suggest that Americans are concerned about rising economic inequality, yet the same polls reveal popular opposition to redistributive tax policies that would help mitigate inequality. Numerous commentators have drawn attention to this paradox, attempting to explain why voters would support policies contrary to their pecuniary interests. This chapter connects the debate over U.S. tax attitudes with research on the role of expressive preferences in electoral choice. An expressive account of political behaviour emphasizes the low likelihood that any one voter's views will influence policy outcomes and thus locates her cost-benefit calculus in the expression itself rather than its effect on policy outcomes. Expressive considerations include the reputational consequences of taking sides in popular debates, especially as those consequences bear on the voter's effort to portray herself to the people that matter in her life—her family, friends, co-workers, and most of all, herself. The author explains how an expressive account resolves the supposed "paradox" of popular opposition to redistributive tax policies and discusses the implications of this view for U.S. tax politics.

11.1 Introduction

In his 1835 treatise on American democracy, Alexis de Tocqueville observed that the redistributive activity of government, through taxes and spending, was likely to increase with the extension of the franchise to persons less capable of sharing in the cost. "As the great majority of those who create the laws are possessed of no property upon which taxes can be imposed," he wrote, "all the money which is spent for the community appears to be spent to their advantage, at no cost of their own" (de Tocqueville 1835). Presaging the insights of public choice theory a century plus later, de Tocqueville was suggesting a seemingly inescapable political

K. J. Stark (✉)
School of Law, University of California, LA, Hilgard Avenue 405, Los Angeles, CA 90095, USA
e-mail: stark@law.ucla.edu

H. P. Gaisbauer et al. (eds.), *Philosophical Explorations of Justice and Taxation*,
Ius Gentium: Comparative Perspectives on Law and Justice 40,
DOI 10.1007/978-3-319-13458-1_11

logic of redistribution—as the number of voters with below average income grows, democracy through majority rule, especially when coupled with universal suffrage, should result in a greater redistribution of income. This logic was later formalized and incorporated into an influential theory of democracy and redistribution (Meltzer and Richard 1981).

Something akin to de Tocqueville's political logic of redistribution underlies the sense of puzzlement expressed by many twenty-first century observers of American tax politics. In ongoing debates about various redistributive tax policies, it is commonly described as "perplexing" or "baffling" when beneficiaries of redistribution indicate opposition to policies that would benefit them (Sheffrin 2013). Numerous examples from the U.S. political experience illustrate this phenomenon—e.g., grassroots enthusiasm for property tax revolts, popular antagonism toward the estate tax, middle-class support for tax cuts chiefly benefiting the wealthy. The supposed irony of these political stances was captured with hilarious satirical precision in a 2003 Nick Anderson cartoon showing Homer Simpson celebrating his own meager $ 2 tax cut, while his wealthy boss, Mr. Burns, quietly gathers several bags full of tax cut savings, muttering "Sucker…" under his breath. The research of political scientist Larry Bartels has provided some empirical substantiation for the intuition behind the Homer Simpson cartoon. Interpreting survey data on popular attitudes toward the 2001 tax cuts supported by the George W. Bush administration, Bartels concluded that "it appears that the strong plurality support for Bush's tax cut … is entirely attributable to simple ignorance" (Bartels 2005, p. 24).

The notion that those benefitting from redistribution should support it—or that their failure to do so is attributable to ignorance—is based on the assumption that voters will generally favour policies consistent with their economic self interest, what some commentators have termed the "self-interested voter hypothesis" (SIVH) (Caplan 2008). When that assumption appears not to hold, or obtains only in the most short-sighted sense as in the case of popular support for the Bush tax cuts, we are left shaking our heads in some mixture of pity and disbelief. Our incredulity is only intensified by the increasing disparities in wealth and income over the past half century and the concomitant hollowing out of the middle class through the polarization of labour market opportunities (Piketty 2014; Autor and Dorn 2013). Polling data suggest that Americans are in fact concerned about rising economic inequality, yet the same polls often reveal popular opposition to redistributive tax policies that would help mitigate the effects of that inequality. It is no surprise that we feel perplexed or baffled by these apparent contradictions. Like Bartels, we may find ourselves asking, "Why do millions of ordinary Americans support massive tax breaks for the rich in an era of accelerating economic inequality?" More generally, on questions of taxation and redistribution, why do American voters so often seem to vote against their economic self interest?

My purpose in this chapter is not to answer these questions, but rather to suggest an alternative narrative that puts popular attitudes toward redistributive taxes in a somewhat different light. This alternative perspective takes issue with a second assumption, one that works hand in hand with the self-interested voter hypothesis described above. This second assumption is that political behaviour, including the expression of beliefs through voting, answering a survey, or otherwise, is motivated chiefly by a desire to produce a certain outcome in public policy. If this assumption holds, and voter behaviour is indeed driven by a desire to influence policy outcomes, then our sense of puzzlement at popular support for tax breaks for the wealthy may well be justified. After all, the outcome preferred is one that chiefly benefits a wealthy minority and may well carry with it indirect costs to the non-wealthy voter in terms of reduced government services or a less favourable distribution of the remaining tax burden. Thus, to the extent that one assumes that voter behaviour is driven by a desire to produce outcomes, one might reasonably regard as puzzling or perplexing the apparent support among ordinary Americans of significant tax reductions for the wealthy.

But influencing outcomes may not be the only, or even a primary, motivation for political behaviour. Popular attitudes, whether registered at the voting booth, captured in survey instruments, or shouted across the kitchen table, often have an important expressive dimension, providing a means for individuals to associate themselves with a certain set of beliefs, ideas and preferences. Rather than focusing on how a particular policy outcome may affect voters, an expressive account of political behaviour emphasizes the utility that voters derive from the expression itself. Under an expressive account, self interest is determined not by the effects of policy outcomes (which after all will come about, or not, regardless of any single voter's actions) but rather by the immediate and tangible consequences of taking sides in popular debates, especially as those consequences bear on the voter's effort to portray herself to the people that matter in her life—her family, friends, co-workers, and most of all, herself. Salient considerations might include how a given opinion or vote will contribute to one's reputation as being charitable, self-reliant, open-minded or ambitious—to name just a few possibilities. In an age of digital social media, one's expressive utility might turn on how many "likes" a Facebook post got, or how many times a tax tweet was retweeted. Depending on the context and the nature of the issue about which an opinion is being expressed, we might even expect these considerations of reputation and self-portrayal to overwhelm any thoughts the voter might have about actually influencing policy outcomes. The relative significance of expressive considerations will also be greater when the likelihood of influencing outcomes is small, as will typically be the case with regard to questions of national policy.

The insight that voter behaviour is undertaken for its expressive value has been around quite a while and has formed the basis of important and interesting work at the intersection of political science and economics. Within the literature on expressive preferences, there is even some discussion of how the pursuit of expressive (as opposed to instrumental, outcome-related) benefits might shape the politics of redistribution. Nevertheless the importance of this perspective to the question of how we should understand U.S. popular attitudes toward taxation and redistribution has not been given the attention it deserves. In this essay I hope to take a step in the direction of filling that gap. Section A begins with a brief survey of popular attitudes toward economic inequality and redistributive taxes, highlighting the often puzzling contradictions in survey results that many authors have identified.

Section B discusses the concept of expressive utility and the circumstances under which voters might be expected to vote in accordance with their expressive preferences rather than their instrumental preferences. Finally, Section C extends the analysis to the context of taxation and redistribution, describing how an expressive account of voter behaviour might help explain U.S. popular attitudes thought to be puzzling within an instrumental framework.

11.2 American Attitudes Toward Inequality and Redistributive Taxation

The rise of inequality in income and wealth beginning in the latter half of the twentieth century has been a subject of extensive empirical investigation and debate across numerous disciplines. Indeed, it is hard to identify a topic that has received as much interdisciplinary attention in the past quarter century. Yet the attention on these issues has by no means been limited to the expert community. As Thomas Piketty notes in his recent book on the subject,

> The distribution of wealth is too important an issue to be left to economists, sociologists, historians, and philosophers. It is of interest to everyone, and that is a good thing. … Peasant and noble, worker and factory owner, waiter and banker: each has his or her own unique vantage point and sees important aspects of how other people live and what relations of power and domination exist between social groups, and these observations shape each person's judgment of what is and is not just. Hence there will always be a fundamentally subjective and psychological dimension to inequality, which inevitably gives rise to political conflict that no purportedly scientific analysis can alleviate. (Piketty 2014)

Of course, in a democratic setting, the "subjective and psychological dimension to inequality" should be expected to play an especially important role, exerting pressure on elected representatives to respond to popular sentiments. Thus, it is no surprise that just as research on economic inequality itself has increased, so too has research on popular perceptions of inequality, as well as popular opinion regarding what (if anything) should be done in response to changes in the distribution of economic resources.

Political scientist Larry Bartels, author of the Homer Gets a Tax Cut study mentioned above, provides a useful summary of U.S. attitudes toward inequality, redistribution, and tax policy in his 2008 book on the subject, which includes and extends the earlier study (Bartels 2008). Bartels reviews National Election Study (NES) survey results over a 20 year period covering 1984–2004. Three key findings highlighted in Bartels' analysis warrant emphasis here.

First, on the question of popular support for broadly stated "egalitarian values" there appears to be very strong agreement across the population. Nearly 90% of respondents indicate some measure of agreement (60.2% agree strongly, 27.5% agree somewhat) with the statement, "Our society should do whatever is necessary to make sure that everyone has an equal opportunity to succeed." Of course this statement leaves open several important questions, such as whether "our society" includes government (and if so which level of government), what constitutes an "equality opportunity to succeed" and what sort of metric might help us decide whether everyone has such an opportunity. Surely there are significant cleavages in public opinion regarding those important details. Nevertheless, the willingness of such a strong majority to express agreement with this statement suggests a remarkable level of popular support for egalitarian values at a broad conceptual level.

Second, the NES surveys for 2002 and 2004 also included a question designed to determine the degree of popular awareness of changes in economic inequality over the previous 20 years, the general magnitude of those changes, as well as how those changes should be regarded. More specifically, the survey asked, "Do you think the difference in incomes between rich people and poor people in the United States is larger, smaller, or about the same as it was 20 years ago?" The survey results reveal that a significant majority of respondents (75.7 %) believe that the gap between rich and poor is either "much larger" (44.3 %) or "somewhat larger" (31.4 %). As to how these changes in the distribution of income should be regarded, 43.8 % of respondents indicated that the gap between rich and poor was larger and that this increased gap was "a bad thing" (Bartels 2008). While not as robust as the general endorsement for addressing equality of opportunity, this strong plurality support for the notion that increased inequality is a bad thing again would suggest that policies targeted at reducing the income gap between rich and poor would resonate with many ordinary Americans.

A third feature of the NES survey results identified by Bartels relates specifically to the distribution of tax burdens. In surveys conducted in both 2002 and 2004, a majority of respondents (55.9 %) indicated that "rich people" pay less than they should in federal income taxes, and a plurality of respondents (44.9 %) indicated that "poor people" pay more than they should. Again, these data might be interpreted in a number of ways, but Bartels is surely correct in noting that "if taken at face value, they seem to demonstrate substantial public support for increasing, rather than decreasing, the progressivity of the tax system" (Bartels 2008, p. 140). In combination, then, these three findings provide support for the following statements: (1) almost all Americans are strongly committed to ensuring equality of opportunity, (2) a strong plurality of Americans believes that economic inequality has increased and that this is a bad thing, and (3) substantial support exists for using the tax system to shift a greater federal income tax burden to the rich.

These findings are largely consistent with those identified by sociologist Leslie McCall, whose work also focuses on American beliefs regarding inequality and redistribution. In her 2013 book, McCall considers three separate questions that appear over several years in the Social Inequality Modules of the General Social Survey (GSS) and the International Social Survey Program (ISSP). Like many of the questions from the NES surveys, these opinion polls also ask respondents to indicate their agreement or disagreement with particular statements (including options for neither, as well as strong agreement or disagreement). The three statements highlighted by McCall are: (1) differences in income in America are too large, (2) inequality continues to exist because it benefits the rich and powerful, and (3) large differences in income are necessary for America's prosperity. As McCall explains,

GSS/ISSP survey results over a period of 24 years suggest consistent majority support (that is, combined responses indicating "agreement" and "strong agreement") for the first two statements, as well as strong plurality support, with majority support in some years, for the third statement. These data lead McCall to the conclusion that "half to two-thirds of Americans accepted neither the current level of income inequality nor its stated rationale as a driver of economic prosperity that benefits all Americans and not just the rich and powerful" (McCall 2013).

If the popular perceptions of inequality reported by Bartels and McCall are relatively clear—revealing a broad recognition of rising inequality and substantial support for egalitarian values—the picture regarding specific tax policies is considerably murkier. In his in-depth review of popular attitudes toward the Bush tax cuts of 2001 and 2003, Bartels finds that, while a plurality of respondents indicated that they had not yet formed an opinion, supporters of the tax cuts outnumbered opponents by a factor of two to one. As Bartels notes, this strong popular support for the tax cuts is "especially impressive in light of widespread public suspicion, even before they were passed, that the benefits would go mostly to the rich" (Bartels 2008, p. 172). Bartels reports that an NBC News/Wall Street Journal poll conducted in March 2001, on the eve of enactment of the first Bush tax cut, revealed that 74 % of respondents indicated that they expected the wealthy to benefit more from the tax cut than the middle class, and 57 % expected that the tax cut would not give enough help to those with lower incomes. Perhaps not surprisingly, Bartels also found that respondents in the NES survey were substantially more likely to support the Bush tax cuts if they had also reported that their own tax burdens were too high, even after controlling for partisan and ideological affiliation. This was true even though the benefits of the Bush tax cut went overwhelmingly to the top quintile of the income distribution and, as noted above, most respondents felt that the rich generally paid too little in taxes already.

If nothing else, the juxtaposition of these findings reveal that the cartoon image of "Homer Gets a Tax Cut" at the heart of Bartels' analysis was brilliantly spot on. The distributional properties of the 2001 and 2003 legislation heavily favoured the nation's wealthiest households, yet it faced scant popular opposition (and even enjoyed significant support). As Larry Zelenak noted, "middle-class taxpayers are not demanding tax cuts—not even for themselves, let alone for the rich." Nevertheless, the experience with the Bush tax cuts suggests that "if politicians want to enact tax cuts for the rich, they will not face hostility from their non-rich constituents as long as the big tax cut dollars for the rich are accompanied by a few dollars for the masses" (Zelenak 2004, p. 95).

McCall's analysis on popular attitudes toward taxing the rich offers up its own mysteries. Recall that in her discussion of GSS/ISSP survey results on popular perceptions of income inequality, McCall reported strong majority recognition of rising income inequality and displeasure with the accrual of benefits for the wealthy and powerful. These same surveys included specific questions regarding tax policy towards the rich and it is here that the plot thickens. With regard to questions regarding the tax burden on high-income Americans, the surveys reveal what McCall describes as "a colossal drop in the public's inclination to favor stiffer taxation of the rich in 1996 and 2008, and a still significant but less dramatic decline in 2010" (McCall 2013, p. 201). Thus, while McCall identified a significant baseline level of support for higher taxes on the wealthy (a figure which itself increased in 1992 relative to 1987), that support has shown notable declines, particular in 1996 and the late 2000s during the Great Recession. The reasons for these sharp declines are not entirely clear. Nevertheless, an undercurrent of anti-tax sentiment—even among those not targeted by the tax—runs through McCall's findings. As with the Bartels results regarding popular support for the Bush tax cuts, here again we observe a reluctance among ordinary Americans to "tax the rich" as a means of addressing increasing levels of inequality that they regard as problematic.

In a 2011 study, Rebecca Reed-Arthurs and Steve Sheffrin shed further light on this question by examining American attitudes toward redistribution via taxation (Reed-Arthurs and Sheffrin 2011). The authors report the results of a 2009 Harris poll in which respondents were asked the following question: "Would you support or oppose the government redistributing wealth by a much higher income tax on high income earners?" Of particular interest here is that respondents also provided detailed demographic information, including information regarding annual income. As a result, the study sheds lights on the heterogeneity of preferences among respondents of different income classes. As expected, opposition to the statement is strongest among high-income respondents, with nearly 45 % of those with income in excess of $ 200,000 indicating that they "strongly oppose" redistributing wealth through a higher tax on high income earners. Interestingly, however, there was also significant opposition among respondents with lower incomes (15 % "strongly oppose" taxing the rich), as well as significant support among high income earners (19 % "strongly support" taxing the rich)—both instances where the respondents were, as the authors claim, expressing "views contrary to their direct pecuniary incentives" (Id. 166; Sheffrin 2013).

Popular attitudes toward taxing the wealthy are also reflected in survey results regarding the U.S. estate tax, which was the subject of ongoing legislative debate over the first decade of the twenty-first century. In the 2001 legislation referenced above, Congress enacted a phased-in repeal of the estate tax, with complete repeal scheduled (under the original legislation) for 2010. Because the legislation implementing repeal was itself subject to a sunset provision, the estate tax was technically scheduled to re-emerge in its pre-2001 form as of January 1, 2011. These various provisions effectively ensured that estate tax repeal would figure as a prominent issue for legislative and public debate over a period of several years in the late 2000s. Interestingly, in these debates the general view of most ordinary Americans was in favour of estate tax repeal, despite the fact that the tax applied to an extremely small percentage (1–2 %) of the nation's wealthiest families. In this context perhaps more than any other, commentators have repeatedly described the views of ordinary Americans as "puzzling." Journalist David Brooks joined the chorus, asking "Why don't people vote their own self interest?" (Brooks 2003).

In their in-depth analysis of the politics of estate tax repeal, Michael Graetz and Ian Shapiro describe this state of affairs as a "political mystery" and set out to explain the constellation of circumstances that lead to the paradoxical result of ordinary Americans clamouring for Congress to grant more tax relief to the wealthiest families. As they note, "[f]or more than a century, the estate tax affected only the richest 1 or 2% of citizens, encouraged charity, and placed no burden on the vast majority of Americans. This tax was grounded on a core American value: that all people should have an equal opportunity to pursue their economic dreams." Despite the seemingly stable and robust support for this state of affairs, the estate tax "was transformed, in the space of little more than a decade, into the supposed enemy of hardworking citizens all over this country" (Graetz and Shapiro, 2005, p. 3). For Graetz and Shapiro, the "low intensity" nature of public opinion about tax issues in general, and especially the estate tax, made it vulnerable to an aggressive and creative campaign by a coalition of repeal advocates. It was, in effect, the perfect storm of malleable public opinion and dogged coalitional politics that doomed the estate tax. The central point is that the public at large, whose views on the matter were largely uninformed, was steered by savvy political operatives into supporting estate tax repeal, a policy that in reality served the interests of a small number of extremely wealthy families.

Bartels takes issue with the Graetz and Shapiro analysis, suggesting that the estate tax was unpopular with ordinary voters "long before conservative think tanks, interest groups, and propagandists came along" (Bartels 2008, p. 198). For Bartels, the drama over estate tax repeal during the 2000s reveals a political mystery of a very different sort. Under his view, "powerful public officials pursuing their own ideological impulses" had long sustained the estate tax, despite widespread (and remarkably robust) popular opposition to the tax. The irony for Bartels was that "the powerful public officials happen to have been on the side of ordinary people, while public sentiment has been on the side of the multimillionaires" (Ibid.). Here again we see the sense of puzzlement at the notion that popular sentiment would support the wealthy elite. The fact that Bartels regards this as "strange" (the chapter on this topic is titled "The Strange Appeal of Estate Tax Repeal") seems to suggest that the more logical or natural position for ordinary Americans would be to support the estate tax, not its repeal.

11.3 Expressive Utility and the Veil of Insignificance

The public opinion research summarized above raises more questions than it answers. If Americans recognize rising levels of inequality and find it troubling, and if they generally embrace an egalitarian worldview, even believing that the rich should bear heavier tax burdens, then why do so many Americans support policies seemingly at variance with these normative commitments? What accounts for the broad public support of the regressive tax cuts, including the repeal of the highly progressive estate tax, enacted during the George W. Bush administration? At the state and local level, one might ask a similar question about the pervasive adoption of tax limitation initiatives such as California's Proposition 13. What explains the popularity of these anti-tax measures, especially when the tax most directly targeted for limitation, the local property tax, is levied principally for the purpose of funding K-12 public schools, one of the most important institutions for promoting the goal of equal opportunity that Americans purport to embrace?

Any number of explanations might be offered—and indeed have been offered—in response to these questions. It is possible, for example, that voters actually believe that the adoption of regressive tax policies will promote broader economic benefits that will eventually inure to their own personal benefit through increased employment opportunities or otherwise. McCall's research casts some doubt on this possibility, but does not refute it entirely. Alternatively, where an overall legislative package offers tax cuts across the board, with substantially greater benefits accruing to higher-income taxpayers (as was the case with the Bush tax cuts), it is possible that the availability of even a small tax cut is so valuable to low- and middle-income voters that they are willing to tolerate overall regressivity in order to secure the benefit of a small tax cut for themselves. This is certainly a plausible explanation based on Bartels' research. Yet another explanation is that voters are simply confused or misguided. This is a common explanation for the oftentimes puzzling and contradictory views about tax policy reflected in opinion polls, and with good reason. Taxation is notoriously complex and susceptible to misunderstanding. Moreover, as suggested by the Shapiro and Graetz's characterization of estate tax repeal as a "low intensity" issue, tax matters are typically not at the forefront of public consciousness. Given the complexity of the issues, and the public's limited attention span, it is possible that voters will support regressive tax policies simply because they fail to appreciate how a particular policy will affect relative tax burdens. Finally, it bears noting that other political actors with a more direct and concrete interest in regressive tax legislation will undoubtedly attempt to influence popular opinion in the directions just suggested, touting its benefits to the populace at large (or sowing confusion) as a means of neutralizing political opposition. To use a pejorative term, one might say that interest groups (lobbyists, think tanks, etc…) are out to "hoodwink" the public into supporting regressive tax reforms.

What each of these explanations has in common is that they assume that the voter is acting instrumentally—in the sense of forming an opinion with an eye towards securing a particular outcome in the law-making process. Whether the explanation is rooted in some belief about general economic effects, tangible (albeit small) benefits, or voter confusion about a proposal's consequences, the underlying logic of each explanation is that the voter must be focused on outcomes, the effect of those outcomes on her well-being, or perhaps even the consistency of those outcomes with her beliefs, as suggested by Steve Sheffrin in his recent book on the role of "folk justice" in tax policy (Sheffrin 2013).

It is impossible to disprove any of these explanations. Given the nature of the question we are considering (i.e., why do voters behave in a particular way?), neither empirical verification nor falsification is possible. But I would like to suggest that there is reason to be sceptical of the proposition that policy outcomes are at the forefront of the voter's calculus when formulating their opinions. The basis for this scepticism is the familiar "paradox" of voting, which applies not just to voting but any form of political participation (including expressing opinions on matters of public concern) where the costs of participation are likely to exceed the benefits derived from it. The paradox arises from the fact that any individual voter faces an infinitesimal likelihood of her vote proving decisive in the outcome of an election. This simple, irrefutable reality of mass collective decision-making forms the basis of what Hartmut Kliemt once termed the "veil of insignificance" (Kliemt 1986). Kliemt coined this term in the context of describing how individual decision-makers were likely to behave in what he called "low cost situations"—i.e. those in which an individual decision-maker's decision "has only a negligible effect on expected outcomes" or the decision-maker "has no direct interest in the outcome because she or he will hardly be influenced by the outcome." An example of the latter, not discussed here but relevant to Kliemt's analysis, would be serving on a jury or otherwise standing in moral judgment of others. An example of the former situation, most relevant for our purposes, is the act of voting in a large electorate where the likelihood of casting a decisive vote is effectively zero.

The term "veil of insignificance" (no doubt intended as a poke at the Rawlsian "veil of ignorance") nicely captures a central, defining feature of the circumstances under which individuals express their opinions on matters of broad public concern, as when voting in an election or responding to a survey. Given that the costs of voting are likely to be positive, and the likelihood of influencing outcomes something close zero, one might assume that individuals will simply choose, on the basis of a straightforward cost-benefit calculus, not to vote. While many individuals do indeed choose not to vote, popular political participation is common enough to call into question the simple cost-benefit analysis just described. The paradox then boils down to this: why do so many people vote when it is clearly "irrational" (in the narrow cost-benefit sense) to do so? It bears noting that the paradox also speaks to the content of an individual decision-maker's vote or opinion: what motivates someone to adopt a particular opinion—support for regressive tax reforms in our analysis—when the instrumental/outcome-related consequences of taking that position are, like the act of voting itself, virtually non-existent?

Public choice theorists Geoffrey Brennan and Loren Lomasky provide an extended treatment of these questions in their book, *Democracy and Decision: The Pure Theory of Electoral Preference* (Brennan and Lomasky 1993). Their analysis distinguishes between two possible motivations for political behaviour, instrumental and expressive—terminology which I have adopted for purposes of the present analysis. The instrumental or "outcome-causal" dimension of individual decision-making relates to the likelihood that one's participation or action will bring about a particular outcome. By contrast, the expressive dimension is the "value that the voter places on expressing a preference for a, rather than b, in and of itself (i.e., independent of any effect of the voting act on the electoral outcome" (Brennan and Lomasky 1993, p. 23). The point here is to specify with greater differentiating precision the underlying logic of an individual decision-maker's electoral choice. Rather than focusing solely on the instrumental elements of a decision-maker's electoral calculus, the Brennan/Lomasky approach explicitly incorporates the possibility of "expressive" or "intrinsic" returns the decision-maker may derive from the act of voting or registering an opinion.

The Brennan/Lomasky analysis has some parallels, which the authors highlight early in their analysis, to a sports fan's decision to cheer for a particular team: "Every Saturday afternoon in the relevant season, for example, vast numbers of sporting fans toddle off to the game of their choice or sit glued to the live television coverage." These fans "clearly have a preference as to which team they would like to have win and this is a preference that their cheering and booing unequivocally declare. But even the most enthusiastic partisan does not and cannot believe that his cheering brings about the outcome for which his cheering is expressed" (Brennan and Lomasky 1993, p. 33). Leaving aside the empirical validity of these assertions, which the most ardent New York Yankees fan would no doubt contest, the analogy prompts the question as to why anyone would undertake all the screaming and booing. For Brennan and Lomasky, the explanation is clear: "The fan's actions are purely expressive. They arise from a desire to express feelings and desires simply for the sake of the expression itself and without any necessary implication that the desired outcome will be brought about thereby" (Ibid.).

Building on the Brennan/Lomasky framework, political scientist Alexander Schuessler takes the logic one step further, developing what he calls a "jukebox" theory of electoral choice (a reference to a jukebox analogy similar to the sports fan example Brennan and Lomasky employ). Schuessler's analysis covers much of the same ground as Brennan and Lomasky, emphasizing the centrality of expressive returns to individual decision-making in the low cost context of political participation. Rather than simply modelling individual decision-making, however, he develops a fascinating parallel between the various stages in the evolution of product markets for soft drinks (chiefly Coca-Cola and Pepsi) and the development of mass political campaigning in presidential campaigns over the twentieth century (from McKinley through Clinton). In each case he identifies three stages: (1) a "segmented" phase where product development is chiefly local and advertising/campaigning is product-focused (in the sense of emphasizing specific attributes of the consumer product or the policy platform), (2) a "unified" phase in which technological developments enable advertising/campaigning at a national level, catering to the product preferences of median consumers/voters, and (3) a "expressive segmented" phase where the goal is to pursue a nationwide (or even global) campaign that markets a single product/candidate to multiple constituencies by appealing to different emotions, lifestyles, and imagery.

Schuessler's historical discussion highlights the analytical similarities between certain retail product markets (a domain in which we readily recognize the influence of expressive values and affiliations) and political markets (where those same expressive tendencies have developed, and certainly are widely recognized, though regarded perhaps with a bit more disdain). Whereas Brennan and Lomasky focus on the demand side of the expressive calculus, emphasizing the expressive utility that voters may derive from their political behaviour, Schuessler's account stresses the supply side and the production of expressive opportunities by political entrepreneurs. In this sense, Schuessler's analysis is similar to that of Graetz and Shapiro, who detail the role of political entrepreneurs in cultivating a more antagonistic public assessment of the estate tax. For example, in a chapter entitled "Stories Trump

Science," Graetz and Shapiro describe how those working behind the scenes in the estate tax repeal movement "knew that compelling stories revolve around captivating characters—both heroic figures who evoke empathy and villains who breed outrage" (Graetz and Shapiro 2005, p. 231). This perspective on the battle over estate tax repeal dovetails with Schuessler's discussion of Nixon's "Checkers" speech and the "Pepsi Generation" marketing campaign in the 1960s—each involves an effort to steer the choices/opinions of consumers/voters on the basis of emotion and lifestyle, rather than a substantive engagement with the particular issue or product. In the political context, this appeal to expressive impulses is aided by the paradox of voting. If the opinion itself is unlikely to influence outcomes, then we should expect voters (as well as those attempting to "inform" voters) to find other reasons for taking sides.

11.4 Expressive Preferences on Taxation and Redistribution

If we take as a given that U.S. attitudes on taxation and redistribution are shaped by expressive rather than (or in addition to) instrumental preferences, what is it exactly that Americans are "expressing" via their opinions on these matters? On this question, of particular interest is a passage from the Brennan/Lomasky analysis concerning expressive attitudes toward income redistribution. Brennan and Lomasky posit that voters may adopt a favourable outlook on the question of income redistribution because of the altruistic sentiment that such policies express. "The central notion," they explain, "is that individuals derive direct satisfaction from expressing support for the poor" (Brennan and Lomasky 1993, p. 45). Indeed, according to Brennan and Lomasky, the opportunity to express one's political support for government redistribution is likely to supplant much of the charitable impulse that voters might have had to make direct (and privately costly) transfers to the poor.

This idea was originally developed by Gordon Tullock in his 1971 paper, The Charity of the Uncharitable, in which he suggests that voters inclined to provide income assistance to those in need might vote to have the government do so via coercive taxation rather than taking on the financial responsibility themselves. Tullock writes,

> Suppose that it is suggested that I give \$ 100 to the poor. Suppose further that this proposal is in the form of two options. Option 1 is that I take \$ 100 out of my pocket and give it to some charity. Option 2 is that we vote on whether I should be taxed \$ 100 for the purpose of making this charitable payment. The cost to me of making the direct payment is \$ 100. The cost to me of voting for the tax, however, is \$ 100 discounted by my estimate of the influence my vote will have on the outcome. Granted the constituency is 100,000 or more, the discounted cost to me of voting for this special tax on myself is vanishingly small. Thus, if I feel just a little bit charitable, I would not make the \$ 100 payment but I would vote for the tax. I would make this vote in full awareness of the fact that many other persons are also voting on the same issue and that my vote will make very little difference in the outcome. Thus the cost to me of casting my vote is small. Putting it differently, the act that I am called

> upon to perform in voting is very low cost, even though it refers to a $ 100 gift; the private gift is high cost. Under the circumstances, one would predict that I would be more likely to vote for charitable activity than to undertake it myself. (Tullock 1971, p. 388)

Tullock's central claim here is that a vote in favour of redistribution expresses a charitable impulse, satisfying the voter's psychological urge for altruism and relieving the voter of the private cost of making the transfer himself. Under the veil of insignificance present in all collective decision-making, whereby the individual's vote is inconsequential with regard to the outcome, he can vote for income redistribution with little or no expected cost to himself. Indeed, as the size of the electorate increases, and the likelihood that a single vote will prove decisive declines, one might expect this calculus to shift even more in favour of voting for redistribution. Tullock therefore predicts that redistributive transfers are more likely to enjoy popular support at higher levels of government where the number of voters is the greatest, a prediction for which there is some empirical support (Sobel and Wagner 2004). It is even possible, Brennan and Lomasky suggest, that societies may fall into a "trap" insofar as voters endorse more generous levels of redistribution than they "really" want since each individual decision-maker derives positive expressive utility from doing so.

There may be something to this notion of voters deriving expressive value from supporting redistribution, thereby fuelling higher levels of redistribution than would come about in the absence of such sentiments. The logic has considerable intuitive appeal, though it bears noting that Tullock's project is mostly conjectural, not empirical. He illustrates his point by reference to the typical university professor, whose "expressed opinions are largely in accord with the ethically-given drive toward 'loving thy neighbour and giving all you own to the poor'" but whose actual behaviour entails "few sacrifices for the poor." In Tullock's view (which is probably not inaccurate), the university professor "who said flatly that he is opposed to charity because he likes to spend his money himself would be subject to very large private costs." Support for government charity—taxing the rich to fund transfers to the poor—enables him to substantiate a self image of charity and generosity at the lowest possible private cost (Tullock 1971, p. 389). Thus, government redistribution becomes "the charity of the uncharitable."

But surely this is not the only way (and perhaps not even the most important way) that a presumed desire to maximize expressive utility might influence popular opinions on the question of income redistribution. What other sentiments might be expressed via a particular opinion on the distribution of income, in particular the taxation of higher-income individuals for the benefit of lower-income individuals? As his reference to the university professor reveals, Tullock's analysis—as well as that of Brennan and Lomasky—says very little about the expressive preferences of possible beneficiaries of income redistribution. Indeed, Tullock asserts that "[w]e intellectuals are the primary holders of these attitudes" and that "[t]he blue-collar majority are much less prone to this type of thinking" (Tullock 1971, p. 389). But this seems overly dismissive. Are there not expressive preferences that the rest of the population might hold with regard to questions of taxation and redistribution?

To evaluate this question, let us consider a voter of lesser means, someone who may or may not be a direct beneficiary of the proposed redistribution but in any event will not be among the taxpayers required to fund the new program. To give the hypothetical a bit more context, let's assume that this voter is an assistant manager at a Red Lobster restaurant in Tulsa, Oklahoma and that he is one of three assistant managers positioning himself to become the manager at a new location opening up across town. In this community there is some tax measure that will appear on the ballot the substantive provisions of which would essentially tax the rich in favour of some sort of redistributive expenditure program. To be more concrete still, let's assume that the proposal is to impose a millionaire's tax that will fund the adoption of an earned-income tax credit targeted to benefit low-income workers.

What sort of considerations—instrumental or expressive—might influence how our assistant manager will vote on this proposed measure? As to the purely instrumental considerations, factors that he might take into account would include the likelihood that he (or loved ones) would benefit from the new earned income tax credit. Such considerations are obviously focused on the possible outcome of the ballot measure, and certainly we should not underestimate the role of instrumental concerns in the formulation of popular opinions on tax policy and other forms of government redistribution. Indeed, it would not be surprising to learn that, with regard to most tax issues, instrumental concerns are paramount for the modal voter. But if expressive concerns also play a role, what role do they play?

One possibility worthy of consideration, in my view, is that someone in the position of our assistant manager might utilize the public discourse on tax policy and redistribution as a vehicle for building out his image as an entrepreneurial, self-reliant, up-by-the-bootstraps hard worker who regards taxation, governmental largesse, and redistribution with disdain. Just like the university professor in Tullock's example, who derives private benefits among his colleagues from portraying himself as a charitable proponent of government redistribution, our Red Lobster assistant manager derives private benefits (in terms of the image he portrays to co-workers, family members, future employers, etc…) by signalling that he is an adherent of a Horatio Alger style commitment to hard work, grit and determination. In other words, one need not resort to instrumental irrationality to explain this assistant manager's opposition to the proposed millionaire's tax ballot measure. Instead, expressive self-interest may well be the better, more convincing explanation.

11.5 Conclusion

It is impossible to know the extent to which these types of expressive considerations actually influence voter opinions, but in the version of fend-for-yourself capitalism in operation in the United States, where many millions of families are living paycheck to paycheck, it would not be unreasonable for a stressed breadwinner to regard politics (including her own policy opinions) not as a means of promoting legislative outcomes that alleviate that stress but rather as a costume to be donned in the service of more pressing economic needs. This is the sense in which expressive preferences might help explain the sometimes "puzzling" attitudes of ordinary

Americans toward taxation and redistribution. This is not to diminish the role that instrumental self-interest, or ideology, or even deep seated moral convictions play in the formulation of popular attitudes. Surely all of these considerations are relevant. But our understanding of American tax politics is incomplete without a recognition of the role that expressive preferences can play.

References

Autor, David, and David Dorn. 2013. The growth of low skill service jobs and the polarization of the U.S. labor market. *American Economic Review* 103 (5): 1553–1597.

Bartels, Larry. 2005. Homer gets a tax cut: Inequality and public policy in the American mind. *Perspectives on Politics* 3:15–31.

Bartels, Larry. 2008. *Unequal democracy: The political economy of the new gilded age*. Princeton: Princeton University Press.

Brennan, Geoffrey, and Loren Lomasky. 1993. *Democracy and decision: The pure theory of electoral preference*. Cambridge: Cambridge University Press.

Brooks, David. 2003. The triumph of hope over self-interest. *New York Times,* 12. January.

Caplan, Bryan. 2008. *The myth of the rational voter: Why democracies choose bad policies*. Princeton: Princeton University Press.

De Tocqueville, Alexis. 1835. Democracy in America. Trans. Henry Reeve. London: Saunders and Otley.

Graetz, Michael, and Ian Shapiro. 2005. *Death by a thousand cuts: The fight over taxing inherited wealth*. Princeton: Princeton University Press.

Kliemt, Hartmut. 1986. The veil of insignificance. *European Journal of Political Economy* 2 (3): 333–344.

McCall, Leslie. 2013. *The undeserving rich: American beliefs about inequality, opportunity, and redistribution*. Cambridge: Cambridge University Press.

Meltzer, Allan, and Scott Richard. 1981. A rational theory of the size of government. *The Journal of Political Economy* 89 (5): 914–927.

Norton, Michael, and Dan Ariely. 2011. Building a better america-One wealth quintile at a time. *Perspectives on Psychological Science* 6 (1): 9–12.

Piketty, Thomas. 2014. *Capital in the twenty-first century*. Trans. Arthur Goldhammer. Cambridge: Harvard University Press.

Reed-Arthurs, Rebecca, and Steve Sheffrin. 2011. Windows into public attitudes towards redistribution. Proceedings of the National Tax Association, 165–173.

Sears, David, and Carolyn Funk. 1990. The limited effect of economic self-interest on the political attitudes of the mass public. *The Journal of Behavioral Economics* 19 (3): 247–271.

Sheffrin, Steve. 2013. *Tax fairness and folk justice*. Cambridge: Cambridge University Press.

Sobel, Russell, and Gary Wagner. 2004. Expressive voting and government redistribution: Testing Tullock's 'charity of the uncharitable'. *Public Choice* 119:143–159.

Tullock, Gordon. 1971. The charity of the uncharitable. *Economic Inquiry* 9:379–392.

Zelenak, Larry. 2004. Framing the distributional effects of the bush tax cuts. *Tax Notes* 105:83–95.

Part III
International and Global Taxation

Chapter 12
What Burden Should Fiscal Policy Bear in Fighting Global Injustice?

Gillian Brock

Abstract In this contribution I examine how improvements in our fiscal arrangements could be an important vehicle for realizing key aspects of global justice. I begin by outlining some of the important principles that orient my account of global justice (and, moreover, should be part of any plausible account of what we should aim at in pursuing global justice). Improved institutional quality at both the state and global level has a crucial role to play in achieving global justice goals. In Sect. 2 I outline some of the challenges that must be met to deliver the necessary institutional quality in the area of taxation. Effective and legitimate states, tax morale, and an appropriate fiscal contract are all highly important for creating and sustaining an environment conducive to beneficial development, as I explain. I also sketch some of the particular obstacles for developing countries in trying to achieve the right conditions, including both domestic and international challenges that must be confronted. Section 3 covers some solutions to the problems identified and the important role developed countries can play in addressing crucial problems. For instance, as we come to appreciate, in a context of globalization, robust and equitable fiscal policies require transnational cooperation. Many concerns, such as clamping down on tax evasion and harmonizing corporate tax rates can only effectively be tackled at the global level. As I also discuss, feasible arrangements for tackling such issues are available, as are mechanisms for collecting and disbursing funds in ways that promote accountability and compliance. I outline a range of additional ways in which we can usefully discharge some of our global justice duties by assisting with several tax problems highlighted in this contribution. In Sect. 4 I discuss some positive proposals for levying global taxes that could assist enormously with realizing global justice. Here we discuss taxes that could help create conditions beneficial to development and could provide an important source of funding for core global public goods. Currency conversion taxes seem especially worthy of serious consideration, as do carbon taxes and expansions of the air-ticket tax. Section 5 briefly reviews some of the features that make the global taxes discussed both normatively desirable and politically feasible.

G. Brock (✉)
Faculty of Arts, University of Auckland, SYMONDS ST 14, Auckland 1010, New Zealand
e-mail: g.brock@auckland.ac.nz

H. P. Gaisbauer et al. (eds.), *Philosophical Explorations of Justice and Taxation*,
Ius Gentium: Comparative Perspectives on Law and Justice 40,
DOI 10.1007/978-3-319-13458-1_12

12.1 What does Global Justice Require?

My starting point is the insight, now well-established in political philosophy, that the fundamental institutions that we collectively uphold structure and importantly influence how our lives will go. Rawls makes this a focal point of his theory. The basic structure of society—which includes all the main political, economic, legal and social institutions—is the core focus for theorising about justice because its effects are pervasive, profound, and present from birth. Whether or not we endorse Rawls's particular claim about the impact of institutions, we must at least recognize a version of it: the institutions that govern our lives—whether at state-level or international ones—have an important role to play in structuring our life prospects and so it is important that we ensure that these aim at approximating just ones.

My next presumptively uncontroversial point is to acknowledge the importance of the "Moral Equality Imperative"—we all must acknowledge the moral equality of all human beings. No matter where people are located on the globe they deserve to be treated as human beings that have equal value to other human beings, *ceteris paribus*. All human beings' needs and interests deserve equal respect and consideration, *ceteris paribus*.

What should commitment to the Moral Equality Imperative mean with regard to how we ought to structure the institutions we collectively uphold? In my view, it minimally entails that we should ensure everyone is well positioned to enjoy the prospect of a decent life and I elaborate on this via four central components (Brock 2009). First, one should be enabled to meet one's basic needs. Second, one must have adequate protection for one's basic liberties. Third, fair terms of cooperation must govern one's collective endeavours. And fourth, one must have background conditions (especially social and political arrangements) that support these core ingredients of a decent life. There are various ways to make the point that these four components are important ingredients for a decent life.[1] Like human rights approaches, we might start with the individual human person and consider what she needs to live a life of dignity, fleshing out opportunities, protections, resources, and the like, that are central for such a life, taking account of a wide sweep of variation in human living arrangements. That will get us some distance, but we quickly realise that on such reflection, how that person stands in relation to others is also a key part of enjoying a life of dignity. Is she subject to domination, exploitation, or oppression? Must she endure highly coercive terms of cooperation? If her relationships with others are characterized by marked inequality, this may interfere with the ideal of a life worthy of human dignity. And so we arrive at the necessity of including relational components in our account of what global justice requires such as fair terms of co-operation. The details of my account of global justice need not concern

[1] We can argue that these define the minimum that we can reasonably expect of one another, and we can go on to elaborate these ideas of reasonable expectation by harnessing the power of normative thought experiments, as I do in Brock (2009), Chap. 3, for instance.

us for the purposes of this contribution.[2] For our purposes, we need only note a few key points. First, global justice requires that we must be concerned with everyone's prospects for a decent life in designing just institutions. Second, we all have duties to one another to ensure that we are adequately positioned to enjoy prospects for a decent life.[3] Governments can frequently act as efficient co-ordinators and dischargers of these responsibilities. As this view suggests, governments then have an important role to play in discharging global justice duties.

Let us consider next the relevance of states in my account of global justice. In my view, rather than having little importance (as some cosmopolitan global justice theorists maintain), states are highly relevant for several reasons.

First, states matter to people. People are, for the most part, attached to their fellow citizens and current political arrangements, and care greatly about their state's standing and achievements in the world. Of course, this attachment is socially constructed and is subject to modification, though the mechanisms for modification require careful treatment including managing rather than suppressing identities, at least over a reasonably long time frame (Brock and Atkinson 2008). At any rate, there are good reasons to make space in an account of global justice for defensible forms of such attachments, citizens' commitments to states and, indeed, flourishing forms of civic nationalism, that enhance rather than undermine support for key elements of global justice. States are likely to be a core feature of our world order for many years to come and so to ignore the role they can and should play in transitioning to a more just world is not only myopic but a missed opportunity to further key global justice goals. Even in an ideal world, however, there are reasons to think states might be a robust part of the global institutional architecture and that a world state would be less desirable. The obvious concerns surround the concentration of power and its possible abuse. Multiple centres of power might provide better protection from potential abuse and global institutional derailment.

Second, there are many state-level institutions, policies and practices that should be of concern in ensuring the Moral Equality Imperative is implemented satisfactorily in state-wide institutions. State-level institutions are still highly significant in promoting or retarding human beings' prospects for flourishing lives and constitute an important site of co-operation that ought to aspire to fairness.

Third, in the world we live in, much of the responsibility for ensuring core ingredients necessary for a good life is devolved to states. They are an important vehicle through which many key ingredients of global justice are secured and protected.

Fourth, as an empirical matter, in our current world *effective* states are undeniably important for beneficial development. One of the largest scale global injustices we currently face is the massive extent of poverty. Two billion people currently live below the $ 2 (US) per day poverty line (IDS 2012). Many of these poor people live in developing countries (or countries that are classified as low-income or middle-income ones) and those countries especially need effective states that can actively

[2] Though the interested reader might see Brock (2009), Chap. 12.

[3] For the full moral argument, see Brock (2009).

manage the development process and economic growth in beneficial ways. For instance, Duncan Green remarks:

> Why focus on effective states? Because history shows that no country has prospered without a state that can actively manage the development process. The extraordinary transformations of countries such as South Korea, Taiwan, Botswana, or Mauritius have been led by states that ensure health and education for all, and which actively promote and manage the process of economic growth. After 20 years of erosion by deregulation, 'structural adjustment programs', and international trade and aid agreements, many states are weak or absent. But there are no shortcuts, and neither aid nor NGOs can take its place; the road to development lies through the state. (Green 2008, p. 12)

Effective states are enormously important to beneficial development and considerably assist with it. There are many reasons why states that are effective are indispensable to beneficial development. States, after all, are necessary to underwrite or ensure the availability of key goods including healthcare, education, water, sanitation, infrastructure, security, the rule of law, and at least a minimum level of social and economic stability, all of which are necessary precursors in building a dynamic economy capable of beneficial growth. Furthermore, states are in a unique position to regulate and develop the economy in beneficial ways. Taxation has a tremendously important role to play in creating and sustaining effective and legitimate states with robust domestic institutions and we discuss this issue in more detail in the next section.

12.2 The Important Role of Taxation in Creating and Sustaining Effective States and Robust Domestic Institutions

Edmund Burke, an eighteenth-century philosopher, once remarked that "Revenue is the chief preoccupation of the state. Nay more it is the state" (Dietz 1964, p. 213). Whether or not one endorses Burke's view, taxation is undeniably very important to the state: collecting taxes is typically necessary for the state to function effectively. In addition, how taxes are collected and disbursed is important to state legitimacy and effective state building.

Constructing and maintaining robust taxation systems can be challenging for even the strongest states. Taxation systems should incorporate several desiderata that are sometimes in tension with each other. Ideally, taxation systems should be equitable, efficient, and effective. Equitable tax systems treat taxpayers fairly and promote social cohesion. Effective systems are ones which are administratively capable of delivering desirable policy objectives at the least compliance and administrative cost. Efficient systems raise revenue at least cost and without creating undesirable disincentives, such as to work or invest.

Constructing efficient, effective and equitable tax systems can play an enormously valuable role in creating the ingredients for effective states, helping to sustain the legitimacy of the state and its accountability. Tax collection can strengthen the relationship between states and their citizens, empowering citizens to demand accountability from their states and therefore helping states to be more accountable to citizens. Moreover, a strong tax system is central to a state's financial independence. Ensuring appropriate revenue is available also helps sustain appropriate levels of state sovereignty.

Sustaining efficient, effective and equitable taxation systems is challenging for all states at all levels of development. Developing countries have additional challenges to meet including the following six.

1. Tax administration is often very weak with the result that much taxation fails to be collected.
2. Large informal sectors can seriously restrict developing countries' abilities to tax all citizens fairly. Many developing countries have large numbers of workers who are employed in the informal economy. When workers are not formally employed, it is difficult to track their wages, let alone collect any taxation from that income.
3. Tax morale—citizens' willingness to pay taxes and comply with tax laws—is a key factor that needs to be understood. Perceived unfairness in the collection or disbursement of taxation revenue can significantly undermine such morale. When citizens do not feel that they are getting value for their taxes, they will be less willing to contribute the taxes that are owed. So, for instance, when core goods fail to be provided, when there is a perception that taxes collected will be wasted, squandered, embezzled or otherwise not spent on their legitimate purposes, citizens will again be less likely to want to contribute their legally required taxes. Citizens will generally be unwilling to pay taxes unless they feel that the taxes themselves are legitimate, that services will actually be delivered, and that others are also paying their fair share. When there is a sense of uneven contribution and enforcement this will also undermine tax morale.
4. Related to the previous point, the relationship between the state and citizens concerning tax matters is often described in terms of a 'fiscal social contract'. This contract seems to involve an implicit agreement between citizens and the state that taxes can reasonably be expected in return for good governance. The robustness of the contract can reflect how well governments are performing in delivering good governance.
   Positive feedback loops are created when there is high tax morale (citizens perceive that they are getting fair returns on their tax contributions and there is an even-handed approach to taxation policy and collection) and states are therefore able to discharge their functions effectively. Moreover, negative feedback loops can gain traction when the reverse is the case: low tax morale can lead to insufficient funds for executing core state functions effectively which can further undermine tax morale. Problems with rampant tax escape also damage the social contract in multiple ways, as I discuss in 5) and 6) below.
5. In competing to attract foreign direct investment, states feel pressured to create a favourable tax environment, such as by implementing low (or no) tax rates, "tax holidays", and exemptions. Declaring one's state a tax haven appears to enable

more revenue to flow into the state, however, tax havens create a variety of problems. They support illegal activity including bribery, organized crime, and tax evasion. The World Bank estimates the annual flow of illicit money across borders to be $ 1–1.6 trillion (Baker 2005). Tax havens destabilize the international economy (Keeler 2009). However, most importantly, they divert revenue from governments and facilitate massive tax escape. Developing countries are losing an estimated $ 385 billion per year because of tax evasion and avoidance (Cobham 2005). Tax havens can provide important channels for tax evasion. For instance, economic activity is often declared as occurring in places where taxes are low, rather than accurately recorded where it actually takes place. "Transfer pricing" is a recognized accounting term for sales and purchases that occur within the same company or group of companies. For example, it is not uncommon for a company to produce goods in one country, "sell" them to a subsidiary in a tax haven at cost price, then "sell" them again at an inflated price to a third subsidiary. The end result is that when the product is finally sold to a consumer, it misleadingly registers as a tax loss. These transactions create significant opportunities to disguise profits and instead report losses that attract no fiscal obligations. About half of all world trade passes through tax haven jurisdictions, as profits are shifted to places where tax can be avoided (Christensen et al. 2005).
Tax evasion and avoidance constitutes a grave impediment to development and democracy, especially in developing countries (Oxfam GB 2009). Because large corporations and wealthy individuals are effectively escaping taxation, the tax burden is frequently shifted onto ordinary citizens and smaller businesses. Governments often thereby collect much-reduced sums insufficient to achieve minimal goals of social justice, such as providing decent public goods and services, which can also have a dramatic effect on developing or maintaining robust democracies (Vigueras 2005).

6. In many cases, the revenue that poor, developing countries could obtain from resource sales would be more than enough to finance what is needed for the state to be effective, that is to say, if the revenue were actually received and appropriately disbursed. Assisting countries in receiving such revenue seems especially important and in this respect developed country multinationals and governments have been especially negligent in not demanding more transparency and accountability with respect to resource sales. Non-transparent processes for resource sales have enabled massive corruption and theft of resources, the proceeds of which could have been used to build effective states.
The problem of corruption in the sale of resources is large. McFerson (2009) makes the following estimates of losses from corruption in Africa: $ 1 billion a year has been stolen from the Angolan people since 1996; one third of the Democratic Republic of Congo's oil revenue is not shown in the country's budget; and despite $ 7 billion in annual oil profits, 60 % of Guinea's population live on less than $ 1 per day. Corrupt resource sales harm more than just the economy. For instance, corruption is strongly linked to severe restrictions of political and civil rights (McFerson 2009). Governments (and individuals within governments)

who stand to gain from corrupt deals are apt to take extreme measures to retain their position.

12.3 What Solutions are Available to Problems Identified and How Can Developed World Citizens Assist?

There is much scope for international co-operation in managing the destructive effects resulting from the taxation arrangements canvassed in the previous section. In addressing the problems discussed in Sect. 3, point (5), concerning tax competition, some solutions include developing systems of unitary taxation for multinationals to stop the entirely false shifting of profits to countries with low or no taxes, prescribing transfer pricing formulae which share taxes on profits among all the states in which the corporation engages in economic activity, and, more generally, harmonizing tax rates and policy. There are promising moves in some of these directions. The US Treasury has proposed several international reforms, including the "worldwide formula apportionment" model. This involves assigning the corporate tax base across jurisdictions according to a formula reflecting the global dispersion of firm activity and distributing profits across countries more evenly (Mintz and Weiner 2003). A similar model is being considered by the EU. Under this proposal, companies could choose a single tax base from member states and a formula would be used to distribute profits across countries (Mintz and Weiner 2003).

In addressing problems canvassed in Sect. 3, point (6) above, concerning resources sales that are not transparent, citizens could be considerably assisted in keeping their governments accountable for resource sales through international measures that promote transparency and accountability, such as the Extractive Industries Transparency Initiative (EITI).[4] Approximately 3.5 billion people live in countries rich in resources. Yet all too often many poor citizens do not benefit from the extraction of their natural resources. The EITI promotes transparency of revenue flows at the local level. Companies disclose their tax and royalty payments for resources to governments. Governments disclose what they receive in payments. The tax and royalty payments are then independently verified and made public in a process overseen by several key stakeholders including representatives from governments, companies, and civil society. This initiative allows for the development of consensus-building and helps create trust, stability, coherence, good governance, and confidence in judicious revenue collection and disbursement. The initiative provides mechanisms for relevant information gathering, such that citizens and the private sector in those countries can help improve governance. Citizens of countries in the developed world can assist poor citizens in resource-rich, developing countries by making participation in the EITI mandatory when operating in key organizations under their jurisdiction. For instance, they could require that all multinationals that are listed on developed world stock exchanges comply with transparency practices

[4] See the EITI website at http://eiti.org.

such as those outlined by the EITI. They could make membership of the EITI mandatory for participation in desirable opportunities such as being involved in contracting agreements with the government.

How can developed countries assist developing countries in improving their domestic tax systems to make them more effective, efficient and equitable? How can developed countries assist in strengthening the fiscal social contract and tax morale (problems (3) and (4) discussed in Sect. 3 above)?[5]

Modern tax systems aim to promote voluntary tax compliance through a number of desirable features including good public information, clear and simple laws, low compliance costs, simple tax forms, sufficient enforcement power for competent tax administration, automated processes for filing returns and payments (which limit direct contact between tax administrators and taxpayers), promoting professionalism and integrity in human resource management, and a low tolerance environment for cases of corruption or dishonesty. Developed countries can assist by sharing knowledge related to a number of these features, for instance, they can share knowledge about technological innovations in tax collection, monitoring and auditing. Information Technology solutions can play a very important role. Automation of tax administration processes can not only reduce burdens on personnel, but also provide fruitful areas for reducing corruption and evasion. They can assist in developing human resources for fiscal roles. They can also assist by ensuring tax processes are transparent and largely non-discretionary (in efforts to block corruption opportunities), and they can ensure there are many vehicles for active citizen engagement, such as ensuring that feedback mechanisms like hotlines, corruption report cards, or surveys are a regular part of evaluative processes. There is a clear need in many cases to train suitable personnel and grow local fiscal capacity, and developed countries can assist with training up the necessary personnel. Additional personnel are also needed for a range of other tasks such as improving taxpayer compliance and updating the legislative framework where this is needed to counter tax evasion.

Developed countries can also help organize the international response to issues that benefit from co-operation among tax authorities, especially through sharing of information and supporting those initiatives that facilitate transparency and block tax evasion. Developed countries can also support developing countries in how to apply transfer pricing rules and thereby enable them to collect their appropriate share of taxes owed in multinational enterprises. They can establish "panels of experts" that can provide real time advice on a case by case basis to tax administrators in developing countries trying to adopt and implement transfer pricing rules. They can assist countries with exercises such as "joint transfer pricing audits" where this would enhance effective compliance. In addition, they can assist developing countries in establishing a transfer pricing dispute resolution mechanism and fund the participation of personnel from developing countries. They could also support

[5] Even though many acknowledge that local solutions should be found for a particular country's tax problems, nevertheless there is also widespread insistence that there are some common lessons to be drawn from the experiences of many countries already having travelled on similar paths, and so they can offer to share these experiences.

dialogue networks, and international meetings for tax officials to share information about successful experiences or new ideas in strengthening tax administration that can support tax policy reform.[6]

Why do developed world governments have duties to assist in developing better tax institutions? This is a huge topic that I cannot do justice to here.[7] For the purposes of this contribution I might make just the following remarks. According to my account of global justice, we all have duties to one another to ensure that all human beings are well positioned to enjoy the prospects for decent lives. Governments often act as efficient co-ordinators and dischargers of the responsibilities we have to one another as moral agents. They are in an excellent position to deliver on the responsibilities we have to one another. Since there are several mechanisms—including inadequate tax institutions—that block the ability of citizens in developing countries to enjoy the effective states they need to facilitate better prospects for decent lives, targeting these defective arrangements promises to be an effective way to deliver on our responsibilities to one another.

12.4 Global Taxes for Global Justice

We have seen how reforms to existing fiscal arrangements could have profound effects for developing countries through working on creating more effective states that can better manage beneficial development (and hence effectively tackle some of the most pressing global justice problems today). In addition, global taxation could also be an important tool in shaping policy and raising revenue to address significant global justice problems, especially those posed by inadequate resourcing for global public goods and poverty elimination. Taxes on carbon emissions might be one important policy response to threats posed by climate change. Taxes on speculative currency trading could reduce instability in developing countries and promote beneficial development. Taxes on airline tickets currently support global efforts to reduce global burdens of disease, such as malaria, HIV/AIDS, and tuberculosis. In addition, recent events that triggered the global recession of 2009 have generated increasing public support for the permissibility of more financial transaction taxes, as we see with the "Robin Hood Tax" proposals (The Robin Hood Tax 2010).

Several kinds of global taxes have been proposed including carbon taxes, currency transaction taxes (e.g. Tobin taxes), air-ticket taxes, immigration taxes, taxes on arms trading, e-mail taxes, or taxes on the sale of luxury goods. Here I discuss

[6] Many of these suggestions are drawn from a few helpful reports including OECD, 2008, "DAC Guidelines and Reference Series: Governance, Taxation, and Accountability"; and Informal Task Force on Tax and Development, 2011, "Summary Record from the Second Plenary Meeting of the Informal Task Force on Tax and Development", (OECD Conference Centre, Paris).

[7] For more on this topic see Brock (2009, 2014), Blake and Brock (2015).

very briefly only two; first, the air-ticket tax and, second, currency transaction taxes (of which Tobin may be the most well known).

12.4.1 Air-Ticket Tax

The air-ticket tax may represent the most successful example to date of a global tax levied with the intention of raising poverty-fighting funds. The concept of such a tax is to levy a small "solidarity contribution" on airplane tickets at the point of sale. The tax is intended to pass unnoticed due to the disparity between its small size and the significantly larger cost of the ticket. At present the largest air-ticket tax initiative is that run by UNITAID. Since November 2008, seven countries have implemented a small compulsory airline tax under this scheme: Chile, Cote d'Ivoire, France, Madagascar, Mauritius, Niger and the Republic of Korea. Norway gives part of its emissions tax, while other member countries have chosen to implement voluntary airline taxes. UNITAID also accepts contributions from states and institutions that wish to give lump-sum payments (Gumbel 2009). The funds raised are used to finance medicines required to assist poor countries struggling with the burdens of diseases such as malaria, AIDS, and tuberculosis. To date, the project has been quite successful, raising almost $ 1 billion and commencing projects in 94 countries (UNITAID 2009). Approximately 70 % of funding to date has been raised by air-ticket taxes, making the tax a clear success. Statistics provided by UNITAID show the concrete effect even a small tax can have: the € 4 tax levied on international flights out of France, for instance, funds treatment for one HIV positive child (UNITAID 2009). The achievements of the project are further reflected in the powerful supporters it has attracted, including the WHO, the Clinton Foundation, and the Global Fund.

However, there is scope for further expansion. While UNITAID has proved the viability of the air-ticket tax model, it has to date not attracted widespread international cooperation. A 2010 statement by the organisation shows that increasing the number of participating countries is a key goal. This could be achieved by various institutional design innovations, such as making it a requirement that states implement this tax as a condition of belonging to the International Civil Aviation Organization (the UN body tasked with oversight of international air transport). Alternatively, it could be made a condition of membership to the WHO that one's state agree to the air-ticket tax.

There is also reason to believe that the tax could be substantially increased. A study conducted by Brouwer et al. (2008) on consumer willingness to pay for an additional airline tax found that the average willingness to pay was very high—€ 20. It is notable, however that consumers stated they only supported such a program on the grounds that it was mandatory. This suggests voluntary "opt-in" schemes are less likely to succeed.

12.4.2 Currency Transaction Tax

Unlike the tax previously discussed which is actually in operation, the Tobin tax has not yet been implemented anywhere. Originally proposed by James Tobin in the 1970s, this proposal would impose a miniscule tax on every currency trade. The central benefits of such a tax are twofold. First, a Tobin tax could bring greater stability to the financial system. It is estimated that well over half (on some reliable estimates, 80 %) of the $ 4 trillion in currency transactions that occur every day are speculative and as such are potentially destabilizing to local economies (Global Policy Forum 2011). Local currencies can devalue rapidly, causing major financial crises such as occurred in Argentina in 2001, greatly harming millions of people. Tobin's original idea was premised on the suggestion that a small tax on currency trades would reduce speculation and promote more long-term investing, thereby preventing such crises (Tobin 1974). Secondly, such a tax has the potential to raise immense sums of money that could be targeted towards global poverty programs. Because the foreign exchange market is the largest in the world (in 2009 it was at least $ 900 trillion) a tax on this market has the potential to raise vast sums (Task Force on Financial Integrity and Economic Development et al. 2010). While estimates vary according to the size of the tax and the methodology used, most serious studies have predicted revenue of approximately $ 30–100 billion (Schmidt 2008; Baker et al. 2009; Baker 2008). It is this benefit, rather than the stability argument discussed above, that has been emphasized in recent discussions on currency transaction taxes. Perhaps a minimal tax that raises significant revenue without disrupting markets is likely to be the most effective model (Irish 2010).

The currency transaction tax could be practically and politically workable. Currency deals already carry an administrative charge in the main currency exchange countries, so the administrative feasibility of such a tax is already plain. Because foreign exchange markets tend to be concentrated, a currency transaction tax can be effective even if it is only imposed in a limited number of states. In Europe, for example, 97 % of all such trades occur in either the UK or Germany, so taxes in other states would not be necessary (Schulmeister 2009). Politically, the tax has considerable support not just from NGOs but also from politicians. In September 2010, 60 nations, including Britain, Japan, and France jointly proposed a currency transaction tax before the UN (Irish 2010). Since the financial crisis, the concept of such taxes appears to have gained popularity with the general public, as the "Robin Hood Tax" campaign suggests.

Opponents of a currency transaction tax raise two main objections. First, it is argued that banks will simply alter their systems to avoid the tax. While this is possible, particularly if the tax is imposed in only a few countries, there are a number of factors that suggest this objection should not be given undue weight. The taxes proposed are remarkably low—a fraction of 1 %. Further, there are notable benefits from conducting transactions in established commercial centres. For example, London is widely accepted as holding a "time zone advantage" over other financial centres. In addition, the extreme concentration of financial markets (the UK and

Germany account for 97 % of all exchange transactions in the European Union) suggests the presence of positive network externalities (Schulmeister 2009). There are also important costs associated with choosing less secure alternative routes. Financial and foreign exchange settlement systems such as SWIFT currently assist in the coordination of many millions of trades each day (SWIFT 2011). If a currency transaction tax were incorporated into these services, traders would have little choice but to pay the tax. Any alternative route would be both "difficult and unprofitable" (Schmidt 2008). The UK "stamp duty", imposed on stock transactions, provides support for these arguments. Despite the relatively high rate of that tax—0.5 %—London continues to operate as a major financial centre (Schulmeister 2009).

Secondly, it is argued (e.g. Dolphin 2010) that banks will not be able to afford the tax, resulting in costs being unfairly passed on to consumers. But this argument should not be given undue weight. The crucial aspect of a currency transaction tax is its potential to raise revenues that can be used for development purposes. For this reason we should not be too concerned about whether those revenues are sourced from the profits of banks or from the incomes of their consumers (who, by global standards, are still highly advantaged). Though this concern about passing costs on to consumers is frequently raised within developed countries, such as the United Kingdom, adopting a more global perspective, its force should not derail the proposals, since, even if these relatively small costs are passed on to consumers, it is not unreasonable for the relatively affluent in developed countries to assist the severely disadvantaged of developing countries in these tiny ways.

The argument for a currency transaction tax has only been intensified by recent data that suggests the economic crisis has had a disproportionate impact on the developing world. The Task Force on Financial Integrity and Economic Development (2010) writes: "the financial crisis has done significant economic damage around the globe, but has had the most immediate human impacts in the developing countries which bear least responsibility." As a direct result of the crisis, it is estimated that an extra 120 million people will be living on less than $ 2 a day in 2010. Further, the World Bank has conservatively estimated that the crisis will cause an additional 30–50 thousand infant deaths in sub-Saharan Africa alone (Task Force on Financial Integrity 2010).

12.5 Normative Desirability and Feasibility

The issue of normative justifications for taxation is a huge topic, which I cannot do justice to here. But briefly, in my view, what makes a tax normatively desirable is that it meets at least the following, sometimes partially overlapping, desiderata: (N1) the tax complements or promotes important social, political, and economic objectives, (N2) it is compassionate in that it takes account of the capacity to pay and does not disproportionately burden those whose position makes it particularly difficult for them to bear more of the cost than others far better positioned (i.e., it is not regressive), (N3) it is competitive, that is to say it does not importantly undermine appropriate, fair and non-destructive competition or prevent activities communities should otherwise encourage, and (N4) is one that is competently collected, administered, and disbursed.

Various considerations bear on a tax's feasibility. These include: (F1) Support: (i) there is good public support for the tax, at least in good pockets well positioned to influence implementation decisions, and/or (ii) there is strong backing from influential figures well placed to make progress in advancing tax proposals; (F2) Administrative ease: the tax can be collected easily, which can ensure administrative simplicity (and also good compliance); (F3) Precedent: how many other similar kinds of tax proposals have already met with success, showing that similar taxes work reasonably well in other domains; and, relatedly, (F4) Institutional assistance: the availability of already existing, or partially existing, institutional mechanisms that could facilitate compliance or enforcement. Of these, (F1) is probably the most important, since if there is good support, institutional structure and administration of the tax can easily be created.

Using this list of criteria for judging normative desirability and feasibility of taxes let us consider the ways in which some of these global tax proposals meet the normative and feasibility criteria.

The air-ticket tax clearly promotes important social and political objectives, (N1). Improvements in the health of the global worst off will assist those people to better meet a range of basic human needs, not least of which is their physical health. A tax on air tickets, especially those in business class, would satisfy (N2) as those purchasing or funding the tickets are typically not drawn from the global worst off (nor are there likely to be significant effects for the global poor, of the sort that would undermine entire industries that form an important support basis for the global poor). It is likely that this tax does not have problematic anti-competitive effects, and if a case can be clearly marshalled that such taxes are having an important anti-competitive effect in a particular industry (especially ones that have serious negative repercussions for the global poor), it is possible that exemptions could be allowed in those cases. The air-ticket tax seems to be a model of competent collection, administration and disbursement: collected at the point of settlement for the air-ticket, there is no compliance gap, and since the proceeds are spent on specific goals which have had clear health outcomes, there is no genuine concern about inadequate disbursement.

Turning then to how well the air ticket tax meets the feasibility criteria, the case is really straightforward: an actually existing tax proposal that has been implemented in the world is clearly one that is feasible. Reflecting now on the feasibility of extending the scope of the air-ticket tax, the tax does meet (F1)-(F4) reasonably well. There is important support for the tax, with strong backing growing from both citizens and influential public figures. We saw how the scheme has gained backing from (for instance) the Clinton and Global Funds. We have already seen how the tax meets the criteria of administrative ease (F2) and excellent precedent (F3). There is good institutional framework availability and indeed, the WHO, UNITAID, and ICAO are well positioned to develop more, as needed.

Let us next examine the case for the currency transaction tax using the normative desirability and feasibility conditions, (N1)-(N4) and (F1)-(F4). In aiming at reducing economic volatility and instability, and promoting longer-term investment, and raising revenue for helping to meet the needs of the global poor, we would be promoting a range of worthy social, political and economic objectives. Since currency speculation, which makes up the vast amount of currency trading, is an activity engaged in by the global advantaged, the direct activity is not regressive. While it is possible that much more indirect effects of the tax could be regressive I have not yet found any convincing evidence that this is the case. However, if currency transaction taxes in a particular industry are proving to be regressive, there is scope for exempting such transactions from the currency transaction tax. The minuscule amount of the tax (in the order of 0.1 %) is not anticipated to have important anti-competitive effects. Moreover, the arrangements proposed for collection, even if limited simply to the main currency trading centres, would qualify as plausibly competent. The arrangements for disbursing the funds are not typically as clearly outlined, though there is no reason why such arrangements cannot be modelled on those used for disbursement of the highly effective air-ticket tax.

Turning to the feasibility criteria, currency transaction taxes enjoy good support, so (F1) is well satisfied. Since there are really only a few core currency trading sites that deal with the vast majority of currency trades, the tax can easily be collected and (F2) is met. The stamp tax and commissions on currency trades show that there is relevant precedent, and shows that other similar taxes have worked well in related domains (so (F3) is satisfied). No completely new institutional innovations are required to implement the tax and so (F4) is met too.

All in all, then, the two positive global tax proposals of an air-ticket tax and a currency conversion tax do satisfy the requirements of normative desirability and feasibility reasonably well.

12.6 Conclusions

In this contribution I examined how reforming fiscal arrangements could be an important vehicle for realizing key aspects of global justice. After outlining some of the important principles that orient what we should aim at in pursuing global justice, I argued why improved institutional quality at both the state and global level has a crucial role to play in achieving global justice goals. We saw how developing robust tax systems that are effective, efficient, and equitable is very important for sustaining legitimate and effective states with resilient fiscal social contracts and good tax morale. We saw how developing countries face special challenges in realizing these goals such as weak tax administration and collection capacity and being highly vulnerable to destructive effects of tax competition which also enables vast tax escape. These kinds of challenges undermine effective government and opportunities to develop in beneficial ways. Fortunately, a range of important solutions is available to address the problems canvassed. We saw there was much scope for harmonizing tax rates and policy and that plausible proposals and feasible arrangements for tackling such issues are available. We also saw the powerful ways in which supporting international transparency initiatives can enhance accountability and be a constructive force in improving governance, trust, consensus-building, beneficial development, and effective and legitimate states. Further, we saw how developed countries have an immensely important role to play in assisting developing countries with strengthening their tax and accounting institutions, by offering relevant knowledge transfer, training, support, and help with capacity building.

I also discussed various positive proposals for levying global taxes. In this contribution, I discussed the normative desirability and feasibility of currency conversion taxes and air-ticket taxes. We have seen that there is at least one global tax already in place, namely the air-ticket tax, and that it has resulted in not insignificant gains already. This case is important for several reasons. Perhaps at least part of the success is attributable to the fact that it has very clear goals for disbursement: what exactly the money is spent on is quite clearly specified. This feature is easily replicable in the case of other global taxes. Furthermore, the implementation success of this tax provides a nice response to one commonly voiced objection concerning scepticism about achieving universal agreement in tax matters. Though universal support is desirable, we do not need it to make progress in the right direction. As the air-ticket tax demonstrates, substantial progress is possible with just a few countries' cooperation. Even when we do not have universal support at first, in due course, non-participating states may eventually join a tax regime for several reasons. Citizens of non-participating states may pressure their governments to join. Non-participating states might lose influence in policies related to spending revenue raised. Furthermore, once a successful scheme is in place, there might be pressure from the international community to join as well.

As we have seen in several ways in this contribution, then, in a context of globalization, fiscal policies cannot achieve a range of important goals at national levels alone. Many concerns, such as clamping down on tax evasion and harmonizing corporate tax rates can only effectively be tackled at the global level. As I also discuss, feasible arrangements for tackling such issues are available, as are mechanisms for collecting and disbursing funds in ways that promote accountability and compliance. Given the damage current fiscal arrangements facilitate and the availability of normatively desirable, feasible, and reasonable alternatives, we have important reasons to address these inadequacies as a matter of urgency.

References

Addison, Tony. 2009. War on tax havens. *Indiana Journal of Global Legal Studies* 16 (2): 703–727.

Baker, Raymon W. 2005. *Capitalism's achilles heel: Dirty money and how to renew the free-market system*. Hoboken: Wiley.

Baker, Dean. 2008 The benefits of a financial transactions tax. Centre for Economic and Policy Research.

Baker, Dean, Robert Pollin, Travis McArthur, and Matt Sherman. 2009. The potential revenue from financial transactions taxes. Centre for Economic and Policy Research.

Baker Raymond, W, and Eva Joly. 2009. *Illicit money: Can it be stopped?* New York Review of Books.

Bank Information Centre and Global Witness. 2008. Assessment of international monetary fund and world bank group extractive industries transparency implementation.

Blake, Michael, and Gillian Brock. 2015. *Debating brain drain*. Oxford: Oxford University Press.

Brock, Gillian. 2009. *Global Justice: A cosmopolitan account*. Oxford: Oxford University Press.

Brock, Gillian. 2010. Reforming our taxation arrangements to promote global gender justice. *Philosophical Topics* 37:141–160.

Brock, Gillian. 2014. Global poverty, decent work, and remedial responsibilities: What the developed world owes to the developing world and why. In *Poverty coercion, and human rights,* ed. Diana Meyers. New York: Oxford University Press.

Brock, Gillian, and Quentin D. Atkinson. 2008. What can examining the psychology of nationalism tell us about our prospects for aiming at the cosmopolitan vision? *Ethical Theory and Moral Practice* 11:165–179.

Brouwer, R, Brander, L, Van Beukering, P. 2008. A convenient truth: Air travel passengers willingness to pay to offset their CO_2 emissions. *Climate Change* 90:299–313.

Chen, Shaohua, and Martin Ravallion. 2008. The developing world is poorer than we thought, but no less successful in the fight against poverty. World Bank Development Research Group.

Christensen, J., P. Coleman, and S. Kapoor. (2005). Tax avoidance, tax competition and globalisation: Making tax justice a focus for global activism. In *MORE TAXES! Promoting strategies for global taxation,* eds. J. Penttinen, S. Ville-Pekka, and M. Ylonen. Helsinki: ATTAC.

Cobham, Alex. 2005. Tax evasion, tax avoidance, and development finance. Queen Elizabeth House Working Paper no. 129.

Dharmapala, Dhammika. 2008. What problems and opportunities are created by tax havens? *Oxford Review of Economic Policy* 24 (2): 661–679.

Dietz, Frederick. 1964. *English government finance 1485–1558*. London: F. Cass.

Dolphin, Tony. 2010. Financial sector taxes. Institute for Public Policy Research.

Freedom House. 2006. Countries at the cross roads. http://freedomhouse.org/template.cfm?page=140&edition=7. Accessed 10 Nov 2012.

Financial Stability Board. (2010). Mandate. http://www.financialstabilityboard.org/about/mandate.htm. Accessed 10 Nov 2012.

Global Policy Forum. 2011. Currency transaction taxes. http://www.globalpolicy.org/global-taxes/currency-transaction-taxes.html. Accessed 10 Nov 2012.

Green, Duncan. 2008. *From poverty to power: How active citizens and effective states can change the world.* Oxford: Oxfam International.

Green, Duncan. 2012. *From poverty to power: How active citizens and effective states can change the world.* 2nd ed. Rugby: Practical Action Publishing.

Gumbel, Peter. 2009. New airline-ticket tax to aid the developing world. TIME Magazine, 18 September 2009. http://www.unitaid.eu/en/. Accessed 10 Nov 2012.

IDS. Institute of Development Studies. 2012. IDS in Focus Policy Briefing. Issue 26 August 2012.

IMF. 2010. World economic and financial surveys, http://www.imf.org/external/pubs/ft/weo/2009/02/weodata/weorept.aspx?sy=2007&ey=2014&scsm=1&ssd=1&sort=country&ds=.&br=1&pr1.x=56&pr1.y=7&c=001&s=NGDPDgrp=1&a=1. Accessed 10 Nov 2012.

Informal Task Force on Tax and Development. (2011).Summary record from the second plenary meeting of the informal task force on tax and development, (OECD Conference Centre, Paris).

International Accounting Standards Board. 2009. Extractive activities (draft) discussion paper.

Irish, John. 2010. 60 states to lobby U.N. for currency transaction tax. Reuters.

Juan Hdez. Vigueras. 2005. *Tax Havens: How offshore centres undermine democracy.* Spain: Akal.

Keeler, Rachel. 2009. Tax havens and the financial crisis. *Dollars & Sense* 21–25.

Kudrle, Robert T. 2009. Ending the tax haven scandals. *Global Economy Journal* 9 (3): 1–11.

Larudee, Mehrene. 2009. Sources of polarization of income and wealth: Offshore financial centres. *Review of Radical Political Economics* 41 (3): 343–351.

McFerson, Hazel. 2009. Governance and hyper-corruption in resource-rich African countries. *Third World Quarterly* 30 (8): 1529–1549.

Mintz, Jack, and Johann M., Weiner. 2003. Exploring formula allocation for the European union. *International Tax and Public Finance* 10:695–711.

OECD. 2008. DAC guidelines and reference series: Governance, taxation, and accountability.

Oxfam GB. 2000. Tax havens: Releasing the hidden billions for poverty eradication. http://publications.oxfam.org.uk/display.asp?k=002P0036&sf1=sort_series&st1=OXFAMBRIEFINGPAPERS&m=13&dc=448. Accessed 10 Nov 2012.

Oxfam GB. 2009. Money for nothing. http://publications.oxfam.org.uk/display.asp?k=002P0728&keyword=tax+havens&x=0&y=0&sort=SORT_DATE%2Fd&m=1&dc=2. Accessed 10 Nov 2012.

Schmidt, Rodney. 2008. *The currency transaction tax: Rate and revenue estimates*. New York: United Nations University Press.

Schulmeister, Stephan. 2009. WIFO working papers: A general financial transaction tax: A short cut of the pros, the cons, and a proposal. Austrian Institute of Economic Research.

SWIFT. 2011. http://www.swift.com. Accessed 10 Nov 2012.

Task Force on Financial Integrity and Economic Development, Christian Aid UK, Tax Justice Network International, Trade Union Congress of the UK. 2010. Taxing banks. Norfolk, UK: Tax Research LLP.

The Robin Hood Tax. 2010. www.robinhoodtax.org. Accessed 10 Nov 2012.

Tobin, James. 1974. *The new economics, one decade older. The Eliot Janeway lectures on historical economics in honor of Joseph Schmpeter*. Princeton: Princeton University Press.

Unitaid. 2010. www.unitaid.eu. Accessed 10 Nov 2012.

US Government Accountability Office. 2009. International taxation: Large US corporations and federal contractors with subsidiaries in jurisdictions listed as tax havens or financial privacy jurisdictions.

US Senate, Committee on Homeland Security and Governmental Affairs. 2008. Tax haven banks and U.S tax compliance. Staff report.

Van Parys, Stefan, and Sebastian James. 2010. The effectiveness of tax incentives in attracting investment: Panel data evidence from the CFA franc zone. *International Tax and Public Finance* 17:400–429.

Wahl, Peter, and Peter Waldrow. 2001. Currency transaction tax- a concept with a future- chances and limits of stabilizing financial markets through the Tobin Tax. Bon, WEED.

Chapter 13
The Global Luxuries Tax

Timothy Mawe and Vittorio Bufacchi

Abstract This chapter proposes a policy to tackle the problem of global poverty, the Global Luxuries Tax (GLT). The GLT is a levy collected whenever a person, anywhere in the world, purchases a certain luxury good or service. The money collected will go towards a Global Poverty Fund to be used to alleviate the worst cases of global poverty. The tax is a miniscule percentage of the price of the good or service being purchased, so that the GLT raises money for the Global Poverty Fund by virtue of the high number of transactions taking place. The first part of the chapter will highlight two main pitfalls faced by any potential solution to the problem of global poverty, the Unintended Consequences Objection and the Implementation Objection. The second and third parts will introduce the idea of a Global Luxuries Tax, first in theory and then in practice. Examples of luxuries to be taxed by the GLT include air travel, financial transactions, texting on mobile phones, and procreation. In the final part some objections to the GLT will be considered, and appeased.

13.1 Introduction

Poverty is not a natural phenomenon but the result of human-made policies and institutions, therefore the solution to the problem of poverty must also be sought in social, economic and political policies and institutions. Furthermore poverty is a global social scar, not merely in the sense that it is present in some form in every corner of the world, but because it is the product of global affairs and institutions. It follows that we must look at global policies for a remedy. This chapter proposes a policy to tackle the problem of global poverty. In putting forward our policy proposal, the Global Luxuries Tax (GLT), we are aware that the challenge of global poverty is too complex and entrenched in the basic structure of global society to

T. Mawe (✉) · V. Bufacchi
Department of Philosophy, University College Cork, Elder-wood 2–4, Cork, Ireland
e-mail: 109457721@umail.ucc.ie

V. Bufacchi
e-mail: v.bufacchi@ucc.ie

H. P. Gaisbauer et al. (eds.), *Philosophical Explorations of Justice and Taxation*,
Ius Gentium: Comparative Perspectives on Law and Justice 40,
DOI 10.1007/978-3-319-13458-1_13

harbour the hope of a quick-fix solution. We put forward this proposal in the hope that the GLT can play some role, albeit small, in moving the agenda in the right direction.

The first part of the chapter will highlight two main pitfalls faced by any potential solution to the problem of global poverty; these are objections that any policy solution must be able to avoid or respond to if it is to be taken seriously. The second and third parts will introduce the idea of a Global Luxuries Tax, first in theory and then in practice. In the final part some objections to the GLT will be considered, and appeased.

13.2 One of Many

A number of ingenious solutions to the problem of global poverty have been put forward in recent years. Apart from the well-trodden path of raising domestic taxes to subsidize a 1 % GDP redistribution of resources from the wealthy nations to the poorer nations, other propositions include the Global Resources Dividend (Pogge 2008 and 2011); the Global Fund (Steiner 2011); the Global Share (Casal 2011); extensive reforms of the global tax system (Brock 2008); or even free-movement across borders (Barry and Goodin 1992). All of the above are important contributions to the debate, and all contain valid intuitions that should not be dismissed lightly.

As one might expect, there is no unanimous agreement as to which of these solutions is likely to bring about the best results. They all have their strengths but also their alleged weaknesses. There is a case to be made for advocating a pluralist approach whereby all these solutions are defended, recommended, and to the best of our ability implemented. The assumption being that these solutions can complement one another, the shortcomings of one policy being compensated by the strength of an alternative policy, making each policy only one factor in a pluralist, comprehensive, multi-pronged solution.

Pogge's Global Resources Dividend (GRD) is arguably the most talked about proposal on the table at the moment, and rightly so. Pogge envisages the GRD as a levy paid at source by resource extracting firms: as they extract resources, they pay a certain amount to a world fund. There is something normatively significant about the GRD. Pogge is to be praised not only for suggesting an ingenious solution to the problem of global poverty, but for starting from the assumption, too often conveniently neglected by champions of the status quo, that fairness demands some form of compensation from those who make more extensive use of the planet's resources to those who, involuntarily, use very little.

This proposal is more moderate, or less radical, than the view that holds that all natural resources belong to everyone, globally, to an equal degree, therefore we should not assume that artificial constructs such as sovereign nation states have a prior moral claim over the full extent of all the natural resources. This position was reiterated in 1994 by Hillel Steiner in *An Essay on Rights*, in his account of the

Global Fund, which in many ways can be seen as a precursor of the GRD.[1] Following Locke's claim that 'the earth, and all inferior creatures, be common to all men,' Steiner (1994, p. 236) argues for "an equal share of initially unowned things". What Steiner is telling us here is that we do not have to go along with the widely held assumption, never justified but seldom challenged, that the natural resources below the ground are the legal and moral rightful property of the arbitrary political outfit above the ground.

In this chapter we are going to bypass the Steiner-Pogge controversy regarding the moral (and legal) ownership of unused natural resources, not because it is not an important debate, since it clearly is, but merely because our proposal does not rest on the resolution of this dispute. Instead, we want to highlight two potentially problematic issues that any global policy intent on alleviating global poverty ought to be sensitive to: the Unintended Consequences Objection, and the Implementation Objection.

13.2.1 The Unintended Consequences Objection

This objection suggests that some solutions may not be as effective as it may seem at first, since the policy has unintended consequences that take away from its merits. For example a policy may trigger inflationary pressure which would indent on the funds raised for the benefit of the global poor. The GRD is possibly susceptible to this line of critique. Let's assume that the GRD imposes a $ 3 dividend on every barrel of oil that is extracted from the ground. The $ 3 will in turn be passed on to the consumers, who will be asked to pay more for the petrol they buy. But since oil is needed for the production of many other goods, the unintended consequence of the GRD is that it will put inflationary pressure on the cost of basic goods worldwide.

The global price of food is a case in point. There is ample empirical evidence to suggest that the price of food worldwide follows closely, and is determined by, the price of crude oil. The World Bank calculated that food prices increased by 8 % from December 2011 to March 2012, and they quote higher oil prices as a key factor.[2] As World Bank Vice President for Poverty Reduction and Economic Management (PREM), Otaviano Canuto, warns us: "After 4 months of consecutive price declines, food prices are on the rise again threatening the food security of millions of people. Putting food first must remain a priority for the international community and in our work in developing countries." [3] According to the quarterly Food Price Watch report, maize prices increased by 9 %, soybean oil by 7 %, wheat by 6 %, and sugar by 5 %. Crude oil prices rose by 13 %. The risk here is that the GRD will increase the price of crude oil, which in turn will generate inflationary pressures on

---

[1] The same intuition can be found in Thomas Paine's Agrarian Justice, written in 1795.

[2] Two other factors mentioned by the World Bank are adverse weather conditions and Asia's strong demand for food imports.

[3] The World Bank. Press Release No:2012/411/PREM.

food and other basic products. As a result, those worst affected by the food price rise are precisely the people that the GRD is supposed to help in the first place, namely the global poor.

The unintended consequences of inflationary pressures generated by the GRD are not a fatal blow to Pogge's policy. It may be possible for measures to be put in place to counteract these tendencies and prevent the price of basic goods from rising more than is warranted. Nevertheless, the Unintended Consequences Objection remains a worry, if only because it threatens to make the GRD less effective than it might seem at first. The same objection could also apply to other possible solutions.

13.2.2 The Implementation Objection

Any policy recommendation being put forward as a solution to the problem of global poverty must not only be within the scope of international politics as it operates today, but it should also be conceivable to put it into practice. One problem is to work out exactly who, on grounds of justice, should pay for the dividend. If the global poverty tax takes the form of a tax on the extraction of natural resources, like in the case of the GRD, it is imperative to work out in detail exactly where the burden of the GRD will fall. A related issue is how to ensure that this tax applies universally, without exceptions. For example, given the existence of financial tax havens around the world, there is reason to worry about potential global poverty tax havens too.

13.3 The Global Luxuries Tax in Theory

The GLT starts from the basic assumption that the world is divided into two groups of people: the global poor and the global wealthy. These two groups are differentiated by the fact that while the global poor have only enough resources to cover their basic needs (and often not even that), the global wealthy have at their disposal enough resources to cover their basic needs and also enjoy luxuries. The assumption behind the GLT is that the burden to do something about global poverty should fall, first and foremost, on those with an overabundance of resources, namely the global wealthy.

The reason for expecting the global wealthy to bear the burden when it comes to helping the global poor should be obvious to many, one would hope, but it may nevertheless be necessary to briefly reiterate the argument. Even a rudimentary knowledge of world history should be sufficient to remind us that anyone today who has resources at their disposal to spend on luxuries has come upon those resources in a way that somewhere, in the past, involved an injustice. Of course this does not mean that all the wealthy people in the world are criminals; that would be absurd, and inaccurate. We are merely suggesting that the global wealthy are lucky, to the extent that they find themselves at the end of a line of descendants that has benefitted from historical injustice more than it has suffered from it. As Thomas Piketty (2014) has demonstrated on formidable empirical grounds with devastating clarity and rigour, wealth (and capital) has a tendency to multiply over time, and grows faster than other forms of income. Furthermore as Martin O'Neill (2007) points out it also passes down the family line in a way that is arbitrary and therefore ultimately unjustified.

The key question is how, and when, the original bundle of resources that has been passed down from benefactor to benefactor, generating the inequality between the global poor and the global wealthy, was originally acquired. We will never know of course, and no one can trace their wealth to that moment in time which Robert Nozick refers to as the 'initial acquisition'. But while historical accuracy on individual wealth accumulation will always remain a mystery, there is a great deal we know about historical injustice (See Daniel Butt 2009 and Spinner-Halev 2012). The wealth of the industrialized countries has been accumulated over the centuries in no small part thanks to a long history of colonization, imperialism, slavery and military expansion. It is much too convenient to lay claim over our individual wealth today while forgetting all the injustices of yesterday. So, to use Nozick's terminology once again, targeting the global wealthy is merely the simplest way to enforce some semblance of rectification of injustice. Another way of stating this point is that the burden of proof should be on those who claim or believe that they have acquired their wealth via a fair initial acquisition, not on those who want to justify the redistribution of resources.[4]

A great deal more can and ought to be said about historical global injustice as a determining cause of contemporary inequality and poverty, but that is a debate for another day. However even if we assume the validity of this initial supposition, and we accept that the global wealthy should be at the forefront of the efforts to solve the problem of global poverty, the mechanism according to which wealth is to be appropriated from the global wealthy and redistributed to the global poor needs elucidation. The GLT is a policy that could perform this redistributive manoeuvre.

The idea behind the GLT is simple: this is a levy collected whenever a person, wherever they happen to live (bar a few exceptions), accesses a certain luxury. The money collected will go towards a Global Poverty Fund to be used to alleviate the worst cases of global poverty.[5] The tax is a miniscule percentage of the price of the goods or services being purchased, so that the GLT raises money for the Global Poverty Tax by virtue of the high number of transactions taking place.

As the name suggests, there are three aspects of this policy that require further explanation: What do we mean by 'tax'? Why does it target 'luxuries'? And in what sense is it 'global'? The global dimension of the GLT should be obvious, given the

[4] For a defence of the opposite view, namely that past wrongs should not be rectified, see Perez (2012).

[5] According to Thomas Pogge $ 506 billion per annum would suffice to help the 3.08 billion people (47% of world population) who currently live below $ 2.50 per day. See the interview with Pogge on Policy Innovations, 31 May, 2011: http://www.policyinnovations.org/ideas/briefings/data/000201.

growing process of international integration, especially at economic and financial levels. This is nothing new of course: trade and expansion have been a feature of the world ever since technology made it possible for people and goods to be transported, and all great empires throughout history were built on strategies spanning beyond the domestic sphere, often of a violent nature. The nature and sources of poverty today are not something that can be understood exclusively at the local level, therefore the solution to this problem must also be sought at a supranational level. Poverty is caused by our global institutional arrangements. As Thomas Pogge argues, current global institutional designs are the major impediment to radical changes that would eradicate global poverty. The GLT has global aspirations not only in recognition of the global nature of the causes of poverty today, but also as a reminder that historically wealth accumulation came about as a result of acts of international injustice: imperialism, colonialism, slavery and military expansion.

With the risk of making this proposal unpopular, it is worth emphasizing that the GLT is a tax. We think this is a positive feature of the scheme, as the ability to make a monetary payment for public purposes should be seen in a positive light. Too much has been made in recent years of Nozick's melodramatic claim that taxation is on a par with forced labour. There is another way to think about taxation, which stems from the principle of solidarity rather than individual egoism: namely, that a tax is a contribution towards the common good.

One of the advantages of this scheme is that the tax in question is progressive, to the extent that those who access luxuries repeatedly will contribute more to the GLT than those who do so less frequently, if at all.[6] Furthermore, there is a voluntary element to this type of taxation, as one is required to make the payment only when choosing to purchase certain luxury goods. Someone who does not want to pay this tax has the option of not indulging in the purchase and consumption of luxuries.

Finally, by directing its attention towards the global wealthy, the GLT targets the consumption of luxuries. This requires that we agree on the definition of a 'luxury', and on a list of luxuries to be taxed. The concept of luxury has a long history. As Christopher Berry (1994) explains, over the centuries luxuries have been associated with goods that are refined and positively pleasing, goods that have a transient status, goods that are superfluous, and goods that enjoy high income elasticity of demand. We can perhaps go along with Berry (1994, p. 41) and adopt what he calls 'almost a definition' of luxury: "a luxury good is a widely desired (because not yet generally attained) good that is believed to be 'pleasing', and the general desirability of which is explained by it being a specific need". The 'specific need' in question is not to be confused with a 'basic need'. Another way of distinguishing luxury goods from other goods is that we have a 'categorical desire' to satisfy certain specific needs, in the sense of the term used by Bernard Williams (1973), but not for basic needs.

The fact that certain luxuries are being taxed should not be interpreted as a punitive measure. This is not like a tax on alcohol or tobacco, where the aim of the tax

[6] The history of the concept of taxation, and the justice of a progressive taxation, are perfectly captured by Helmut P. Gaisbauer, Gottfried Schweiger and Clemens Sedmak (2013).

(apart from raising money for the public coffers) is to give an incentive to people to stop consuming certain goods. The luxuries being taxed by the GLT are not morally or medically problematic, or at least not more so than any other goods being consumed, and the tax is not intended to act as a disincentive. On the contrary the idea behind the GLT is that the tax is so small that it will not make a difference to the consumer, so that they will continue to buy the luxury, and in the process raise more funds for the global poor.

To recap, the GLT has a global reach, it targets luxuries, and it generates funds for the global poor by way of taxing the global wealthy. Before we look at some practical implications of this tax, it is necessary to make a further distinction between a Universal GLT and a Partial (or Restricted) GLT. A Universal GLT applies to everyone across the globe who enjoys certain luxuries, even if the person in question lives among the global poor. A Partial GLT applies only to certain areas of the world, namely those countries where the GDP is above a certain threshold. The GLT entails both Universal and Partial components, depending on the luxury. A Universal GLT targets the individual (and their wealth) wherever they happen to be, indeed the majority of luxuries being taxed by the GLT are Universal. The GLT is not a tax on rich states, but on the consumption of rich individuals. As we shall see, the fact that it does not rely on the compliance of a national government for its implementation, and success, is crucially important. This is one of GLT's main attractions. At the same time, in the case of certain luxuries, it may be desirable to make further distinctions based on location, in which case it becomes a case of a Partial GLT.

13.4 The Global Luxuries Tax in Practice

On the basis of this working definition of what constitutes a luxury, we can now speculate on the list of luxuries to be taxed by the GLT. After all, the GLT will work if and only if we agree on a list of goods, deemed to be luxuries, which can be the subject of the global tax.

The luxury goods to be taxed by the GLT are not those that come to mind when we think of luxuries. This is not about taxing products and services that are expensive simply because they are expensive. The GLT is not interested in exclusive items of food, drink, clothes and jewellery so expensive that they can be enjoyed only by the very few, or the very foolish. Instead, two criteria determine the items to be taxed by a GLT.

First, because the tax is going to be extremely small, the goods and services being taxed will generate revenue for the Global Poverty Fund as a consequence of the high demand they enjoy, and therefore the subsequent high volume of transactions. From that point of view the luxuries of the GLT are the exact opposite of the very expensive (because very rare) goods and services that hardly anyone can afford to enjoy.

Secondly, the GLT will want to tax goods and services that are not already the subject of taxes at the national level. In other words the GLT should not compete with nation states for the right to tax certain goods. This is important because consumers should not be subjected to multiple regimes of taxation, furthermore it is important that people know that when they pay a GLT they are making a contribution towards the end of global poverty.

With these two criteria in mind it is possible to make a stab at a list of potential luxuries to be taxed by the GLT. Needless to say this exercise is merely speculative, in the sense that its aim is merely to act as a starting point for discussion, therefore we leave open the possibility of more items being added (and perhaps a few subtracted) from this list.

Universal GLT	Partial GLT
Air travel	Procreations
Financial transactions	Texting on mobile phones

We will start with the list of Universal GLT, as these do not allow for exceptions. We will then look at the Partial GLT, and explain why in certain cases the tax should not be universal.

13.4.1 Air Travel

In the twenty-first century we all travel via airplanes more than we ever did before and a lot more than we strictly need to, with half a million people in the air at any one time. Bar a few exceptions, the bulk of air travel is either for reasons of work or leisure. The latter has grown at a much faster rate than the former over the last 50 years, when going abroad for a holiday was the prerogative of a very small selected (lucky) few. Anyone today who gets on an airplane to go on vacation is clearly exercising their desire for a luxury good, hence they would be a good candidate for contributing to the GLT. Accidently, this will also go some way towards solving the moral dilemma, originally set by Ted Honderich, of whether someone should go on holiday to Venice or give the money to Oxfam instead. Honderich wants to convince us to forego the trip to Venice, but of course few people are prepared to make that kind of sacrifice, and understandably so. The GLT on air travel allows us to go on vacation to Venice, enjoy the city immortalized by Canaletto, while in the process contributing to the solution of global poverty. A rare case of having your moral cake and eating it too.

Adding US $ 5 per air ticket would generate a considerable source of revenue for the Global Poor. If we take the EU as an example, between 2009 and 2010 the total number of passengers travelling by air in the EU increased to 777 million. If each passenger was charged an extra $ 5 for the pleasure and convenience of travelling by air, this tax alone would contribute US$ 3885 million to the global fund.[7]

[7] The idea of air-ticket taxation to pay for climate change has been raised before. The International Institute for Environment and Development calculates that a small tax of just US$ 6 per economy-

Of course not everyone travels for pleasure. There are many who also travel for work, in which case it might seem odd to include their activity as a luxury. These concerns can easily be countered. First of all, adding US$ 5 per air ticket will not make much difference to business travellers, since in the majority of cases those who travel for work related reasons don't pay for their travels out of their own pocket, instead the business they represent picks up the bill. In fact, there is an argument to be made that anyone travelling business class should pay an added global luxury tax of US$ 30.

Secondly, it could be argued that adding air travel to GLT may have the unintended consequence of giving an incentive for businesses to find an alternative to sending their employees on long journeys that require taking to the air, for example by investing in video-conferencing technology. If this was indeed an unintended consequence of a GLT on air travel, then this development is to be welcomed, as it would contribute towards cutting carbon emissions and therefore make a positive impact on the environment, and indirectly on the global poor who are most at risk from climate change. The fact that video-conferencing technology is an alternative to work-related air travel only strengthens the argument that air travel is a luxury, in the sense that a luxury good is superfluous, something we can do without. Whether it is for leisure or for business, air travel is a choice, not a necessity.

13.4.2 Financial Transactions

The idea of an international tax on financial transactions has been on the agenda for a while, for example in the form of a Tobin Tax. Originally defined as a tax on all spot currency conversions, the Tobin Tax is now no longer confined to the currency markets, but includes trading in shares, bonds and derivatives.[8]

It may be necessary to distinguish between two types of financial transactions, namely transactions that are necessary and those that are speculative. Necessary Transaction are those performed by any citizen in the modern world, for example buying foreign currency—perhaps before travelling by air to an academic conference in Venice. The levy on these transactions can be minimal, so much so that one would not even notice this at the end of the month, although they would add up. After all, units are made up by fractions, so even an insignificant amount of tax on a single transaction, even as small as US$ 0.05 can make a difference. The money for the global fund will be generated by the volume of transactions, so that the ordinary citizen will not even notice they are being taxed.

The GLT on financial transactions undertaken for speculative reasons would be much greater, in part because the motivation behind the transaction is not a necessity (hence by definition a luxury), and in part due to the much higher number of

class ticket and US$ 62 for business class tickets could generate as much as US$ 10 billion. See Tom Birch and Muyeye Chambwera, 'Fundraising Flights: A Levy on International Air Travel for Adaptation', IIED, March 2011.

[8] For an endorsement of the Tobin Tax, see Brock (2008).

transactions incurred by financial institutions. It is crucial that GLT on financial transactions are Universal rather than Partial, in order to avoid the risk of Global Luxury Tax havens in remote parts of the world.

It is unlikely that the GLT on financial transactions will have the unintended consequence of giving individuals and institutions an incentive to hold back from doing a transaction, since the cost per transaction will be extremely small, and even the higher tax on speculative transactions levied will not deter the investors, given that financial institutions are among the richest groups in the world. Also, in a perverse way global financial institutions may even welcome a GLT on financial transactions, as this would make it possible for them to take the moral high-ground, and remind anyone listening, especially the activists of the Occupy Movement, that they are not always the bad guys, instead they are doing their part to help solve the problem of global poverty. For international finance institutions a GLT is a small price to pay for some moral capital.

13.4.3 Procreations

Apart from Universal GLT, we must also consider Partial GLT. These are taxes that are levied only in certain parts of the world, specifically countries that enjoy a GDP per capita above a certain threshold.[9] According to the International Monetary Fund, in 2010–2011, the country with the highest GDP per capita is Luxembourg (US$ 160,000) and the one with the lowest is the Democratic Republic of the Congo (US$ 217). For example, we could draw the line at US$ 10,000 per capita, hence Malaysia would be above the line at US$ 10,085 and Lebanon would be below the line at US$ 9,862.

All the countries within the EU are above this threshold. According to Eurostat, approximately 5.4 million children were born each year in the 27 countries of the European Union between 2008 and 2010. The GLT on procreation would tax each family for the birth of their child, perhaps as little as US$ 5. This would generate US$ 270,000,000 for the global fund from the EU alone.

The basic assumption behind this tax is that choosing to have a child is a luxury. This idea has a long history, indeed as Marx argued in his Economic and Philosophical Manuscripts of 1844: "There are too many people. Even the existence of men is a pure luxury; and if the worker is 'ethical', he will be sparing in procreation". More recently Paula Casal and Andrew Williams (1995) convincingly argue that procreation may cause a public bad, since adding another human being to the planet will only worsen resource scarcities, in which case it may be legitimate to tax those who have children (See also Casal and Williams 2004). It may seem counterintuitive to classify having a baby as a luxury, since procreation is an integral part of the

[9] There is of course a serious problem with relying too much on GDP as an indicator of poverty, especially in poor countries – see Morten Jerven, 'Lies, Damn Lies and GDP', The Guardian, 20 November 2012.

natural cycle, and what is natural cannot be a luxury. But closer analysis suggests otherwise. Even if one were to accept the dubious claim that having a family is a human need, it is important to distinguish between having a family and having a baby (or procreating). Having a baby is only one way to have a family; another way of having a family is by adoption. The difference between procreation and adoption is morally significant. In an era defined by overpopulation each addition to the human race carries negative externalities on non-consenting third parties, which is why having a baby should be taxed, while adopting a baby should not. In fact, a case could be made for parents to be given a financial incentive to adopt rather than procreate.

The GLT on procreation may need to be more nuanced than some of the Universal GLT we have considered so far, since it may not apply across the board as easily as a tax on air travel. For example, it may be desirable to exempt some people from the GLT on procreation. One group that should be exempt from GLT is victims of rape, for obvious reasons, or families whose newborn dies within the first year. Another group is women who live in countries where abortion is illegal, since they do not have the option of interrupting their pregnancy, although in such cases there may be some merit in making governments of countries where abortion is illegal pay for the GLT on procreation. But we don't need to get too concerned about this issue here.

13.4.4 Mobile Phones

Mobile phones are another modern luxury, even though anyone under the age of 20 will probably vehemently object. Just because mobile phones have made modes of communication terribly convenient, indeed too convenient sometimes, it does not mean that they are not a luxury. We know that they are a luxury because it is possible to live without mobile phones (many of us did until recently, and a few still do), and our general proclivity to use our mobile phones incessantly is nothing more than a desire to satisfy a yearning, not a basic need.

The GLT on mobile phones would work by adding an almost insignificant charge on every text message sent via mobile phone, say US$ 0.01 per message. When one considers that in 2003 in Europe 16 billion messages were sent each month, that in 2009 in the USA 152 billion texts were sent each month (an average of 534 messages per subscriber per month), and that in China in 2007 about 700 billion messages were sent, the GLT on mobile phones could prove to be very lucrative for a global fund.

As in the case for procreation, there are good reasons for making this a partial tax, since some groups should be excluded from paying it. In Africa for example there is simply no alternative to using mobile phones, since the network of landlines is extremely small and inadequate. It would be unfair to tax people for using a form of technology where no alternative exists. This is why mobile telephony is truly revolutionary in Africa.[10] The fact that there are apps widely used in Africa for monitoring the gestation periods of dairy cows, and likely birth dates of calves (iCow), and for verifying the legitimacy of medicines, and checking for expiry dates, given that Africa can be a dumping ground for counterfeit pharmaceuticals (Pedigree), suggests that mobiles phones perform a vital function in African society.[11]

But apart from these exceptions, the rule should be that anyone who texts could make a contribution to the global fund. The contribution per person would be minimal, even for the most enthusiastic text users, but it could make a considerable impact in the fight against global poverty. For example in the Republic of Ireland in 2006 on average 114 messages were sent per person per month. At US$ 0.01 per text that would mean US$ 1.14 per person per month.[12] A small cost for the average Irish person, but a potential life-safer in many parts of the world.

13.5 Objections to the Global Luxuries Tax

If GLT is to be a serious contender as one of the policies that could, if enacted, make a difference to world poverty, then any potential weaknesses must come under scrutiny. In Part I above it was suggested that any solution to global poverty is susceptible to two objections: the Unintended Consequences Objection and the Implementation Objection. We must consider how the GLT fares on these two issues.

The first issue is the Unintended Consequences Objection, namely the idea that this tax would not help the global poor as much as we may anticipate. As we saw in Part I, the unintended consequence of Pogge's GRD is that it would have inflationary pressure on global prices, therefore the money raised and passed on to the global poor would not have the purchasing power required to push people out of the poverty trap. Are there similar unintended consequences to the GLT? We do not think so, or at least not to the same extent compared to the GRD. There is no reason to suspect that GLT will have the same impact on general prices, since the GLT taxes luxuries. Unlike natural resources, luxuries do not feed into the production line of other goods. Thus, the fact that the price of a luxury like airfare or financial transactions or a text on a mobile phone or a new baby goes up will not affect the price of other goods. Compared to GRD, the GLT has the advantage of taxing consumers at the moment when goods are being purchased and enjoyed (or in the case of procreation at the moment when a child is born), which suggests that the tax will affect only those targeted by the GLT, and the GLT will not have further unintended consequences.

The Implementation Objection raises issues of a more complex nature. According to this objection, any policy recommendation being put forward as a solution

[10] 'Digital Revolution Lights up Africa with Maps, Mobiles, Money and Markets', The Guardian, Tuesday 30 October 2012.

[11] 'Africa's Apps: Farming to Gaming', The Guardian, Tuesday 30 October 2012.

[12] RTE News, Tueday 26 September 2006.

to the problem of global poverty must not only be within the scope of international politics as it operates today, but it should also be easy to put in practice. In other words, it must pertain to the discipline of political science rather than science fiction. The fact that the tax of the GLT is miniscule goes some way towards alleviating some concerns one may have. Of course one could still object that what are luxuries for some are necessities for others, therefore taxing luxuries is potentially unfair to those who have no choice in the matter. The GLT gets around this objection by introducing the distinction between the Universal GLT, which applies to everyone across the globe, and the Partial GLT, which applies only to certain areas of the globe where the GDP is above a certain threshold.

Unlike Pogge's GRD, the GLT is not vulnerable to certain implementation objections, such as: How can we identify the relevant sum of economic value of any given resource that the tax would be applied to? At which point of the primary production should the tax be applied? How can we generate enough goodwill among rich nation-states that they would be willing to commit themselves to supranational institutional reforms?[13] The GLT imposes a tax based on consumption. This means that we do not need to get involved with the difficult question of quantifying the economic value of a resource. All that is required is to come up with an (admittedly arbitrary) amount for this tax. For example, we suggested US$ 5 for each economy-class air ticket. Of course this amount can be revised, but as long as it is inconspicuous and will not be resented by the consumers, it can be more or less than the US$ 5 being suggested. Since the tax applies at the point of consumption rather than production, we do not have to worry about the complexities of the production process. The tax will be paid by the consumers at the moment they pay for the goods they purchase. When it comes to solving the problem of global poverty, issues regarding the goodwill of rich nation-states will never go away, since rich nations are not only responsible for the poverty but they also stand to lose most from any solution to the problem. Yet the GLT does not need the compliance of nation-states, since the international organization responsible for collecting the GLT will deal directly with the multinationals that produce the goods being taxed, without having to go through any intermediate third-party. The issue of natural resources is of course a much more complex issue, since sovereign states will claim to have a right over their natural resources. The fact that the GLT is not taxing natural resources makes it possible to get around this potential stumbling block.

There are, however, two further issues regarding the implementation of the GLT that need to be considered. How can we be sure that the correct amount will be paid to the global fund? What punishment can be meted out if those who are supposed to pay fail or refuse to do so?

The items listed as susceptible for a GLT are chosen in part with an eye to what is practical in terms of collecting the tax. There are many goods that qualify as a luxury which will not be taxed, merely because it would be much messier to know with any precision how many goods were in fact consumed. Hence, we are suggesting taxing air-travel rather than caviar, texting via mobile-phone rather than e-mails,

[13] For incisive critiques of the GRD, see Fuller (2008); Hayward (2005); Haubrich (2004).

procreation rather than champagne, etc. The point is that it would be extremely easy to have access to the information concerning the consumption of luxury goods being taxed. Statistics on air travel, financial transactions, babies born and even texting are readily available. This is in part because the manufacturers or service providers not only declare their output, but have an incentive to boost their numbers. When an air carrier reports back to their shareholders, they will have an incentive to show that passenger numbers on their airline carrier have gone up compared to the previous year. So the statistics on air-travel exist already. The expectation is for the GLT to be passed on directly to the consumers, so that the private companies selling a good being taxed by the GLT will not be affected by this tax. As for procreation, anyone in the process of giving birth will have other things on their mind than the GLT, so it is unlikely that they will object to a minimal flat tax. Not to mention the fact that compared to the cost of raising a child, the flat tax imposed by the GLT is almost laughably small.

Finally, what can be done if the multinationals involved decide to pocket the GLT and not pass it on to the global fund? We believe that this is highly unlikely, since the risk of being 'named and shamed' would not make it worth their while. The harm to the reputation of a company that kept the revenue of a GLT meant to fight global poverty would be so great that it would be irrational for any company to entertain that thought, even in the cut-throat competitive world we live in. However, in order to give an incentive to these companies to pass on the GLT to the global fund, we could agree that these companies get to keep 10% of the funds being raised through the GLT. This would give them an added incentive to market their luxury products even more than before.

13.6 Conclusion

There is a tendency in academic circles for scholars to present their ideas as radical and original alternatives to the existing body of literature. Academics feel compelled to dismiss all competing ideas before offering their preferred solution to a specific problem. This tendency is unhelpful and should be resisted. In this chapter we put forward a policy that we believe could contribute to the fight against world poverty, the GLT. We are not suggesting that this is the only or even the best solution to the problem. Instead, we believe that the most effective approach to the problem of global poverty requires the problem to be tackled via a whole range of different measures, from reforming the international tax regime to taxing natural resources to reforming the global rules that dictate the interactions between nations at a political and economic level. The GLT is simply one measure amongst many others that can deliver for the global poor.

We have also argued that to be taken seriously, any policy recommendation has to respond to two possible objections, namely the Unforeseen Consequences Objection and the Implementation Objection. We believe that the GLT deals adequately with these objections, and it has some advantages with respect to other possible solutions to the problem of global poverty. But of course there is still much work to be done. Raising the funds to fight global poverty is a huge challenge, but even if one were to succeed on that front, another issue arises around the fairness and practicality of distributing the funds. How to distribute the resources in the Global Poverty Fund raises more difficulties than raising the funds in the first place, but precisely how to deal with this issue is for another day.

References

Barry, Brian, and Robert Goodin, eds. 1992. *Free movement*. Pennsylvania: Pennsylvania State University.

Berry, Christopher J. 1994. *The idea of luxury: A conceptual and historical investigation*. Cambridge: Cambridge University Press.

Brock, Gillian. 2008. Taxation and global justice: Closing the gap between theory and practice. *Journal of Social Philosophy* 39 (2): 61–184.

Butt, Daniel. 2009. *Rectifying international injustice*. Oxford: Oxford University Press.

Casal, Paula. 2011. Global taxes on natural resources. *Journal of Moral Philosophy* 8 (3):307–327.

Casal, Paula, and Andrew Williams. 1995. Rights, equality and procreation. *Analyse und Kritik* 17:93–116.

Casal, Paula, and Andrew Williams. 2004. Equality of resources and procreative justice. In *Dworkin and his critics,* ed. Justine Burley. Oxford: Blackwell.

Fuller, Lisa. 2008. Poverty relief, global institutions, and the problem of compliance. In *The global justice reader,* ed. Thom Brooks. Oxford: Blackwell.

Gaisbauer, Helmut P., Schweiger Gottfried, and Sedmak Clemens. 2013. Ethical obligations of wealthy people: Progressive taxation and the financial crisis. *Ethics and Social Welfare* 7 (2): 141–154.

Haubrich, Dick. 2004. Global distributive justice and the taxation of natural resources—who should pick up the tab?. *Contemporary Political Theory* 3:48–69.

Hayward, Tim. 2005. Thomas pogge's global resources dividend: A critique and an alternative. *Journal of Moral Philosophy* 2 (3): 317–332.

O'Neill, Martin. 2007. Death and taxes: Social justice and the politics of inheritance tax. *Renewal: A Journal of Social Democracy* 15 (4): 62–71.

Perez, N. 2012. *Freedom from past injustices: A critical evaluation of claims for inter-generational reparations*. Edinburgh: Edinburgh University Press.

Piketty, Thomas. 2014. *Capital in the 21st century*. Cambridge: Harvard University Press.

Pogge, Thomas. 2008. *World poverty and human rights*. Cambridge: Polity.

Pogge, Thomas. 2011. Allowing the poor to share the earth. *Journal of Moral Philosophy* 8 (3): 335–352.

Spinner-Halev, Jeff. 2012. *Enduring Injustice*. Cambridge: Cambridge University Press.

Steiner, Hillel. 1994. *An essay on rights*. Oxford: Blackwell.

Steiner, Hillel. 2011. The global fund: A reply to Casal. *Journal of Moral Philosophy* 8 (3): 328–334.

Williams Bernard. 1973. *The makropulos case: Reflections on the tedium of immortality. Problems of the self.* Cambridge: Cambridge University Press.

Chapter 14
Taxation: Its Justification and Application to Global Contexts

Teppo Eskelinen and Arto Laitinen

Abstract The article focuses on the justification of taxation, in other words the principled rather than the technical aspect of taxation. We first show how, on the one hand, democracy is required for taxation to be legitimate, and how on the other hand democratic communities are dependent on taxation, and argue that this does not constitute a vicious circle. We then present a typology of ways of justifying taxation, according to which taxation can base its legitimacy on (1) meeting basic needs, (2) financing public goods, (3) redistribution, or (4) (dis)incentivising certain types of conduct. We then discuss the applicability of each of these types of justification, arguing that all of them do apply at a global level. The article further concludes that different normative justifications guide us towards different designs of taxation in practice, so the background justification has to be made clear, especially when designing new taxation systems.

14.1 Introduction

14.1.1 Global Economy and Global Morality Call for Global Politics—and for Global Taxation

The growing interest in global taxation reflects the observation that a worldwide economic system, which transcends the borders of any single political community—the traditional site of handling public finances—seems to have evolved. To put it crudely, economy is global, while political government, as it stands, is not. In addition, while within welfare states certain kinds of voluntary charitable activity are made almost redundant by institutions of social security, in the global setting moral

T. Eskelinen (✉)
Department of social sciences University of Eastern Finland, PO Box 111, 80101 Joensuu, Finland
e-mail: arto.laitinen@staff.uta.fi

A. Laitinen
School of Social and Political Philosophy, University of Tampere, Tampere, Finland
e-mail: leila.haaparanta@uta.fi

H. P. Gaisbauer et al. (eds.), *Philosophical Explorations of Justice and Taxation*,
Ius Gentium: Comparative Perspectives on Law and Justice 40,
DOI 10.1007/978-3-319-13458-1_14

or humanitarian concerns, although widely perceived as pressing, are addressed chiefly via voluntary NGOs, along with development aid interventions. In simple terms, humanitarian morality is global, while political government, as it stands, is not.

There are various reasons why the situation is unsatisfactory from the viewpoint of the aims which political communities are set to serve. The system of competing nation-states, engaging in a plethora of bilateral and areal treaties and a set of confusing semi-binding obligations, proves unsatisfactory for the growing number of global political concerns. The situation might also be unsatisfactory from the viewpoint of the economy: the economic system would work better if it was held more in check by political forces—this is one of the lessons of welfare societies. In addition, the situation is unsatisfactory for moral reasons: the shoulders of humanitarian aid are far too narrow to meet global needs. For such reasons, global taxation might be a fitting, even necessary, solution.[1] It would help global politics to complement global morality and global economy, in order to better serve the constitutive aims not only of political communities, but also of economy and morality.

In this article, we analyse the justification of global taxation at the level of guiding principles. Thus, the main question is not what kinds of detailed systems of tax collection ought to be designed, how tax evasion ought to be tackled, or what the technically best process for deciding how to use the tax revenue is. Rather, our main question is on what kinds of grounds the legitimacy of a tax can be assessed.

This principled level is to a surprising extent neglected in the discourse on tax policy. Rather, governments aim to optimize their tax revenue, for example, by identifying the level at which increasing the capital gains tax percentage would decrease its revenue because of capital flight. Taxation becomes a technical issue, seen through the prism of economics and the rationale of filling the funding gaps in public finance. This leads to the risk of losing the fundamental understanding of what makes taxation desirable in the first place.

Awareness of the choice of justification of the taxation system is especially important when designing completely new tax regimes. Global taxation is a case in point. Even though no individual tax is designed without reference to other taxes, and to its effects in the overall taxation system—an inevitably complex system of money streams and incentives—the lack of certain basic economic functions in the global sphere forces the normative questions to the forefront. It is symptomatic in the political discussions on global taxation that they tend to begin by pointing out the need for a specific tax, such as the "Tobin tax" (Tobin 1978, Patomäki 2001), without first arguing for the justification of taxation, which would give the rationale for implementing the tax. This inverse political logic also tends to blur the design

[1] There are of course risks involved in creating a centralized global political power, but it might also serve to decentre global power from economic and military centres. In any case, the downsides of global taxation are to be weighed with the advantages. [because 'pros' are normally only used in contrast with 'cons'.]

of ideas such as the Tobin tax, as the tax can take very different forms depending on which justification is given most weight.[2]

14.1.2 *The Aims of this Chapter*

So we need to start from the philosophical basis: first, as taxation presupposes a political society, presumably the basic legitimacy or permissibility of taxation (within a single political society) will partly depend on the legitimacy or authority of that political society. Democratic political society with its implied equality is a superior way of arranging human relations in comparison to subordination and dominance of some (14.2.1). But second, mere permissibility is not yet a reason in favour of doing something. What justifies taxation in the first place? One observation is that taxation is a way of creating economic and democratic community. Taxation is required to bring about legitimate political society in the modern form (14.2.2). Over and above that, we will discuss four further purposes that taxation is especially fitted to serve. First, some reasons derive from the universal human claims to a basic standard of living. Institutions funded by taxation provide a principled alternative to charity as a way of ensuring that everyone's basic needs and entitlements are met (14.3.1). Second, taxation is needed to see to it that "public goods" are provided (14.3.2). Third, some reasons derive from distributive justice. Taxation—especially progressive—provides a means of promoting social justice and economic equality. (14.3.3). Fourth, taxation provides further normative guidance on people's behaviour.[3] Normative guidance can be understood as the collective self-direction of society: what kind of conduct does the political community choose to encourage or discourage amongst its members. Pigovian taxes are sometimes suggested as providing normative guidance on the behaviour of individuals. We will suggest that this needs to be understood to be an aspect of all taxes, affecting the reasons for or against certain kinds of taxation (14.3.4).

In the contexts of analysing each justification of taxation we will ask whether that kind of justification can also be applied at a global level. Our main argument is that none of the justifications for taxation "stop at the border"; in other words, they all provide a justification for implementing global taxation, were a global democratic community to set such taxation.

[2] Currently, the Tobin Tax is gaining political popularity, but apparently mostly because of the indebtedness of European governments, not because of its original rationale—the need to curb financial speculation and fund global public goods.

[3] Raz's (1986, p. 53) "normal justification thesis" can be used for justifying the existence and authority of such guidance.

14.1.3 What do we mean by Taxation?

As for the definition of taxation, we need to note two things. First, taxation takes place within an established society or state. Private insurance schemes, in an (imaginary) state of nature, or for example land rent in an (equally imaginary) geoanarchistic context, do not count as taxes. Taxes are legally stipulated, mandatory, and universal. Universal does not mean that everyone is taxed an equal sum or necessarily even that everyone is taxed at all, but that the tax is not determined by the identity of the subject to be taxed: everyone in the same (legal, financial) position pays equally.[4]

Second, in the context of established societies, for example user fees of various stripes, are not taxes. This is because funds derived from taxation are (theoretically speaking) never earmarked. This does not mean that there could not be a wide consensus on always using public money for certain purposes. A tax can even be proposed for meeting a certain funding gap. It does mean, however, that being taxed is not identical to paying for using a service. For instance, one can pay a fee for seeing the doctor within a partially subsidised healthcare system. The public subsidisation of the healthcare system is paid for by money derived from taxes. Even though both amount to making a payment to the very same account (the health care facility), the fee is a direct payment for using a service and the collection of a tax is detached from its final use, and mediated by some political body.

The implication in regard to the global society is that membership fees are not taxes. The difference between the current state of affairs and global public finances is that currently all supranational bodies (UN, World Bank, EU) are funded by membership fees, not taxation. Thus proposing global taxation means proposing legally stipulated and mandatory taxes, which would bring funds to a body functionally independent of the decisions of individual nation-states.

14.2 The Chicken and Egg of Taxation and Democratic Community

14.2.1 Taxation Presupposes a Political Society, Legitimate Taxation Presupposes a Legitimate Political Society

For taxation to be justified, the ordered societies or states implementing taxation must themselves be justified. They must possess legitimate authority over individuals in general in order to tax these individuals. Everyone would agree that, at least in some cases, a putative government lacks legitimacy, even if there is disagreement about which cases would be such. For example, a colonial power after an unjust aggressive war may be a case of an illegitimate power-holder, so it does not

4 For a definition of taxation, see for example (Black 1979)

have a proper right to force taxes on the colonized people (yet of course taxation has always been one of the chief interests of the colonisers). Alternatively, a local mafia can be strong, organised, and systematic enough to be seen as some kind of tax-collecting entity. It serves as a prime example of taxation which is unjustified on the basis of the illegitimacy of its implementer, even though it would succeed in producing social goods such as stability.

Legitimate authority derives not only from the beneficiality of the social arrangement to the individuals involved (say, when people are better off within a society than in a state of nature), but also from considerations of democratic participation: democratic decisions have content-independent authority (i.e. whatever the decision is, it binds everyone because it is democratically made) Raz 1986). This authority has certain normative limits: as long as the rights and entitlements of everyone involved are respected, and as long as the content of the decisions is not intolerably unreasonable, the public decisions are binding independently of their content (Christiano 2010).

Consequently, the justification for a given tax, or for a tax system, can be approached at two levels: first, a legitimate taxation scheme has content-independent justification as a result of the legitimacy of the community exercising its democratic authority—as long as the tax does not violate the fundamental rights of individuals, and as long as it is not too foolish. Second, a legitimate taxation scheme has content-dependent justification due to its purposes and actual content. Below we will discuss four basic purposes that taxation serves, and all these purposes are relevant at the global level. The content-dependent justification of any scheme will depend on its details: naturally, some ways of promoting the four purposes will be better, more justified by their content, than others.

However, before discussing these four purposes, let us tackle the permissibility of taxation in the light of the limits of democratic authority. So, first of all, does taxation violate fundamental rights of individuals? The libertarian and anarchist slogans "taxation is theft" and "taxation is slavery" protest against the legitimacy of all taxation exactly on the grounds of violation of individual rights (Nozick 1974; Narveson 1988; Schmidtz 1991). This interpretation of rights can be easily contested, though. Here it will suffice to briefly go through the line of argument provided by Liam Murphy and Thomas Nagel among others: private possession of money (or property in general) is possible only in the context of societal institutions. Such societal institutions need to be funded by taxation, and thus taxation is not a way of "stealing" existing private property, but rather an inalienable part of the institutions making private property possible in the first place.[5]

The very move that protects private property is at the same time constitutive of community. The move is familiar, for example, from the writings of Rousseau: either some individuals are dependent on and subordinate to some other individuals, or the subordination is cancelled by everyone being dependent on common norms whose co-authors they all are. The opponents of taxation sometimes take taxation

[5] "There is no reality, except as a bookkeeping figure, to the pre-tax income that each of us initially 'has' which the government must be equitable in taking from us" (Murphy 2004; p. 36).

to be a form of subordination, but precisely because it binds everyone, and in the legitimate cases where it expresses the general will, taxation is causally and constitutively relevant for the latter option. The contrast case of a democratic community is undemocratic, unprincipled subordination—say, in terms of economic or military power. In a world of unconnected individuals such subordination would not exist, so this kind of conditional argument for a democratic community (that it is needed to combat subordination and domination) would not get foothold. Nevertheless, as soon as there is dependence between individuals, a normative requirement rises to turn this into mediated freedom in mutual relations to others (Neuhouser 2000). Democratically agreed forms of taxation have by default content-independent justification, whereas a tyrant collecting money, for even what appears to the tyrant to be the collective good, is a case of an illegitimate use of force. This point applies directly to the global setting: global taxation has a *prima facie* content-independent justification if a global democracy sets it. If it is set by a global tyrant, it lacks such a justification (even when it is for what the global tyrant takes to be the good of the humankind).[6]

Naturally, while the content-independent justification will be part of the story of the legitimacy of taxation, it does not yet address the whole issue. *Mere permissibility* is not as such a sufficient reason in favour of something. The content of a proposed tax scheme is naturally relevant in answering such questions and in providing *content-dependent* justifications for some proposals. The evaluative features of the proposed content justify the decisions to impose taxes of the proposed kind. Below, in four subsections, we discuss four aspects of the point of taxation. However, before going to these purposes of taxation, we can point out an even more general consequence of taxation, which might be a desirable general telos as well, namely the fact that taxation is a way of creating economic and political community.

14.2.2 On the Other Hand, Taxation Goes to Create Economic and Democratic Community

The previous section argued that legitimate taxation presupposes legitimate democratic community. Yet curiously, in some sense the logical relation goes both ways. Taxation can indeed be seen as a condition of the creation of a democratic community in the modern sense.

[6] Presently there is nothing at a global level which could be meaningfully called taxation—global institutions such as the World Bank or UN, or transnational bodies such as the EU, are funded on membership fees rather than anything resembling taxation. Indeed, there is nothing like a global political society either. Thus the question of the content-independent justification of global taxation is speculative by nature: we can ask what the minimum criteria for the existence and legitimacy of a global political community would be, yet we really cannot evaluate the present global order in terms of content-independent justification for taxation.

Is this a vicious circle? If we need democracy (just) for legitimate taxation, and taxation (just) for democracy, why would it be better to have both rather than neither? Of course, democracy is desirable for various reasons over and above merely giving content-independent justification for taxation—for one thing, it is an intrinsically valuable realization of collective freedom and a desirable alternative to domination and subordination—and taxation is desirable for various reasons over and above promoting democratic community, or so we hope to argue below. But how is it that taxation promotes community?

First, taxation creates an economic community. By means of taxation, the members of a given community come to use the same currency. The monetary power of government lies exactly in the government's capacity to enforce the use of the government's currency by demanding tax payments in that currency. The subjects are free to use any currency of their preference, but needing government currency for tax payments creates a demand for the government's currency, which makes it the general unit of exchange. This, in turn, creates an economy as a social unit: everyone can rely on other subjects, strangers included, accepting the same currency. This mutual trust fundamentally creates money.[7] Thus taxation is the means of creating co-operation—by coercion, perhaps–but co-operation nevertheless (Wray 1998).

Second, taxation creates a political community. By paying taxes people bond in a political way, and become more mutually interdependent than they would be otherwise. Taxation creates a pool of public resources. This, ideally, creates solidarities, as there are resources the wise use of which is in everyone's interest. But also, conflicting ideas and interests regarding the use of public money (and the question of to what extent taxes should be collected in the first place) create the political discourse on public finance. For politics to exist meaningfully, there has to be something at stake in politics. The use of public funds collected by taxation is perhaps the most important of such issues. In short, taxation strengthens, and to some extent even creates, membership in a political community, as it gives strong reasons to care about political decisions. By taxation, the public political sphere is created. (Of course, this is speaking about ideal cases, as political communities come in many forms and in some forms taxation can be totally irrelevant for democracy).

Curiously, such community—shared political institutions and discourse, the idea of a common market etc.—seems to be highly relevant functionally or instrumentally, and not only because of the intrinsic value of democracy and community. For instance, tax avoidance seems highly detrimental to the institutional core of the society, and not only because of the immediate lost funds.[8] The existence of functioning, transparent and widely trusted "shared institutions" remains one of the most viable explanations of why some countries are rich while some are poor (Risse 2005, de Soto 2003). Further, democracy is often seen as the key to overcoming poverty[9],

---

[7] On money as a social relation, see (Ingham 2004).

[8] See Commission on capital flight from developing countries: Countries (2009).

[9] For the discussion on democracy and the economy and a defence on the importance of democracy see (Sen 1999b).

implicating that the "political" problem of democracy and the "economic" problem of poverty might not be as distant as the disciplinary division insists.

Implementing the idea of community on the global level is more complex. It is a relevant argument to state that there is and will be no "global community". And surely there is no global currency. Yet clearly the world is economically more interconnected than ever, with no corresponding democratic mechanisms in existence Patomäki (2005). Thus it can be argued that global taxation would create meaningful politics on a global scale, that is, something at stake to agree or disagree about within the framework of an established institution. As is the case of any government, global public finances would give a reason to care about global politics. The relationship between global taxation and global democracy goes both ways: global taxation is causally and constitutively relevant for global democracy, which in turn is relevant for the legitimacy of global taxation: if there is taxation, ideally everyone affected ought to have a say about the decisions.

Of course, it can be asked whether a global political entity is needed for global taxation. Do not nation-states form political communities, which are, at least mostly, relatively legitimate, and take care of the functions of public finance? Why does, for instance, global poverty call for global taxation, rather than for particular nation-states to perform their functions properly? Two points are relevant here. First, as noted in the introduction, the economy is currently largely global. As major democratic decisions concern the division of material goods, a global economy needs to be accompanied by global democracy. (Whether the global analogue for a political community, with the powers to collect taxes, would need to be a world-state with individual citizens as its members, or whether a federation of states with taxation powers would be enough, or whether we should approach global democracy in terms of democratizing existing international institutions is a further issue not discussed in this chapter. The crucial point is that there would be a genuine tax in place, and not a voluntary, unilateral membership fee; see above). Second, material basic goods are entitlements on the basis of humanity itself, not on the basis of particular citizenships. The logical conclusion from entitlements on the basis of humanity (which is one of the four justifications we discuss below) is that a global system of public funds is needed to see that these entitlements are met. If impoverished governments cannot guarantee meeting the basic needs of their citizens, global funding is needed.

14.3 Are there General Purposes for which Taxation is an Especially Fitting Solution?

Now we turn to discuss four purposes for which taxation is an especially fitting solution. These four reasons for taxation are arguably each applicable to the global setting.

14.3.1 Reasons for Taxation 1: Minimum Claims (the Entitlement to a Decent Minimum)

A very common and clear moral justification for a taxation system is that it is a function of the government to ensure that everyone's basic needs are met. This can be seen as a response to fundamental human rights. These rights imply universal secured access to basic goods such as food, water, housing and schooling.[10]

Of course, "basic needs" is an ambiguous concept, leaving room for interpretation. For example, education and health care are typically seen as belonging to the scope of basic needs, and it is open to debate what level of these is enough for basic needs to be met (Braybrooke 1987). Yet in the context of several developing countries, in which children get no schooling and where easily curable diseases are lethal due to the lack of ridiculously cheap medication, one can be excused for bypassing these conceptual ambiguities: whatever the philosophical disputes, it seems clear that in cases of extreme poverty the basic needs and corresponding rights of individuals are not met. Taxation is called for, since government funds for public services and also cash transfers are necessary, if meeting basic needs is to be guaranteed.

Needs-based accounts are often criticized for stressing the aspect of humans as recipients, as centres of well-being, rather than as free agents—a point made e.g. by Sen (1999a). There are however various ways to articulate the claim to the "basic minimum" which avoids this theoretical problem.[11] Although they draw from

---

[10] Or more precisely, every adult has a human right to feed herself rather than a human right to be fed—it is not a duty of the government to bring food to your doorstep, yet it is its duty to see that such conditions prevail in which people can get enough to eat (typically by working or cultivating food rather than receiving food packages). (Künnemann 1998; Moore Lappé 1998)

[11] First, one can start with Martha Nussbaum from a list of essential capabilities of human persons, and argue that everyone is entitled to a minimally decent living standard, compatible with the means to human dignity. One can then argue that, insofar as anyone can, they share the responsibility for having everyone's basic needs and entitlements met. In welfare states taxation has replaced direct "aid", alms, and dependence on the goodwill of donors, with very welcome effects. The same ought to be done globally (Nussbaum 2006). Or, in a more Kantian constructivist manner, one can start from Rainer Forst's "basic right of justification" (Forst 2011). According to this argument, if all norms are human constructions, including the moral norms concerning the basic minimum, it is of vital importance that everyone capable of taking part in the critical evaluation of these constructions is in a position to do so. An appeal to the capacity of critical evaluation is an attempt to explicate what it takes for human beings to be agents capable of functioning in society. This is thus a notion demanding more than merely basic needs, yet it entails, similarly to Nussbaum, that meeting basic needs is a prerequisite for functioning. Third, in addition to such universalist claims which are in some sense ahistorical and abstracted out of political context, one can make a historical point that the poorest participants of the global society have been wronged by the global structures. Their entitlements and rights have been significantly violated, they have been harmed by these unjust structures, implicating specifically those who have benefited from these arrangements. These better-off participants actively violate their negative duty not to harm the worst-off by sustaining these structures (Pogge 2005); for further discussion about identifying institutions that harm the poor, see Reitberger 2008, Eskelinen 2011. Thus, meeting basic needs universally is not primarily a matter of suitable level of resources, but of compensating ongoing harm. These three argumentative lines converge in seeing basic subsistence as a universal right.

different philosophical traditions, and differ in their background philosophical assumptions, they converge on the claim that meeting basic needs is of utmost urgency (and consequently, public funds need to be used for seeing that this happens), and is a universal right.

Universal rights are quite straightforwardly related to global taxation, which is a possible way of funding the efforts to guarantee that these rights are met. As human rights are declared at a global level, it would make sense to argue that some global agent or body ought to see to it that such rights are met, if the local government is unable to do this. Individual governments cannot in all cases see to it that these rights are met.

A general point in favour of taxation is the fact that institutional, tax-funded support to the poor is superior to voluntary, unorganized charity. This is so because, first, human rights pronounce a strong claim as such, with no excuses or utilitarian considerations trumping them, and charity is by definition not the best system of responding to human rights—charity should begin only after basic entitlements have been met.[12] Also, from a functional point of view of poverty reduction, reliable systems which allow people to plan their life are superior in poverty reduction to arbitrary systems even if the provided goods would be of same value. In other words, the poor need to be able to *count on the fact* that they get certain services and guaranteed minimum income not only this year, but also next year. For their rightful claims to be met on an ongoing basis, there needs to be an institution or institutions from which the goods or services can be *claimed*. It is naturally not necessarily that this institution is the *local* government.

Currently, the most important agents taking care of the basic needs of impoverished people in least developed countries are, apart from charities, global organizations. The motivation and rhetoric of some such organizations, such as UNDP or UNICEF, clearly point to the direction of universal responsibility. Yet these organizations do not have the power and potential to be agents responsible for *seeing to it that such rights are met*. Even if, say, a poor peasant in rural Zambia might receive support from these organizations, the poor peasant cannot make a claim on them on the basis of her rights.[13] Needless to say, charities and small NGOs have even more restricted duties. Further, charity implies that, because of the lack of any rightful claim to the service, the recipients cannot take part in its design by any established institutional arrangement.

On this argumentative basis, there have been some initiatives for global public finance schemes. For example Thomas Pogge (2002) has argued for a "Global

[12] Or is it perhaps so that charity can, conceptually speaking, start only when the basic entitlements have been met? That may be an exaggerated view. In a situation where everyone's basic entitlements have not been met, and in the absence of global or local institutions providing the relevant services, an individual benefactor can first meet his or her own duties, and then engage in supererogatory support for charitable organizations to help the needy. This would not be needed if everyone would do their duties, or if adequate institutions would be in place, but in the less optimal situations, there is conceptual room for charity even when everyone's basic entitlements have not been met.

[13] On the allocation on duties see e.g. O'Neill 2001.

Resources Dividend", suggesting that nations ought to pay a kind of tax on any resources they use or sell, justified by the fact that such gifts of nature are completely undeserved and in some sense common property. The key normative idea behind the proposal is not the payment, though, but the idea that this money would be directed to a fund with the mandate to alleviate global poverty.

While Pogge carefully avoids the term "taxation", the argumentative structure is open for the defenders of global taxation. Indeed, conceptually taxation would be more appropriate than "a dividend", since the benefits actually gained from resources vary considerably.[14] Further, while Pogge does not discuss the details of the operation of the fund and even hints that the fund would follow the logic of development aid, there is no reason why such a fund, given that it is large enough, could not be designed to promote the possibility of the poor presenting claims on their basic social and economic human rights.

14.3.2 Reasons for Taxation 2: Public Goods

Apart from creating community by shared institutions and political practices, taxation is also the condition of the continuing existence of a society in some sense. Namely, any society needs some basic infrastructure and services to function, and these cannot be provided by the market, as there is no profit to be gained from these by anyone. These are called public goods. Public goods are, then, by definition such goods, the existence of which is dependent on government provision. A classic example, used already by John Stuart Mill, is the lighthouse—it is totally essential for safe maritime travel, but asking for a fee from passing ships would make little sense (Mill 1909/[1848]; book 5, Chap. 11, par 57). No market-rational agent will therefore ever construct a lighthouse. Other examples of public goods include the police, the jurisdiction, pavements and streets, sewage systems, and so on.

Some researchers have suggested that several globally relevant goods can be seen as "global public goods" (Sagasti 2001; Lesage 2009). Indeed, the concept of public goods by no means presupposes the context of nation-states. What is supposed, rather, is that the good in question is necessary, and it cannot by nature be privately funded. According to Dries Lesage's definition, global public goods are "goods that can be consumed by the entire world and in principle also by future generations, in a non-rival and non-exclusive way" (Lesage 2009; pp. 204–205). A possible way to think about public goods would even be that the lack of a necessary public good would be a reason as such to install a government.

When thinking of goods which would fall under the category of "global basic goods", the most common examples relate to the environment. For instance, we all need the Amazonian rainforests to be able to breathe and eventually survive as

[14] Incidentally, this also brings forth a strong counter-argument against Pogge. Namely, while some countries indeed enjoy natural resources as a kind of gift—revenue without economic effort—some countries have faced considerable challenges exactly because of their vast resource base, as demonstrated by the notion of the "resource curse"; see Ross 1999.

a species, so there has to be some global mechanism for ensuring that the rainforests are protected. Protection practically implies some funding. Other issues sometimes discussed under the concept of global public goods include financial stability, peace, and prevention of lethal transmittable disease" (Lesage 2009; p. 214).

No individual is to gain from providing this funding, and it is difficult to allocate the responsibility for this funding to any individual government. Government contributions would be some kind of semi-voluntary donations—as if donations were asked to maintain the lighthouse, just hoping that enough payments would be received. Global taxation would therefore be very logical for this purpose.

14.3.3 Reasons for Taxation 3: Affecting Distribution

Another key function of taxation is to affect the distribution of income and wealth. This relates to social justice in general and not only to guaranteeing social minima or creating a political community. Taxation is a very effective tool in adjusting distribution according to (any) understanding of fairness. Especially the practice of progressive taxation is based on the idea that a socially just distribution of income requires redistribution by taxation.

Justifying taxation for the purpose of affecting income distribution is grounded on two premises. First, it has to be established that an outcome without redistribution by taxation is indeed unjust. Second, it has to be established that taxation is a good way of promoting social justice.

The first argument is often presented in terms of "free-market outcome" versus redistribution. Yet the notion of "free-market outcome" is misleading. As noted in the beginning of this article, a "pre-tax income" is not a description of an actual state in the sense that there could be a modern economy without taxation, but rather a mere accounting measure. In addition, inequalities are not necessarily caused by *markets*, they can be a result of the ongoing effects of historical injustices, for example, along with other possible causes. Therefore the real issue is what kind of taxation system would best serve the ideals of distributive justice; should the taxation system be made more progressive, for instance?

When it comes to establishing what levels of inequalities of income are acceptable, there are two possible rival takes on the "measure" or "currency" of justice. Income distribution can be taken as an issue of social justice as such, or as an indication of problems which ought to be assessed by some other "real currency" of social justice. As an example of the first, Rawlsian theory, argues for a criterion for justified income distribution—that inequalities in incomes (and other primary social goods) are to be for the benefit of the worst off (in terms of incomes and other primary social goods) (Rawls 1971). Alternatively, for example capabilities can be seen as the essence, or "currency", of social justice (Sen 1992; Robeyns and Brighouse 2010). From this perspective, it is the distribution of capabilities that is a measure of justice: if some people need more resources (income and other primary social goods) in order to obtain an equal level of capabilities, then justice requires that they get them—even though measured in terms of resources (income and other primary social goods) they get more than others. Here, too, it is income and other resources that are distributed, but the just pattern of distribution is measured in terms of capabilities. So in this model as well, distribution ought to be corrected by taxation (See Robeyns and Brighouse 2010).

One central attempt to defend the justice of what are perceived to be "free market outcomes" appeals to the notions of desert, merit or contributions. The individuals who contribute more deserve more, and the market outcomes reward them accordingly; therefore taxation is not needed to realize justice. Both parts of this claim have been criticized and need to be qualified. First of all, meritocratic distributions can hardly go all the way. It seems that in any case some basic goods are to be distributed equally, irrespective of merits (say, basic minimum in terms of rights and goods for all; one vote per citizen etc.). Secondly, if the individual contributions matter, then so do the collective ones. Some level of taxation is justified as a reward for the shared contributions of the community.[15] Thirdly, even if individual merits and contributions were to be the sole basis of justice (and all the relevant goods were exchangeable on the market), the market is too dependent on luck and economic domination for it to be even a close approximation of the relevant merits. Thus the unqualified individualist meritocratic view is not as much of a counterargument to redistribution as initially might seem.

Yet it should be argued further, that taxation is indeed the best choice for a mechanism of affecting the distribution. For instance, positive discrimination, guaranteeing services relevant to future incomes, such as schooling for all, government employment programmes and so on, have a significant impact on income distribution. Why is taxation more effective than these policy measures? First, its impact is imminent, and second, it affects the top of the income scale, while most other policy measures only affect the bottom of the scale. This is significant, if income distribution is really taken as important as such, and not only because of the moral problem of poverty.

Of course, the distributional issue gets considerably more complicated when taken to the global level. Should the very same principles of income distribution be applied to the global community? This would, frankly, revolutionise global society as we know it, as in global terms, income disparities are remarkable. The question has been discussed in theories of justice to some extent. Thomas Pogge has argued that the principles of just distribution ought to be applied as such to the "global society". This would mean contemplating the world as a society, the income distribution of which would be roughly similar to Brazil's, and adjusting the preferred distributive mechanisms accordingly (Pogge 2002). On the other hand for example Rawls himself thought that the subjects of global justice should be seen to be "peoples" rather than individuals; meaning a considerably less demanding call for redistribution (Rawls 2001). A mediating position is that global distributive justice has a universal cosmopolitan basis, but memberships in local societies are also relevant for justice in addition to the cosmopolitan basis.

---

[15] See Feinberg, 1973 for the basic positions on this.

Pogge's basic argument regarding the generalisability of principles of distribution is indeed difficult to refute: there simply do not seem to be clear reasons why the principles of distributive justice should only be applied within a domestic setting. Yet this justification for global taxation is perhaps most unclear in regard to what the practical form of implementation would be. The institutional design of taxation is quite unclear. Also, there are problems arising from the resources/capabilities problem. While global income disparities are unacceptably large, there are also social settings with very different levels of monetization of social life, and therefore equal levels of income can be related to very different levels of capabilities. This would mean considerable difficulties for the design of a global tax justified by its redistributive function. Practically, a tax based on redistributive purposes would most likely take the form of an additional income or wealth tax for the extremely rich. This would be well grounded, as the extremely rich today have a relatively low tax burden due to their capability to use the complex system of domestic laws for the purposes of tax avoidance.

14.3.4 Reasons for Taxation 4: Normative Guidance via Incentives and Disincentives

Apart from affecting income distribution, taxation can be used to incentivize certain patterns of economic behaviour and dis-incentivize others. Because no tax is fully "socially neutral,"[16] each and every tax is based on some implicit valuation of certain activities over others. These activities can include working vis-à-vis leisure, saving vis-à-vis consumption, and so on. Practically, any choice of taxation is an implicit choice to value a form of conduct over others even though this is not always evident. Thus, for instance, a decision to increase the VAT instead of increasing income tax, encourages saving over consumption (people have more money but objects of consumption are more costly).

In their most visible form, such valuations concern valuing some objects of consumption over others. For example highly employment-generating consumption can be (partly) exempt from taxes as a part of economic policy strategy. Or some more desired object of consumption (say, theatre) can be taxed on a lower VAT percentage than some less desired object of consumption (say, candies).

The most common form of designing taxation to dis-incentivize some economic behaviour is the use of so-called Pigovian taxes. This means that the consumption of a good is seen to cause negative externalities to an extent that the government ought to minimize such activities by affecting the price of such good. The use of hazardous goods (i.e. alcohol), or environmentally problematic goods (scarce resources, pollutive goods) are often subject to Pigovian taxes.

Following this line of argument, taxation is justified as an economic policy interpretation of moral norms. Any human community will have an idea (negotiated and

[16] The problem of neutral taxation is discussed for example in Thorndike 2002.

based on some consensus, even if always contested by some) of plausible conduct. The community has also several ways to ensure that its members live according to these codes of conduct. One way is mere peer pressure: one will feel uneasy when others react to implausible conduct. Another way is legal enforcement: the subject will be punished for the transgression. Dis/incentives by taxation can be seen as a necessary method in between. They are an articulation of moral norms, with a kind of enforcement, yet without enforcement by the threat of punishment.

Yet the question of the global function of taxation remains, if the role of taxation is interpreted to be dis/incentivizing patterns of consumption. Globally, the justification of Pigovian taxes seems most clear. It is easy to give examples of externalities, which can be curtailed to a reasonable extent by taxation, yet not by taxation within particular and competing nation-states. Examples could include financial speculation, pollution, and overuse of key natural resources.

In the case of Pigovian taxes it ought to be remembered, that there are always alternative means of achieving the same ends, most importantly that of outlawing the activities which are seen to be harmful.[17] If, for example, a certain kind of pollution is harmful, why not outlaw it rather than merely tax it? This clearly would be logical—if some activity is unwanted, then a coherent approach would be not to accept it at all. This applies especially to such cases in which the Pigovian tax is practically a means to outlaw the activity. In such a case, the tax is designed to find its optimum or long-time yield is zero. Thus the activity under tax becomes so expensive, that practically no-one is willing to continue it.

Thus cases in which the use of Pigovian taxes is clearly justified are restricted to cases in which the activity is not seen as undesirable enough to be halted altogether. For example the Tobin tax is not designed to do away with all currency transactions, but to curb some of the harmful (speculative) effects of currency trading. Neither would a carbon emissions tax intend to do away with all greenhouse gas emissions, but to cap them to an environmentally sustainable maximum. The rationale is very different from the Pigovian tax on, say, smoking: at least from a medical point of view, there is no acceptable "cap level" to smoking other than zero.

As the economy and the externalities become more global, and awareness of the global nature of several issues and of the interdependency of humanity grows, there will be ever more political thinking in terms of "desired conduct of humanity". Such issues concern a wide range of areas from finance to new forms of energy, from the extinction of species to issues of war and peace, from climate change to genetics. It is only natural that some, while certainly not all, of such normative ideas find their most natural expression in the form of (suggested) Pigovian taxes. The justification for taxes as a form of society's expression of moral ideas seems fairly unproblematic, and it is appropriate to apply this on the global level. Further, as already noted, any tax has some function of dis/incentivizing some conduct vis- à -vis another, so it is very natural for the global community to express political ideas about the future of humanity in the form of global taxes.

[17] Compare to the idea that not everything is for sale, cf. e.g. Walzer 1983.

14.4 Conclusions

In this chapter we have sought to justify global taxation from the principled point of view. Our strategy has been to analyse different forms of legitimation of taxation, leaning on the observation that no actual system of taxation relies on only one form of legitimation and thus one function. As we also noted in the beginning, the choice of the forms of justification for a tax is highly important, as it has considerable impact on the form the tax eventually takes. Especially with regard to novel ideas such as initiatives for global taxation, the justificatory basis ought to be clear.

As for the structure of our argument, we first argued that taxation is in principle permissible and showed how taxation and democratic community are interrelated. Subsequently we pointed out four positive normative reasons for the justification of taxation. In the moral or humanitarian task of guaranteeing basic minimum for everyone, taxation is superior to voluntary donations or charity, and in fact the only way to *guarantee* anything. In providing public goods, there is no alternative to public funding. In the aim of realizing distributive justice, taxation is perhaps the best-known tool for redistribution—while of course equalising "starting points" and opportunities is of high importance as well. In addition, in the aim of guiding behaviour, taxation proves to be a necessary way for a community to express and institutionalise its moral ideas about plausible conduct, when middle-ground between legal enforcement and peer pressure is needed for this expression.

Further, we have aimed to show in regard to each of the four types of justification what the implications of globalising taxation regimes would be from the point of view of the particular justification. We conclude that each line of argumentation can also be relevant in justifying global taxation. Most likely, the biggest issue will be finding a balance between forming a global political community, (and henceforth a global political arena where decisions are made), and the need to find reliable and fair ways to fund some necessary functions of global society—reduction of extreme poverty and provision of global public goods. In any case, awareness of the partially conflicting plurality of arguments behind the justification of any tax makes resolving such dilemmas at least a little easier.

Naturally, our argument has been restricted to very principled issues. Even though we believe we have shown that any justification for taxation is generalizable to the global sphere, this still says little if anything about the actual design of global taxes. Would the subjects to be taxed always be individuals, could they be governments, too? What kind of body would decide about the use of global public funds, and how would representation function in the body? How would the double relation between taxation and the democratic community be dealt with—which should come first in the implementation of global taxes? These questions call for thorough future research on the subject.

References

Black, Henry Campbell. 1979. *Black's law dictionary*. 5th ed. St. Paul: West Publishing.

Braybrooke, David. 1987. *Meeting needs*. Princeton: Princeton University Press.

Christiano, Thomas. 2010. *The constitution of equality: Democratic authority and its limits*. Oxford: Oxford University Press.

Countries, Commission on Capital Flight from Developing. 2009. *Tax havens and development*. Oslo: NORAD.

de Soto, Hernando. 2003. *The mystery of capital. Why capitalism triumphs in the west and fails everywhere else*. New York: Basic Books.

Eskelinen, Teppo. 2011. Harming the global poor. On the causal and moral role of institutions. *SATS North-European Journal of Philosophy* 12 (1):89–103.

Feinberg, Joel. 1973. *Social philosophy*. Englewood Cliffs: Prentice Hall.

Forst, Rainer. 2011. *The right to justification: Elements of a constructivist theory of justice*. Translated by Jeffrey Flynn. New York: Columbia University Press.

Ingham, Geoffrey. 2004. *The nature of money*. Cambridge: Polity Press.

Künnemann, Rolf. 1998. Violations of the right to food. In Boven, T.C., van Flinterman, C & Westendorp, I (eds.) *The Maastricht guidelines on violations of economic, social and cultural rights*. Netherlands institute of human rights, SIM special no 20, Utrecht, pp. 165–191.

Lappé, Frances Moore, Joseph Collins, Peter Rosset, and Luis Esparza. 1998. *World hunger: 12 myths*. 2nd ed. Grove/Atlantic and Food First Books.

Lesage, Dries. 2009. Public finance for global public goods. In *Tax justice. Putting global inequality on the agenda,* eds. Matti Kohonen and Francine Mestrum, London: Pluto Press.

Mill, John Stuart. 1909/[1848]. *Principles of political economy with some of their application to social philosophy*: London: Longmans, Green & Co. Original edition, 1848.

Murphy, Liam, and Thomas Nagel. 2004. *The myth of ownership. Taxes and justice*. Oxford: Oxford University Press.

Narveson, Jan. 1988. *The libertarian idea*. Philadephia: Temple University Press.

Neuhouser, Frederick. 2000. *Foundations of Hegel's social theory: Actualizing freedom*. Cambridge: Harvard University Press.

Nozick, Robert. 1974. *Anarchy, state, and utopia*. New York: Basic Books.

Nussbaum, Martha. 2006. *Frontiers of justice: Disability, nationality, species membership*. Cambridge: Harvard University Press, Belknap Press.

O'Neill, Onora. 2001. Agents of justice. *Metaphilosophy* 32 (1–2): 180–195.

Patomäki, Heikki. 2001. *Democratising globalisation. The leverage of the tobin tax*. London: Zed Books.

Patomäki, Heikki, and Teivo Teivainen. 2005. *A possible world. Democratic transformation of global institutions*. London: Zed books.

Pogge, Thomas. 2002. *World poverty and human rights: Cosmopolitan responsibilities and reforms*. Cambridge: Polity Press.

Pogge, Thomas. 2005. Severe poverty as a violation of negative duties. *Ethics and International Affairs* 19 (1): 55–83.

Rawls, John. 1971. *A theory of justice*. Cambridge: Cambridge University Press.

Rawls, John. 2001. *The law of peoples*. Cambridge: Harvard University Press.

Raz, Joseph. 1986. *The morality of freedom*. Oxford: Clarendon Press.

Reitberger, Magnus. 2008. Poverty, negative duties, and the global institutional order. *Politics, Philosophy and Economics* 7 (4): 379–402.

Risse, Mathias. 2005. What we owe to the global poor. *The Journal of Ethics* 9 (1–2): 81–117.

Robeyns, Ingrid, and Harry Brighouse. 2010. Introduction: Social primary goods and capabilities as metrics of justice. In *Measuring justice: Primary goods and capabilities,* eds Harry Brighouse and Ingrid Robeyns. Cambridge: Cambridge University Press.

Ross, Michael. 1999. The political economy of the resource curse. *World Politics* 51 (2): 297–322.

Sagasti, Fransisco, and Keith Bezanson. 2001. Financing and providing global public goods. Expectations and prospects. Stockholm: Ministry of Foreign Affairs Sweden.
Schmidtz, David. 1991. *The limits of government*. Boulder: Westview.
Sen, Amartya. 1992. Inequality re-examined. Cambridge: Harvard University Press.
Sen, Amartya. 1999a. Development as freedom. Oxford: Oxford University Press.
Sen, Amartya. 1999b. Democracy as a universal value. *Journal of Democracy* 10 (3): 3–17.
Thorndike, Joseph, and Dennis Ventry, eds. 2002. *Tax justice. The ongoing debate*. Washington DC: Urban Institute Press.
Tobin, James. 1978. A proposal for international monetary reform. *Eastern Economic Journal* 4 (3–4): 153–159.
Walzer, Michael. 1983. *Spheres of justice*. New York: Basic Books.
Wray, L. Randall. 1998. *Understanding modern money. The key to full employment and price stability*. Cheltenham: Edward Elgar.

Printed by Printforce, the Netherlands